HABIB GIRGIS

Coptic Orthodox Educator and a Light in the Darkness

Coptic Studies Series

The Coptic Studies Series at St Vladimir's Seminary Press was conceived with a two-fold purpose: to increase the accessibility of the many treasures of Coptic Orthodox Christianity to a wider English-speaking audience; and to cross-pollinate the spiritual minds of Coptic Orthodox Christians and their Eastern Orthodox brethren with the knowledge of a common faith in the incarnate Word of God—who is the true source of all wisdom and knowledge.

Series Editors:
Bishop Suriel and John Behr

BOOK I
The Life of Repentance and Purity
Pope Shenouda III

BOOK II
Habib Girgis: Coptic Orthodox Educator and a Light in the Darkness
Bishop Suriel

Habib Girgis

Coptic Orthodox Educator
and a Light in the Darkness

BISHOP SURIEL

ST VLADIMIR'S SEMINARY PRESS
YONKERS, NEW YORK
2017

Library of Congress Cataloging-in-Publication Data

Names: Suriel, Coptic Bishop of Melbourne, 1963- author.
Title: Habib Girgis : Coptic Orthodox educator and a light in the darkness / Bishop Suriel.
Description: Yonkers, NY : St Vladimir's Seminary Press, 2017. | Includes bibliographical references.
Identifiers: LCCN 2017003286 (print) | LCCN 2017008593 (ebook) | ISBN 9780881415667 | ISBN 9780881415674
Subjects: LCSH: Habib Girgis, Saint, 1876-1951. | Coptic Orthodox Church--History.
Classification: LCC BX139.H32 S87 2017 (print) | LCC BX139.H32 (ebook) | DDC 281/.72092 [B] --dc23
LC record available at https://lccn.loc.gov/2017003286

SACPRESS
100 Park Road, Donvale, Vic 3111
www.sacpress.com.au

ST VLADIMIR'S SEMINARY PRESS
575 Scarsdale Road, Yonkers, NY 10707
1-800-204-2665
www.svspress.com

ISBN 978–088141–566–7 (paper)
ISBN 978–088141–591–9 (hardback)
ISBN 978–088141–567–4 (electronic)

PRINTED IN THE UNITED STATES OF AMERICA

Dedication

THIS BOOK IS DEDICATED to the memory of His Holiness Pope Shenouda III, the 117th Pope of Alexandria and Patriarch of the See of St Mark, who was a contemporary of St Habib Girgis and also one of his disciples.

As a wise father, writer, poet, and bishop of Christian education, you were my inspiration throughout this fascinating journey. I can still hear your voice teaching me:

> *My child, do not let these escape from your sight:*
> *keep sound wisdom and prudence,*
> *and they will be life for your soul*
> *and adornment for your neck.*
>
> (Prov 3.21–22)

Contents

Acknowledgments

I WISH, FIRST OF ALL, to thank the Lord Jesus Christ for granting me the strength to complete this work.

This book began as my doctoral dissertation, written under the direction of my supervisory committee: Professor Gloria Durka, Professor Emeritus John Elias, and Associate Professor Maged Mikhail (Deacon Severus). I consider all three to be my mentors. The insights and continued support that I gained from Professors Durka and Elias over the nine years of this project have been invaluable. Whenever I had doubts that I could complete this enormous task, both of them believed in me and continued to strengthen me along this arduous journey. Therefore, I thank them. Additionally, Dr Mikhail has been instrumental throughout. As a scholar of Coptic Church history, his vast knowledge of sources and his encouragement assisted me immensely in gaining the necessary knowledge to support my arguments. My deep gratitude goes to all of them for their fine scholarship, which has enriched my work and life.

These acknowledgments would not be complete if I did not remember my spiritual father, His Holiness Pope Shenouda III, of blessed memory, for his encouragement, for allowing me full access to the Coptic Patriarchal Archives, and for allowing me the opportunity to interview him about his experiences with Habib Girgis.

A special group of people worked closely with me in cataloging the documents of the Coptic Patriarchal Archives: George Shahid, Roman Abdel-Massih, Ezzat Zachary, and Dr Nicholas al-Jeloo. They worked hundreds of hours, if not more, on that monumental task, and parts of their work feature prominently in this book. I thank them for their dedication. Further thanks are due to Dr al-Jeloo, who edited my text at the dissertation stage and worked into the early hours of the morning on many occasions to meet deadlines. His dedication and moral support helped me through those most difficult of days.

I would also like to extend my heartfelt gratitude to Bassem Morgan, who tirelessly and painstakingly spent hundreds of hours, over many years, digitizing countless books and articles so that I could carry my research with me wherever I travelled. Having those sources at my fingertips made my task much easier. Bassem also worked on the photographs in the book. I also thank Hani Gadoun for photographing historical items now housed at St Mark Coptic Orthodox Cultural Center at Dayr al-Anbā Ruways.

There are many other people who supported me. In particular, I would like to acknowledge Bishop Ermia, Bishop Martyros, Father Athanasius Farag, Professor Nelly van Doorn-Harder, Associate Professor Paul Sedra, Father Dr Gregorios Awad, Dr Saad Michael Saad, Associate Professor Heather J. Sharkey, Mary Farag, and George Kaldas for graciously sourcing relevant texts and articles that were pertinent to my research, as well as for their thoughtful insights.

My deep gratitude also goes to several people who read drafts of my work and assisted me in sorting through the wealth of material that I had collected over the years. In particular I would like to acknowledge Father Abanoub Attalla, Ralph and Ann Marie Toss, Abraam Mikhail, Chris Ghali, George Makram, and Lisa Agaiby.

The interlibrary loan staff at Fordham University worked diligently and professionally to source books and articles for me over the years, and for this I am grateful. I also appreciated the hospitality of the master and staff at the Catholic Theological College in Melbourne (Australia) for allowing me to use their wonderful facilities whenever I needed a place of solace to work.

As I was nearing the end of my research, the talented iconographer Ashraf Gerges painted a beautiful first icon of St Habib Girgis, which was presented to His Holiness Pope Tawadros II on Tuesday, January 14, 2014. I also thank His Holiness for his encouragement and prayers for me to complete this work.

Many friends and members of my diocese have stimulated me along the way. Furthermore, I acknowledge my 22,000 Facebook friends and 32,000 Twitter followers who supported me with their prayers and inspiration.

I also wish to thank my editor, Dr Belinda Nemec, for her editing of the manuscript as it was transformed from dissertation to book. Her attention to detail and invaluable suggestions were vital. The outstanding quality of Belinda's editing skills is reflected in the book you now have before you.

Finally, I am very grateful to Michael Soroka, Fr Benedict Churchill, and the entire team at St Vladimir's Seminary Press for their encouragement and support throughout the publishing process, and for their many helpful insights. This is the second book in the new Coptic Studies Series initiated by St Vladimir's Seminary Press and jointly published with St Athanasius College Press.

Bishop Suriel
Coptic Orthodox Bishop of Melbourne
Dean of St Athanasius Coptic Orthodox Theological College
25 January 2017
Feast Day of Sts Maximus and Domatius

The first icon of St Habib Girgis, written by Ashraf Gerges in Melbourne and presented to His Holiness Pope Tawadros II on Tuesday, January 14, 2014.

Habib Girgis is depicted holding a Bible, open at Isaiah 27.2–3: the verses printed on the cover of each issue of his monthly magazine al-Karmah *[The Vine]. Beneath this are two scenes from Girgis' life: on the left he is delivering a lecture at Ḥārat al-Saqqāyīn Church in the presence of Pope Kyrillos V, while on the right he is teaching at the seminary; on the chalkboard is one of his famous sayings: "the greatest need for any community, after bread, is education." (Photograph by Bassem Morgan.)*

Introduction

Our teacher Archdeacon Habib Girgis, pioneer of religious education in our generation, started his life in an age that was almost void of religious education and knowledge. "The earth was without form, and void, and darkness was on the face of the deep," as the Book of Genesis describes. Then, God said, "Let there be light," and there was light. And the light was Habib Girgis.[1]

—His Holiness Pope Shenouda III

On June 20, 2013, the Holy Synod of the Coptic Orthodox Church canonized Archdeacon Habib Girgis Manqariyūs (1876–1951) as a saint of the Church.[2] That momentous event has led to a new and heightened interest in Girgis among members of the Coptic community generally, and also among scholars.

Girgis was a prominent figure in the Coptic Orthodox Church in the first half of the twentieth century. He played a significant role in many aspects of Church life, particularly as a prolific writer and educational reformer. Nonetheless, during his lifetime the Church was not yet fully ready for such a reformer, and until recently the Coptic community has largely overlooked his achievements. Since his canonization, however, growing numbers of people wish to learn more about his life, educational philosophy, and vision for reform in order to appreciate his legacy. Thus, the time is ripe for a full account of Girgis' life and his role in the reform of the Coptic Orthodox Church.

Girgis deserves to be studied rigorously and his work and vision scrutinized, analyzed, and understood. He was a man ahead of his time that deserves to be afforded his rightful place in the history of the Coptic Orthodox Church as a prominent educationalist, reformer, and writer, an eloquent preacher and poet, a trusted advisor of popes, the founder of the Coptic Sunday School movement, and dean of the Coptic Orthodox Seminary in Cairo. The recent

[1] His Holiness Pope Shenouda III, "Our Teacher Archdeacon Habib Girgis," *Watani International* 43.2062 (August 26, 2001): 2.

[2] Habib Girgis may also be spelled Ḥabīb Jirjis.

discovery at the Coptic Orthodox Patriarchate in Cairo of thousands of archival documents pertaining to Habib Girgis has made it possible to give a fuller account of this great man's vision, achievements, and legacy.

Habib Girgis' life spanned a period of radical change and turmoil in the world at large and for Egypt and the Coptic Orthodox Church in particular. For most of Girgis' life, Egypt was under British control (1882–1952). He lived through the demise of the Ottoman Empire, World War I, the Great Depression, and World War II, events that caused many financial and other hardships for Egypt and the Church. Moreover, this was a period during which significant numbers of Europeans and Americans settled in Egypt, further influencing the nation with both secular and religious Western ideas.

The only post-secondary academic qualification that Girgis acquired was a diploma of theology from the Coptic Orthodox Seminary, where he later served as dean for more than thirty years. Despite his relatively limited graduate training, he had an innate love of learning that led him to realize the potential value of education for the Copts. He believed that education would eventually lead them to desire and work toward reform in order to regain their Coptic identity and prominent place in society, both in Egypt and abroad.

Girgis faced many challenges and obstacles throughout his career. Tensions between Church hierarchy and laity caused deep conflicts, once even resulting in the banishment of the pope for several months to a desert monastery. Girgis deeply respected the hierarchy and maintained a close relationship with Pope Kyrillos (Cyril) V. However, he also sympathized with the reforms sought by the educated laity, who viewed the hierarchy as ignorant and poorly educated. This tension often obstructed Girgis' work, particularly during his time as a student, teacher, and dean of the seminary.

Girgis' vision for reform embraced the entire Coptic community. Although for most of his career he was the dean of a seminary focused on training priests, preachers, and cantors, he advocated free education for all, including the poor and illiterate. He constantly reached out to those who were seeking to strengthen their faith and well-being. In his booklet on rural education, for instance, he reminded Sunday School teachers of their duty to marginalized people: "For this is a simple matter that does not require more than our feelings toward those members in the body of Christ, whom we neglected for a long time to be knocked around in their darkness, left to stumble in their ignorance, and to perish as sheep with no shepherd."[3] Girgis' innate sense of social justice convinced him that everyone deserved an education. He worked to combat illiteracy using internationally tested pedagogical methods, and helped train blue-collar workers and tradespeople so that they could find suitable jobs or begin their own small enterprises.

Girgis was a tireless advocate of religious education for children and youth. Through the Sunday School movement that he founded, he aspired to teach children the fundamental truths of their faith and instruct them in the history, doctrines, and rites of the Coptic Orthodox Church and the lives of its heroes. He sought to train them to sanctify Sunday, to worship regularly, partake of Holy Communion, and lead a Christian life. Girgis cared for their spiritual and physical health and intended for Sunday School to prepare them to become useful members of their Church and nation.

Through the Coptic Youth League, founded in 1918, Girgis sought to confirm Coptic youth in their faith, consolidate their spirit of unity and general fraternity, and engage them in spiritual, cultural, social, and sporting activities. His aim, in short, was to train young people to embrace virtue and combat vice while preparing them to carry out charitable and social projects to meet the needs of the Church and the community. Young people were encouraged to confront the dangers that targeted the unity of the Church, both internally and externally.

It was because of Girgis' admirable vision for the Sunday Schools that thousands of children received sound religious education and pastoral care. In Girgis' eyes, Christian education in the Coptic Church had long been deficient, lacking both appropriate teaching materials and suitably trained teachers. He believed that Christian instruction for children in the schools and churches was essential for the revival of a spiritually healthy Coptic community. He petitioned for the introduction of Christian education into the state-run schools and lobbied parishes to provide it for their children and youth.

Girgis gave urgent priority to disseminating Orthodox doctrines when educating the young in an attempt to counter the widespread influence of

[3]Habib Girgis, *Iftiqād al-'āmm lil-qaryah* [General Visitations to the Village], 2nd ed. (Cairo: al-Lajnah al-'Ulyā li-Madāris al-Aḥḥad al-Qibṭiyah al-Urthūdhuksiyah, 1949), 29.

Western missionaries, whether Catholic or Protestant. He spoke out strongly against these foreign missions, particularly in his book *The Orthodox Rock* (1948). He wanted young Copts to know the history of their own Church and to be empowered by the lives of their saints—to emulate their actions and virtues. He spoke repeatedly of the importance of teaching virtue and training the young to live spiritual lives. He published many of his rich teachings in books such as *Spiritual Perspectives for Christian Living* (1946), and also in articles for his monthly publication *The Vine*.

The Liturgy figured prominently as a central teaching tool in Girgis' educational philosophy. Because the Liturgy is central to Orthodox Christian life, Girgis asked priests to take the holy altar-board into remote villages where no churches existed and celebrate liturgies with the Copts who lived there.[4] His purpose was to help these Christians become accustomed to liturgical worship and understand its importance as they joined with Christ by partaking of his body and blood in the Eucharist.

The Liturgy also became a vehicle of popular education for Girgis—"popular" in the sense of pertaining to the people, as opposed to the more common meaning of being in favor with or well liked by the majority. Girgis worked with underprivileged and disenfranchised people in rural Coptic communities. His form of popular education primarily sought to stimulate the senses through liturgical worship, hymnology, and the use of icons and religious pictures. He placed particular importance on this last element. For instance, over a period of nine months from July 1948 to March 1949, he organized the printing or importing from Europe of 3.25 million religious pictures, at a cost of EGP 715.[5] Of these, 2.27 million pictures were actually distributed—a staggering number considering that the number of Copts in Egypt at that time was only around one million.[6]

[4]The holy altar-board is a consecrated rectangular wooden panel set into a special slot on the surface of the altar. Usually it is decorated with a cross and bears the Coptic signs for Jesus Christ, Son of God in the four squares between the arms of the cross.

[5]EGP = Egyptian Pounds. Each pound comprised 1,000 millims. All sums have been rounded to the nearest pound.

[6]Habib Girgis, Report of the Higher Central Committee of Sunday Schools and the Coptic Youth League, July 1948–March 1949. Coptic Orthodox Patriarchal Archives, Cairo (hereafter "Patriarchal Archives"), (May 1949): 4–1.218–227, 400–409/30, Sunday School Grants Part 1.

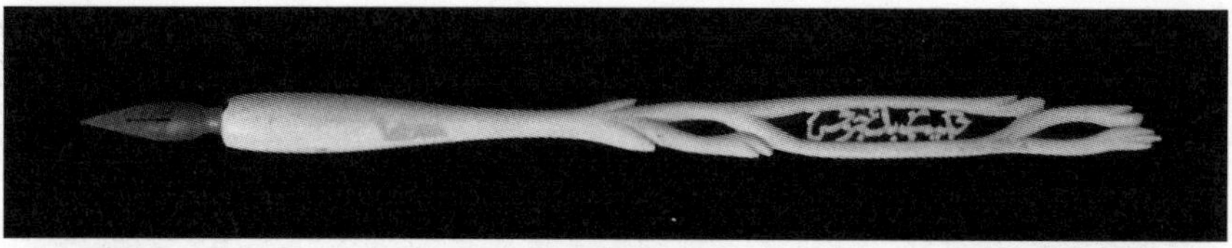

Habib Girgis' ivory pen, with his name carved into the handle. (St Mark Coptic Orthodox Cultural Center, Dayr al-Anbā Ruways; photograph by Hani Gadoun.)

Girgis' educational vision included the imparting of fundamental religious truths to the young through hymns. As a poet, Girgis authored several hymnals for Sunday School students as well as for use in spiritual gatherings. Notably, he used many of the ritual melodies well known to the faithful, writing new texts to fit those familiar tunes.

Girgis was also aware of the need to educate women and girls. He wrote in detail about the requirements of women's education and formulated programs suited to their particular circumstances.

* * *

Did Habib Girgis succeed in implementing his grand vision for reform in the Coptic Orthodox Church? This question deserves careful consideration. At first glance, one is tempted to respond with an emphatic "yes." Certainly, there is much evidence to support such a claim, including Girgis' books and the annual reports of the seminary and Sunday School movement. One can argue that Girgis succeeded at various levels. He managed, for example, to have religious education included in Coptic schools. He also developed the physical infrastructure of the Coptic Orthodox Seminary and sent out students and graduates to preach the word of God in many parishes, dioceses, and Coptic societies. He disseminated religious curricula throughout Egypt and Sudan, raised the profile of religious and theological education in the Church, and much more.

However, by delving deeper and listening more carefully to Girgis through his writings and systematically reading the documents in the Patriarchal Archives, we discern a different picture—one not so bright and, indeed, full of frustration on Girgis' part. He faced a constant struggle, and the resistance he met at many levels and from many quarters ultimately curtailed the unqualified successes that he might otherwise have enjoyed.

Habib Girgis' ornate inkwell, with containers for blue and red ink. (St Mark Coptic Orthodox Cultural Center, Dayr al-Anbā Ruways; photograph by Hani Gadoun.)

This book discusses the subtle nuances of Girgis' success and consistently addresses several vexing questions. For instance, did the seminary ever attain the international standards to which Girgis aspired? How effective were the Sunday School movement and the Coptic Youth League in bringing young Copts back to their faith? To what extent did Girgis manage to stamp out illiteracy (especially in the villages), teach the Copts their ancient language, and help them reclaim their Coptic identity?

Girgis died before he could see all his plans come to fruition, but he hoped and dreamed of a brighter future for the Coptic Orthodox Church. His life continues to inspire the Copts to dream with him, urging a new generation to claim his legacy and soar with it.

Postscript: I recently came across new significant material pertaining to Habib Girgis that requires further research. I hope that this material will shed more light on the life and work of Girgis, which can be published in a future second edition of the present book; it will likely add several new chapters. In addition, at the time of publication further information has come to light concerning correspondence from an American to Habib Girgis in the form of over thirty postcards. Further research will be presented in a future edition of this book.

CHAPTER ONE

Teacher, Reformer, Theologian, and Shepherd: The Life of Habib Girgis

You were not an ordinary man. You were great, and your greatness was true. Your children felt this greatness as well as the rest of the people. You showed forth your idea to all. Everybody knew that the person who owns this idea could be nothing less than a great man. For he passed through a generation of incapable devious leaders who could only resist, and their resistance was fierce.[1]

—Sulaymān Nasīm

Habib Girgis Manqariyūs was born at 65 Shāriʿ al-Qubaysī bi-al-Ẓāhir (شارع القبيسى بالظاهر 65) in the suburb of al-Fajjālah in al-Azbakiyyah district of central Cairo, in 1876. His father, Girgis Manqariyūs, was from the city of Ṭimā in Upper Egypt, and his mother was from al-Bayāḍiyah.[2] At that time both cities were part of the directorate of Jirjā (Girga), and are now part of the Sūhāj (Sohag) governorate. Unfortunately, little is known about Habib's childhood and upbringing, and his own writings mention nothing of that period of his life. We do know that his father worked as a chief clerk in the most important government departments associated with the interior administration during the reign of Khedive Ismāʻīl (1863–1879). He died in 1882, when Habib was only six years old. Habib's mother, Miriam, who died in 1939, continued raising her three sons and her daughter, Martha, in a Christian manner. She enrolled Habib in the Great Coptic School in Cairo,[3] where he excelled and completed both his elementary and secondary

[1]Sulaymān Nasīm, "Rāḥilnā al-ʻAẓīm" [Our Great One who has Departed], *Majallat Madāris al-Aḥḥad* [Sunday School Magazine] 5.9–10 (November–December 1951): 85–88, at 85.

[2]It is customary in Egypt to use a father's given name as the son's surname.

[3]The school, which is discussed further in Chapter 2, officially opened in 1855 as an elementary school, to which secondary education was later added.

Girgis Manqariyūs, the father of Habib Girgis. c. 1880. (St Mark Coptic Orthodox Cultural Center, Dayr al-Anbā Ruways; photograph by Hani Gadoun.)

Habib Girgis' mother, Miriam Girgis (d. 1939). (St Mark Coptic Orthodox Cultural Center, Dayr al-Anbā Ruways.)

Habib Girgis' mother, Miriam Girgis (d. 1939). (St Mark Coptic Orthodox Cultural Center, Dayr al-Anbā Ruways.)

Habib Girgis and his sister, Martha, c. 1930s. (St Mark Coptic Orthodox Cultural Center, Dayr al-Anbā Ruways.)

Ghālī Girgis, brother of Habib Girgis, who died at a relatively young age. (St Mark Coptic Orthodox Cultural Center, Dayr al-Anbā Ruways.)

Kāmil Girgis, older brother of Habib Girgis. (Private collection, courtesy of Emad Asad—Helwan, Egypt.)

schooling. One brother, Ghālī, died at a young age, while the other, Kāmil, eventually became an employee of the railway authority.

The Coptic Orthodox Seminary in Cairo, established in 1893 by Pope Kyrillos V,[4] would become central to the life and work of Habib Girgis. He was among the first students to enroll in 1893. During his first four years there, the seminary had no teacher of theology. The educational level of most incoming students was minimal, and the curriculum was inadequate. Nevertheless, being an astute young man thirsty for learning, Girgis read extensively in the Patriarchal Library. To a large extent he educated himself, as well as gaining much knowledge from Father Fīlūthā'us (Philotheos) Ibrāhīm Baghdādī (1837–1904), the only erudite Coptic preacher of his day.

[4]This institution was established in 1893 as the Clerical School (al-Madrasah al-iklīrīkiyah, المدرسة الاكليريكية) and placed under the leadership of its first principal, Yūsuf Manqariyūs. In 1927, the position to which Girgis had been appointed in 1918 was designated as that of "dean," and in 1946 the name of the institution changed to the Coptic Orthodox Seminary (Kulliyat al-lāhūt al-Qibṭiyah, كلية اللاهوت القبطية). For the sake of clarity, the institution is referred to throughout this book as the Coptic Orthodox Seminary (or a shortened version thereof), and its academic leader is referred to as the dean.

Habib Girgis as a seminarian, wearing his cassock and tarboush (fez). (St Mark Coptic Orthodox Cultural Center, Dayr al-Anbā Ruways.)

The young Habib Girgis, probably while a student at the Coptic Orthodox Seminary in the late 1890s. (St Mark Coptic Orthodox Cultural Center, Dayr al-Anbā Ruways.)

The young Habib Girgis, probably while a student at the Coptic Orthodox Seminary in the late 1890s. (Private collection, courtesy of Emad Asad—Helwan, Egypt.)

As a result of his efforts, Girgis was soon placed at the top of his class. For this reason, and because of the continuing shortage of theology instructors, he was appointed by special decree on March 17, 1898, to teach religion at the seminary on a temporary basis while still in his final year of study. He graduated shortly thereafter and, having shown great potential and success as an instructor, was promptly appointed to a full-time position, teaching theology and homiletics (the art of preaching).

In 1897, while still a student at the seminary, Habib Girgis delivered an impressive two-part lecture on the subject of "Christian religion" over two successive Sundays at the Great Coptic School. Tādrus Bik Shinūdah al-Manqabādī,[5] the owner and editor-in-chief of *Miṣr* newspaper, attended both lectures and was so impressed by the bright young preacher that he

[5]"Bik" and "Afandī" were titles given to notables in Egyptian society during Habib Girgis' era. Lucie Ryzova explains: "The *efendis* are well known to have been the major actors of modern Egyptian nationalism in its many forms: they were the makers, as well as the primary consumers, of modern Egyptian political life, social institutions, and cultural production. Products of modern education, and thus consensually imbued with modern habits and expertise, they were the white-collar workers who ran the modern bureaucracy, the

sought his permission to publish and distribute thousands of copies of his lecture.

Girgis began the lecture by asking, "Is there among us anyone who is capable of responding to those who ask him about his religion and why he is a Christian? I am sure that most of us do not have an answer, except to say that we were born from Christian parents and hence we are Christians."[6] The lecture reflected the pain caused him by the current ignorance and lack of religious education in the Coptic community. He aimed to enlighten his listeners by starting with the basic tenets of the Christian faith and to ignite their interest in learning more.

Tādrus Bik Shinūdah al-Manqabādī (1857–1932), owner and editor-in-chief of Miṣr *newspaper (established 1895). (Girgis,* The Coptic Orthodox Seminary.*)*

Girgis divided the lecture into three sections: "How did it begin?," "What are its benefits and effects on the world?," and "What are the characteristics of true Christians?" He gave a long discourse on the mission of the disciples, who became the instruments of the Holy Spirit although they were merely ignorant fishermen. He detailed the persecution suffered by the Church under Roman rulers in the early centuries of Christianity in Egypt, the era of the great martyrs. The conclusion of the lecture stirred the conscience of his listeners:

> Why do we find the state of our people so deteriorated to this extent after this ascension and honor? Isn't this due to our negligence of duty toward our religion and our loss of determination and the generosity of

experts who supervised its everyday policies, and the policy-makers who formulated it." Lucie Ryzova, *The Age of the Efendiyya: Passages to Modernity in National-Colonial Egypt*, Oxford Historical Monographs (New York: Oxford University Press, 2013), 4.

[6]Habib Girgis, Khuṭbah dīniyah fī al-diyānah al-Masīḥiyah [A Religious Lecture on the Christian Religion] (Cairo: Maṭ ba'at Miṣ r, 1897); a lecture given at the Great Coptic School, 1–2.

> our fathers? Each one of us needs to place in front of him a statue of the characteristics of such men who struggled for the truth and defended it with a death-defying defense, and to make our lofty goal to be to walk a walk worthy of our kinship to Christ. We ask God to plant in us the love of virtue and to remove from our hearts the thorns of sin, in order for us to bear fruits worthy of repentance—and he is capable of rescuing us from the pit that we are in, for he is capable of all things.[7]

Girgis described the suffering and martyrdom of mighty figures from the early centuries of the Coptic Church in order to make his listeners ashamed of the low state to which they had fallen. By means of this comparison, he hoped to inspire his listeners and move them to act to return the Church to its former glory. In Girgis' time ignorance and lack of piety affected not only illiterate laypeople, but also the clergy. For centuries, the Coptic priesthood had been a predominantly hereditary function, particularly in Upper Egypt. A priest automatically handed his church post to one of his sons, whether or not that son had any education beyond an ability to recite the Liturgy.

Girgis' many quotations from philosophers and the Fathers of the Church—Tacitus, Tertullian, Justin Martyr, Clement of Rome, and Montesquieu, to name but a few—show that he was well read. He concluded that the characteristics of a true Christian were fourfold: to be Christ-like, to be saintly and pure, to be a light to the world, and to walk according to the vocation to which one is called.

Girgis gave another important address, this time at the Ḥārat al-Saqqāyīn Church in the presence of Pope Kyrillos V, who was so impressed that he remained standing throughout the lecture. Girgis later recalled: "I cannot forget to mention here the joy that the late pope expressed, when he stood for a full hour, which was the time in which I presented my address. He blessed every word I was saying and blessed the congregation at every significant moment in my address."[8] Kyrillos' reaction revealed his hope that

[7]Habib Girgis, *Khuṭbah dīniyah fī al-diyānah al-masīḥiyah* [A Religious Lecture on the Christian Religion] (Cairo: Maṭba'at Miṣr, 1897), 23.

[8]Habib Girgis, *al-Madrasah al-Iklīrīkiyah al-Qibṭiyah al-Urthūdhuksiyah bayn al-māḍī wa-al-ḥāḍir, 1893–1938* [The Coptic Orthodox Seminary: Past and Present, 1893–1938], (Cairo: Jam'iyat al-Ta'āwun al-Iklīrīkī, 1938), 22.

preaching had returned to the pulpits of his churches, and that a new spirit had budded through this young preacher.

In the 1890s Girgis began teaching religion to children in al-Fajjālah, Cairo. He published a simple catechism that marked the beginning of his mission to establish Coptic Sunday Schools throughout Egypt. Even as a young man, Girgis was willing to devote his life to educating his fellow Copts and defending Orthodoxy. He feared that the attempts of Western missionaries to convert the Copts to Catholicism and Protestantism would ultimately lead to the disappearance of Egypt's rich Coptic tradition. This led him in 1900 to travel to Upper Egypt to give a series of lectures in churches in the dioceses of Minyā, Asyūṭ, and Qinā. His lectures on comparative theology gave a defense of Orthodox doctrine and were published in 1948 as *The Orthodox Rock*, one of Girgis' most important books.

Early in his career, Girgis was instrumental in setting up several Coptic societies. In 1900 he established *Jam'iyat Isha'āt Ḥubb Yasū'* (Society of the Rays of the Love of Jesus), later known as *Jam'iyat al-Maḥabbah* (Society of Love), which had branches in most areas of rural Egypt. In 1905 Girgis focused the work of the society in Cairo on serving Coptic youth and teaching the Christian faith to students at government schools. The society also wished to educate girls living in poverty, so it set up a small school for this purpose that operated at no cost to the students. Two other Coptic societies to which Girgis gave particular attention were *Jam'iyat al-Īmān al-Qibṭī* (Society of Coptic Faith) and *Jam'iyat aṣdiqā' al-Kitāb al-Muqaddas* (Society of the Friends of the Bible). Since there were not enough churches to serve all of Egypt's Coptic community, these and many other such societies took on the essential work of spreading the faith among Copts, establishing schools for boys and girls, building infirmaries and hospitals, and alleviating poverty. Girgis would regularly send students from the seminary to preach to those societies. In 1938 he wrote: "The Coptic societies are the strong moral spirit that works at the heart of the Coptic people. They are the incentive power working toward good and success, while their members are philanthropists that work toward the reform of the state of the people, raising them up and spreading the word of God among them."[9]

[9]Ibid., 120.

Archdeacon Habib Girgis with Pope Kyrillos V, 1913. (St Mark Coptic Orthodox Cultural Center, Dayr al Anbā Ruways.)

Many people mistakenly believed that Habib Girgis was a layman, whereas in fact he held the ecclesiastical rank of archdeacon, one step below the priesthood. He chose to lead a celibate life, and as archdeacon was fully involved in Church ministry according to his rank. However, he did not usually wear a cassock in daily life, donning liturgical vestments only during church services. Wahīb 'Aṭā'-Allāh, the late Bishop Ghrīghūriyūs and a student who graduated from the seminary in 1939, recalled Girgis saying to him: "After a ministry of thirty-five years in my Church, [there was] one lesson I did not yet discern. . . . I did not know that until now I was not reckoned among the men of the cloth."[10] Although the exact date of Habib Girgis' ordination is unknown, he was certainly an archdeacon by January 1912. He went on to earn the trust of Pope Kyrillos V, who appointed him as his personal archdeacon and disciple, and he worked closely with other patriarchs after the departure of Kyrillos V: Pope Yu'annis (John) XIX (1928–42), Pope Macari (Macarius) III (1944–45), and Pope Yusāb (Joseph) II (1946–56).

On September 14, 1918, Pope Kyrillos V appointed Girgis as dean of the Coptic Orthodox Seminary, a position he would hold for the rest of his life, dedicating his energy, ability, time, and health to the task. Not only was he an energetic administrator, he was the most prominent theology professor at that institution and, indeed, the leading Coptic theologian of his time.

In that same year Girgis was chosen to serve on the newly established General Sunday School Committee, and in 1927 became general secretary

[10]Wahīb 'Aṭā'-Allāh, "al-Arshīdyākūn Ḥabīb Jirjis fi al-majlis al-millī al-'āmm" [Archdeacon Habib Girgis in the Lay Community Council], *Majallat Madāris al-Aḥḥad* [Sunday School Magazine] 5.9–10 (November–December 1951): 34–38, at 35.

of that committee. In 1928, following the death of Pope Kyrillos V in August of the previous year, Girgis was nominated to the papacy. He was also nominated as a bishop on various occasions, but these nominations were rejected because of the fact that he was not a member of a monastic order.

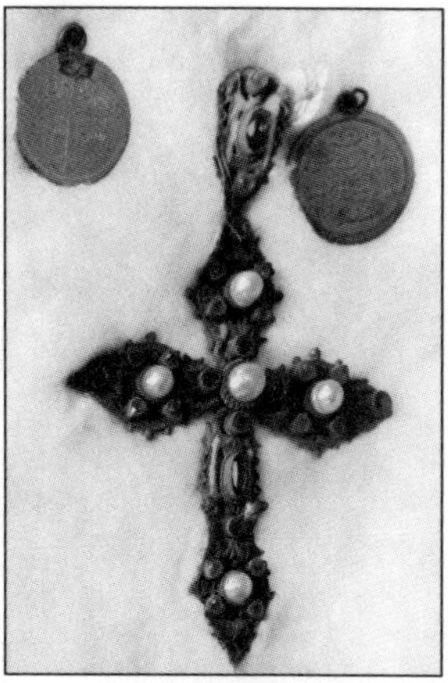

A medallion commemorating the golden jubilee of the enthronement of Pope Kyrillos V, which Girgis presented to the pope at the great celebration at Mahmashah on November 30, 1923. (St Mark Coptic Orthodox Cultural Center, Dayr al-Anbā Ruways; photograph by Hani Gadoun.)

The written word played a significant role in Girgis' life, and he began writing early in his career. He published more than thirty religious, theological, educational, and historical books, as well as numerous sermons and educational studies. His publications include a series of four books on Bible studies, books on liturgy and Church songs, lives of saints, spiritual books, curricula for Sunday Schools and youth, a book on the importance of preaching, six volumes detailing educational methods to help teachers prepare their lessons, an important book on Church reform, and another on the history and work of the Coptic Orthodox Seminary. His two great theological works, *The Orthodox Rock* and *The Seven Sacraments of the Church*, have been reprinted several times. Girgis served on the committee of four that produced a critical edition of the four Gospels, and he published a short treatise titled "Is There Divorce in Christianity?" He was chief editor of *The Vine*, a religious, moral, and historical journal that he published from 1904 to 1931 at his own expense. (Seventeen volumes were produced, although not in consecutive years because of financial constraints.) As well as publishing contemporary theological thought, *The Vine* represented the first effort in centuries to revive Coptic patristic theology and to publish literary treasures from the Patriarchal Library. The journal also served as Girgis' personal mouthpiece through which he expressed his views on a variety of topics, such as the education of women, patristics, the seminary, recent religious publications, important Church news, and the Sunday School movement, to name but a few. His position as dean of the seminary lent authority to his

The Right Reverend Arthur Foley Winnington-Ingram, KCVO, PC (1858–1946, Bishop of London 1901–39), with a Coptic delegation clothed in liturgical vestments alongside Anglican clergy. Habib Girgis was part of this Coptic delegation to Sudan in 1912 for the consecration of an Anglican Cathedral. (Yūsuf Manqariyūs, Tārīkh al-ummah al-Qibṭiyah *[History of the Coptic People in the Last Twenty Years from 1893 to 1912]. Old Cairo: s.n., 1913.)*

writings, and he invited other prominent Coptic figures to publish articles as well. One of Girgis' disciples, Fu'ād Bāsīlī, said: "If you can read the seventeen volumes of *The Vine* you will find wisdom and philosophy, deep spirituality, science and religion combined together, theology and history, legislation and law, news and comments, all written in a sober palatable style and in strong pious language."[11]

Habib Girgis was elected to the Lay Community Council (*Majlis millī*) three times—in 1933, 1938 and 1943—with the highest number of votes, demonstrating the great confidence that the Coptic community had in him. (Ill health prevented a fourth nomination.) Relations between the Church hierarchy and the council were fraught for many decades with power struggles over various aspects of Church life and law. Girgis believed that the Lay

[11]Rudolph Yanney, "Light in the Darkness: Life of Archdeacon Habib Guirguis (1876–1951)," *Coptic Church Review* 5.2 (1984): 47–52, at 50.

Habib Girgis (right) with Pope Yu'annis XIX during a trip to Ethiopia in 1930. (St Mark Coptic Orthodox Cultural Center, Dayr al-Anbā Ruways.)

Community Council should comprise members who were in harmony and agreement with each other, who understood the limits of their duties, and who would not infringe upon the authority of the clergy. He also believed that the clergy should have a voice on the council to deal in particular with questions of marital law. In 1942 he wrote: "We know that the clergy are commissioned by God Most High in the administration of the Church, and they are responsible in front of the Most High for the pastoral care of the flock. How then can they not have a say in this?"[12] Girgis believed that the marriage laws approved by the Lay Community Council in 1938 contradicted scriptural teachings, arguing: "Is it permissible that a priest should confirm a marriage contract that cannot be dissolved, and then later see the laity discharging this honorable bond that God sanctified and ordered that it not be loosened except for one reason?"[13]—that is, adultery.

[12]Habib Girgis, *al-Wasā'il al-'amaliyah lil-iṣlāḥāt al-qibṭiyah* [The Practical Means toward Coptic Reform: Hopes and Dreams], (Cairo: Self-published, 1942), 14.

[13]Ibid.

Habib Girgis (right) with Pope Yu'annis XIX during a trip to Ethiopia in 1930. (St Mark Coptic Orthodox Cultural Center, Dayr al-Anbā Ruways.)

Habib Girgis accompanied Pope Kyrillos V on his visit to Sudan in 1909, and he represented Kyrillos V there again in 1912 at the consecration of an Anglican cathedral. On that occasion the pope was unable to travel, and Girgis was chosen to represent him and deliver a lecture on his behalf. He also accompanied Pope Yu'annis XIX on a trip to Ethiopia in 1930. Because he was a respected thinker and religious and theological educator, the popes considered Girgis central to the success of their pastoral visits.

In 1941 Girgis was an important participant in the first conference for Sunday School teachers, held during the papacy of Yusāb II. He also participated in the second conference in 1949.

Girgis was a man of wide reading, well versed in French and English. (Because of Britain's governing role in Egypt at that time, English was taught in the schools and occasionally used in public life.) He had an eye for detail, as can be seen from his many meticulous reports on the Sunday Schools and the seminary in particular. A person with such a wide range of skills and talents was rare in the Coptic Church of that day, and perhaps even in Egypt in general. Girgis' combination of skill and hard work enabled him to achieve much in education, Church reform, and theology. Perhaps he spread himself too thinly, but there was no one else who could carry the banner of education and Church reform at a time when broader society was tearing at the very fabric of Coptic identity.

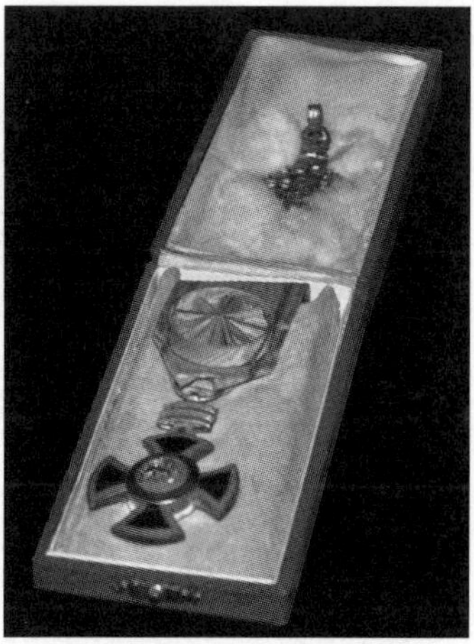

The Medal of Emperor Menelik II, presented to Habib Girgis by the Ethiopian Empress Zewditu I during the visit to Ethiopia of Pope Yu'annis XIX, in January 1930. (St Mark Coptic Orthodox Cultural Center, Dayr al-Anbā Ruways; photograph by Hani Gadoun.)

Girgis was a staunch Orthodox believer, yet he had a deep appreciation for Western methods of education. He adopted and adapted many of these methods as part of his Coptic educational reforms, including his call for the education of girls and women and for education across both urban and rural areas. Moreover, he strongly believed that no man should be ordained to the priesthood without first completing formal theological studies. This point is key to understanding Girgis' life and mission: he believed that an enlightened priesthood and an educated laity could work together in harmony to preserve Coptic faith and culture.

* * *

What type of man was Habib Girgis? Contemporaries described him as meek, simple, and kind-hearted, but he also had a sonorous voice and was an eloquent speaker. As an administrator and leader, he involved both students and colleagues in his vision, yet did so with an authoritative voice that was respected in Coptic circles. His opinions and advice were highly valued. Girgis set aside time every Saturday morning at 9 a.m. to meet with the pope; Kyrillos V even invited him to attend the meetings of the Holy Synod, the supreme ecclesiastical authority of the Coptic Orthodox Church, which was a rare honor for someone who was neither a bishop nor a metropolitan. Kyrillos said, "Invite our beloved [Habib Girgis], as he is a monk like us. Invite him that we may consult him and benefit from his advice."[14] Girgis opened his home to young people as a place of pilgrimage, so that they could

[14]Nasīm, "Rāḥilnā al-'Aẓīm" [Our Great One who has Departed], 88.

Habib Girgis' spectacles and case. (St Mark Coptic Orthodox Cultural Center, Dayr al-Anbā Ruways; photograph by Hani Gadoun.)

learn from that wise teacher. Although he preferred to retire early, he would spend time in the evening talking with his disciples for their benefit. Girgis was both fair and compassionate in his dealings with people, and never bore a grudge toward those (and there were some) who resisted his efforts at educational reform.

An example of Girgis' sense of fairness concerns two preachers who ministered together. One of this pair published three derogatory articles

His Grace Bishop Mārtīrūs (General Bishop, Cairo), left, and the author, His Grace Bishop Suriel (Bishop of Melbourne, Australia), preparing to uncover the relics of St Habib Girgis on January 15, 2014. (Photograph by Victor Farag.)

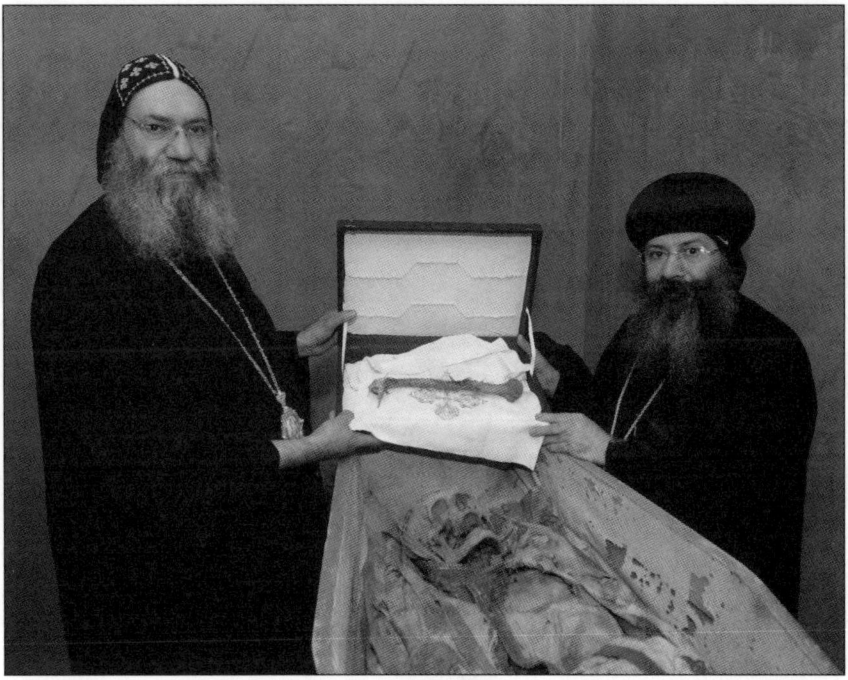

The author, His Grace Bishop Suriel (Bishop of Melbourne, Australia), left, receiving part of the relics of St Habib Girgis from His Grace Bishop Mārtīrūs (General Bishop, Cairo) in Cairo on January 15, 2014. (Photograph by Victor Farag.)

against Girgis. A student of Girgis, Fu'ād Bāsīlī (Father Boulos Bāsīlī) wrote an article in response. However, Girgis tore it up and refused to let it appear in print, saying to Bāsīlī, "Didn't you preach about St Paul's words that say, 'If your enemy hungers, feed him, if he thirsts, give him a drink; for in so doing you will heap coals of fire on his head'?" (Rom 12.20) The second preacher then came to ask Girgis for a raise in his salary; Girgis' response was that both preachers should receive the same raise. When the preacher who had attacked Girgis heard of Girgis' actions toward him, he was embarrassed and full of remorse, and came to beg Girgis' forgiveness.[15]

The death of Habib Girgis on the evening of Wednesday, August 21, 1951, deeply affected both Copts and Muslims. The Church had lost one

[15]Father Boulos Bāsīlī, "My Years with Habib Girgis," *Watani International* 43.2062 (2001): 3.

of its most revered sons—an eloquent teacher, a visionary, an educational pioneer, and a loyal servant of the Coptic Orthodox Church. His contributions to the Church had long been noted. On June 20, 2013, his pious life was officially recognized when the Coptic Orthodox Holy Synod canonized Archdeacon Habib Girgis as a saint of the Church.[16]

The author, His Grace Bishop Suriel (Bishop of Melbourne, Australia) holding part of the relics of St Habib Girgis, which he received on January 15, 2014. The relics arrived in Melbourne on July 8, 2014. (Photograph by Victor Farag.)

[16]The relics of Habib Girgis had been discovered on January 18, 1994, by Father Thī'udusyūs al-Suryānī. On January 1, 2014, they were translated (without much fanfare, due to circumstances in Egypt) back to the site of the Coptic Orthodox Seminary in Cairo, in preparation for the official celebration later that year, when they would be brought to their final resting place in the Virgin Mary Church in Mahmashah. On January 15, 2014, His Grace Bishop Mārtīrūs, General Bishop for the Region to the East of the Railway, Cairo, presented some of the relics to the Coptic Bishop of Melbourne, Australia, to be translated to Melbourne—the only place outside of Cairo to be so honored. These relics included the complete upper right arm bone (humerus), the handkerchief that had been wrapped around the head, an embroidered cross decorated with silver thread, the glove from the right hand, and a section of the liturgical vestment.

CHAPTER TWO

A Time of Doubts and Corrupting Confusions: Historical Background to the Life of Habib Girgis

THE COPTIC ORTHODOX CHURCH is one of the oldest churches in the world.[1] Mark the Apostle, author of the earliest Gospel, founded the church when he visited Egypt around AD 48, converting many to the new faith. He became the first pope of Alexandria and is believed by the Copts to have founded the Catechetical School in Alexandria. This great center of early Christian theological thought also taught secular subjects such as science, mathematics, literature, and the arts. Catechism—the commonly accepted question-and-answer method of teaching religious tenets to people preparing for baptism, communion, or confirmation—began here. Over the centuries many great scholars such as St Jerome (*c.* 347–420) visited Alexandria's school to meet with its teachers and exchange ideas.

The practice of pious men and women removing themselves from general society to concentrate on their relationship with God began with

[1]Secondary sources used in writing this chapter include, in particular: J. Heyworth-Dunne, *An Introduction to the History of Education in Modern Egypt* (London: Luzac, 1938); Majdī Jirjis and Nelly van Doorn-Harder, *The Emergence of the Modern Coptic Papacy: The Egyptian Church and its Leadership from the Ottoman Period to the Present,* The Popes of Egypt 3 (Cairo: American University in Cairo Press, 2011); Afaf Lutfi al-Sayyid Marsot, *Egypt in the Reign of Muhammad Ali* (Cambridge: Cambridge University Press, 1984); Timothy Mitchell, *Colonising Egypt* (Berkeley: University of California Press, 1991); Sulaymān Nasīm, *al-Aqbāṭ wa-al-ta'līm fī Miṣr al-ḥadīthah* [Copts and Education in Modern Egypt], Bishop Ghrīghūriyūs and 'Azīz Sūryāl 'Aṭiyah eds (Cairo: Manshūrāt Usqufiyat al-Dirāsāt al-'Ulyā al-Lāhūtiyah wa-al-Thaqāfah al-Qibṭiyah wa-al-Baḥth al-'Ilmī, 1983); Paul D. Sedra, *From Mission to Modernity: Evangelicals, Reformers and Education in Nineteenth Century Egypt* (London: I.B. Tauris, 2011); Samir Menas Seikaly, "Coptic Communal Reform: 1860–1914," *Middle Eastern Studies* 6.3 (January 1970): 247–75; Joseph S. Szyliowicz, *Education and Modernization in the Middle East* (Ithaca, NY: Cornell University Press, 1973).

Coptic hermits in the Egyptian desert. The first such hermit was St Anthony (*c.* 251–356 AD), who lived in solitude in a cave for forty years. Christian monasticism thrived in Egypt. Visitors to Egypt from other parts of the eastern and western provinces of the Roman Empire observed the practice of monasticism and spread it throughout Christendom. Today, there are Coptic monasteries and convents in Egypt, the United States, Australia, and Europe.

The word "Copt" comes from the Greek word *Aigyptos*, meaning Egyptian. Coptic script combines Greek letters and Egyptian characters. The Coptic language is descended from the language used in the days of the pharaohs. While no longer spoken in everyday life, it is still used in the Liturgy along with Arabic, in the case of countries outside Egypt, and other local languages.

The Coptic Church is one of the Oriental Orthodox churches, alongside the Ethiopian Orthodox Tewahedo Church, the Syrian Orthodox Church of Antioch, the Jacobite Syrian Christian Church, the Malankara Orthodox Syrian Church, the Eritrean Orthodox Tewahedo Church, and the Armenian Apostolic Church. As the main Christian church in Egypt, it has between fifteen and eighteen million members, plus another million members around the world. The Copts are the largest Christian minority of any country in the Middle East, making up between eight and ten percent of Egypt's population.[2] As a minority, Copts have long suffered discrimination both at work and in the political sphere. Few Copts have a role in Egyptian government administration, although there have been some improvements in recent years.

The Pope of Alexandria, who is presently based in Cairo, leads the Coptic Church. He heads the Holy Synod, which is made up of the metropolitans, bishops, abbots, and deputies of the Alexandrian patriarchate.

* * *

Oral learning and popular education are as ancient as the Coptic Church itself. Catechumens (those receiving instruction in the basic doctrines before admission to communicant membership) first began to learn about

[2] *Fanack Chronicle of the Middle East & North Africa:* Egypt: Population, <https://chronicle.fanack.com/egypt/population/>, accessed April 15, 2016.

their new faith in an indirect way, through the Divine Liturgy. Popular education took place by means of the iconography, sacraments and rites, pilgrimages, the feasts and festivals of the saints, and the sacred symbols found throughout Coptic Church life. People also learned through storytelling and music, as well as through the master-and-disciple relationship in Egyptian monasticism. Even listening to Christian hymns had a profound effect on people's spirituality—it was not only the words that educated, but the music too.

These types of popular education were significant in transforming, enlightening, and educating individuals from every walk of life. They served as a form of catechesis for the oppressed and uneducated while touching young and old, rich and poor, simple and wise alike. Furthermore, oral learning meant that catechesis was not limited to those enrolled in formal education, nor to a particular time frame or age group. People of varying ages, life experiences, and educational backgrounds took part in oral and popular education as a continual learning process. As human beings, it is in our nature to learn from our surroundings and collective experiences—even from something as simple as an ant! The whole community educates the whole community, and even non-religious subjects can lead a person to religious experiences.

Following the Arab Islamic conquest of Egypt in AD 641, the Coptic Church kept its catechetical heritage alive in Egypt's native churches and monasteries. In the Nile Valley, this educational tradition persisted in the vicinity of churches as well as in more modest institutions, the equivalent of the medieval scriptoria or writing places. During the late Middle Ages a system of learning called *kuttāb* emerged in Egypt. Practiced in both Christian and Muslim communities, it continued into the nineteenth century. Bishops, priests, and wealthy families organized the *kuttāb* for the Coptic villages and monasteries. The system relied heavily on rote learning, memorization, and popular education. Coptic children learned geometry, arithmetic, religion, good manners, and the reading and writing of Arabic and Coptic. They also had to commit to memory various Scriptures, such as the psalms and St Paul's epistles. Typically, a teacher or cantor played a significant role in enrolling and teaching the students. Often a blind teacher (*'arīf*, pl. *'urfān*) delivered basic level instruction either in the church courtyard or, in the case of girls, in private homes. However, literacy rates among women remained low since many families did not allow females to be educated.

Modernization in Western Europe, which began with the Renaissance, led to a dislocation of values that proved unsettling to the cultures of the Middle East. However, as time went on the region embraced such change and the transformation of ancient societal customs, although to varying degrees and with mixed results. Modernization proceeded at faster or slower rates and by different means in different countries, dependent largely on the degree of interaction with the West.

Education was crucial to modernization in the Middle East. Governments considered education to be a prime catalyst for economic growth, social development, and building the modern nation-state. Modern schools played a fundamental role in spreading fresh ideas and unifying principles, which in turn placed pressure for change on many institutions. In several Middle Eastern societies, the reformers and modernizers who were educated at such schools met with resistance from the uneducated population and the institutionally entrenched personnel, who preferred to maintain the status quo. This was certainly the case in Egypt. Habib Girgis was one of those reformers who received his early education in such a school, albeit one less advanced than some Western missionary schools operating in Egypt at the time.

To a significant extent, education in the Middle East enabled traditional societies to evolve into nations that could both generate and cope with continuous change. Other factors that served either to promote or hinder modernization in these feudal societies were politics and economics.

When Napoleon invaded Egypt in 1798 in an effort to protect French trade interests and obstruct Britain's maritime access to India, the Ottomans still officially governed the province from Istanbul, although the Mamlūk beys (an elite military caste) were effectively in control of Egypt. The French occupation lasted only three years, but it highlighted the vulnerability of Egypt and the ruling Ottoman Empire, while demonstrating the West's military, technological, and administrative superiority. The occupation's effects on Egyptian life included reforms in the administrative and judicial systems. France's advocacy of republican government and the ideals of liberty, equality, and fraternity influenced the Egyptian mindset ever since. While the *ulamā* (the literate and professional elite of Egypt's cities) rejected these new Western notions, perceiving them as a threat to their Islamic values, others were more receptive. This led to the emergence of new leaders who were open to further Westernization, often with a view to bolstering their own authority.

The degree to which the French occupation influenced education in Egypt is a matter for debate. Some historians argue that the French occupiers built schools in Egypt only for the purpose of educating their own children, leaving the Egyptians to their own devices. However, Egyptian religious schools experienced disruption during the occupation, as many scholars who taught there either left Cairo or were arrested or executed by the French.

The Western presence did open the way for the modernization of intellectual pursuits, but only to a degree. The slow pace of progress can be attributed to religious differences that bred suspicion, along with language barriers that may have resulted in misunderstandings.

After the British and Ottomans forced the French to withdraw in 1801, there was a power vacuum in Egypt. Into this vacuum stepped Muḥammad 'Alī Pasha, who in 1805 became governor and self-declared khedive of Egypt and Sudan. Born in Albania in 1770, Muḥammad 'Alī, who came from lowly stock, had earned a military reputation among the Ottoman authorities. He was appointed second-in-command in the campaign against the French before eventually seizing power.

An astute politician who turned to force only as a final resort, Muḥammad 'Alī, unlike his predecessors, was strongly influenced by Western attitudes and had a modern vision for the future of Egypt as a nation-state. He was not a nationalist in the modern sense but is still regarded as the founder of modern Egypt because of the dramatic reforms he instituted in the military, economic, bureaucratic, educational, and cultural spheres. In the educational domain, his main aim was not to educate the masses but rather to form a powerful, educated military bureaucracy through which he would gain control over Egypt and neighboring regions. In 1809, as part of his initial efforts, he sent students to study in Europe. Then, in 1816, he established the first modern Egyptian school, where foreign languages were taught alongside reading, writing, military skills, and the Qur'ān. He then opened

Muḥammad ʻAlī Pasha, who in 1805 became governor and self-declared khedive of Egypt and Sudan. (Bibliotheca Alexandrina's Memory of Modern Egypt Digital Archive, available from Wikipedia Commons, https://commons.wikimedia.org/wiki/File:ModernEgypt,_Muhammad_Ali_by_Auguste_Couder,_BAP_17996.jpg. Accessed January 31, 2017.)

specialized military schools with the aim of creating a modern cavalry, infantry, artillery, and navy. Muḥammad ʻAlī also saw the need to educate personnel to provide the military with auxiliary services, so between 1827 and 1834 he established schools for medicine, pharmacology, veterinary medicine, engineering, signal training, and music (for the training of buglers and trumpeters).

Muḥammad ʻAlī also wanted a strong, professional civil service in Egypt that would pledge total loyalty to him. This particular ambition was pursued to the great detriment of the Copts, who until this time had played a major role in government administration. Muḥammad ʻAlī replaced Coptic bureaucrats with his own Muslim followers, trained in the administrative schools that he had established. He created few opportunities for Copts to study at his schools, while at the same time preventing them from being educated in the West.

The Copts did not remain passive in the face of this discrimination, but sought means to educate their children and equip them for a brighter future and better employment. They established their own private schools excelling in fields such as surveying and accounting, for which the Copts had been renowned since the Middle Ages. These schools were operated either by the Church or by benevolent societies and wealthy Coptic families who endowed land for the purpose.

Muḥammad Alī also set up schools of administration, agriculture, and industry to provide the wider population with skills in these important economic areas. In the course of implementing this network of technical schools, he began to appreciate some of the difficulties and complexities of a modern educational system and the importance of proper planning, particularly in a traditional society such as Egypt. For instance, he was obliged to employ European teachers and translators, but these outsiders did not know Arabic. Besides being an expensive and ineffective way to educate, his system did not produce wholehearted support of his political regime; Muḥammad Alī could never be certain of these teachers' political allegiances. To overcome this, he began sending Egyptians to Europe to be trained as teachers. Their numbers increased until by 1849 over three hundred Egyptians were studying in Europe. Not one of them, however, was a Copt.

Muḥammad 'Alī's next challenge was to recruit more candidates who might benefit from all this modern education in order to replace the cohorts of students coming from the traditional schools that he shunned. So he established new elementary schools, enticing students by offering incentives such as clothing, food, lodging, and financial aid. This was the magic formula that had attracted students to his colleges and, as a consequence, changed the community's attitude toward modern schools significantly. College graduates were guaranteed good employment and salaries, as well as great respect in Egyptian society.

The third major obstacle that Muḥammad 'Alī had to surmount was the lack of educational resources in the Arabic language. To overcome this, he hired translators and eventually established a school for the purpose of translating European educational material. Over a period of thirteen years more than two thousand books were translated—quite an achievement! These translations not only served as teaching resources in schools but also introduced new ideas into the country more broadly, helping to foster the growth of a national consciousness.

Despite these significant achievements, Muḥammad 'Alī's educational plan was haphazard and disjointed in its execution. In 1834, a commission formed to investigate the dire state of the education system recommended a total restructuring and reorganization. For reasons that remain unclear, Muḥammad 'Alī did not adopt its findings and little was done to implement the suggested changes during his reign. Eventually, this inaction led to a situation where Egypt's traditional and modern systems of education ran in parallel, each focusing on different demographics and espousing different values. This situation perpetuated the gap between Egypt's elite and the masses, and also caused a division in the intellectual class itself between graduates of the country's traditional religious schools, the *kuttāb*, and those from the modern institutions.

Nevertheless, Muḥammad 'Alī did succeed in his aim of transforming the nation's social core. He marginalized the Copts, integrated Turco-Circassians into Egyptian society, and used modern education to provide native Egyptians, for the first time, with a mobility that would enable them to secure positions of power and influence. During his reign Western missionaries started to arrive in Egypt in larger numbers. Their mission work took many forms, but a shared aim was to "purify" the Copts from their supposedly archaic beliefs and so-called superstitions, and to convert some of them through missionary schools. Some missionaries even proposed to convert the whole race to Catholicism or Protestantism. This type of proselytism, which sought to take advantage of a struggling Church under attack from all sides, continued well into the twentieth century.

The Church Missionary Society (CMS), a British Protestant evangelistic society, arrived in Egypt in the mid-1820s. Its members began immediately to distribute religious publications—particularly Arabic tracts and the Holy Scriptures—printed at the press the society had set up in Malta. The main target for conversion was the Copts. The CMS established an educational seminary in Cairo in 1843, ostensibly to train candidates for the Coptic priesthood, but with the ultimate aim of "diffusing throughout the Coptic Church such a measure of scriptural truth, that, by means of Copts themselves, it (the Coptic Church) may eventually be purified from the errors that so painfully characterize it."[3] Unfortunately, until the time of Habib Girgis the Coptic Church had no articulate scholars who could respond to such attacks on its faith and doctrines. Nevertheless, the CMS seminary failed, closing its doors in 1848. The Reverend John Lieder, who had conceived the project, claimed that its closure was caused by the fact that "a youth enlightened by an education founded on the Word of God could not enter the service of a deeply fallen Church."[4] In reality, however, the closure was

[3]Seikaly, "Coptic Communal Reform: 1860–1914," 247.

[4]John Lieder, letter published in *The Missionary Register* (1843), 330, quoted in Seikaly, "Coptic Communal Reform," 247.

caused by the Coptic clergy's deep suspicion of this Protestant-inspired institution, despite their pope's apparent approval of it.

The most important of the foreign missionary schools established in Egypt at this time were those founded by Lieder and, from 1854, by the American Presbyterian Mission, which attracted mostly students from lower-class Coptic families. These missionaries viewed with disdain the role of the *kuttābs* and their traditional method of oral learning led by blind schoolmasters. They also ignored the importance of popular education and saw the written word as the only way to enlightenment. Lieder was convinced that the solution was to provide textbooks, part of a broader move by nineteenth-century educationalists in Egypt to eliminate a culture in which the speakers of words, rather than the writers of texts, were the bearers of authority. For this reason, Western missionaries attempted to replace the traditional Egyptian style of education with the formal classroom pedagogy to which they were accustomed. This destruction of the oral culture and its attendant authority was an important step in the efforts to control native Egyptians' morality and behavior—an essential element of the modern state's exertion of control over its subjects.

To some extent the Coptic Church followed suit, accepting this Western ideology and reforming itself accordingly. While oral learning and popular education had been useful in a feudal society, they could no longer be relied upon as the only means of education in the modern era. The Copts, including their clergy, were generally poorly educated, a situation that had led to moral decline and even corruption. For instance, one "Copt of a liberal as well as an intelligent mind" was reported in the 1850s as painting a very bleak picture of his own people:

> He avows them to be generally ignorant, deceitful, faithless, and abandoned to the pursuit of worldly gain, and to indulgence in sensual pleasures; he declares the Patriarch to be a tyrant, and a suborner of false witnesses; and assures me that the priests and monks in Cairo are seen every evening begging, and asking the loan of money, which they never repay, at the houses of their parishioners and other acquaintances, and procuring brandy, if possible, wherever they call.[5]

[5]Edward William Lane, *An Account of the Manners and Customs of the Modern Egyptians*, reprint from 5th ed. (Cairo: The American University in Cairo Press, 1860), 529.

It is true that the Coptic community was in relatively poor shape at this time. Most members of the clergy were badly educated and neglected their religious duties. Drawn from the lower classes of society, they were dependent for their income upon charity rather than a fixed salary, leading many to use church property for personal gain. Some who held both religious and secular positions misused their authority, taking bribes, for example, in their dispensing of justice and charging fees to expedite particular cases.

However, while the harsh assessment quoted above may have been justified in the case of some individuals, it should not have been generalized to apply to all Coptic clergy and parishioners. This type of demonization mainly served the purpose of the missionaries by demonstrating that the fallen Coptic race was truly in need of salvation. Such exaggerated accounts pervaded the mission journals and reports of the day, and probably helped convince those supporting the missions from overseas of the need to continue funding the Egyptian evangelization project. This applied not only to British missionaries but also to the Americans. The rank-and-file American churchgoers who donated money to keep the missions going read these Christian journals along with travelogues, storybooks, and other popular literature about the Middle East. Overzealous missionaries used the stereotypes they conveyed to supporters back home in order to inflate the importance and success of mission work and to keep that money flowing.

For the Copts, there were two struggles for power, one external and one internal. The external power struggle was between the Coptic Church and the Western missionaries, who were far more advanced in their education. The efforts of American Presbyterians, Roman Catholics, and British Anglican missionaries were resented and resisted by Coptic Orthodox leaders as a challenge to their authority. Meanwhile, there was continuous internal struggle between the Coptic laity and Church hierarchy.

The missionaries' ultimate goal was to colonize the Egyptian mind. The missionaries believed that in order for the Copts to convert to an "unadulterated" Christianity, they had to conform to an evangelical mindset rooted in a particular interpretation of the Scriptures. The criteria for such a mindset were industry and discipline. This is where education came into the equation. Reverend Lieder, for example, saw his role as one of "enlightening" the Coptic community through subtle influence via the schools, rather than aggressive proselytizing. For Lieder, Christianity *was* industry, discipline, and order; the spiritual and cultural aspects of conversion were inseparable. Mission schools were thus meant to serve as catalysts for the widespread cultural conversion that Lieder anticipated, namely, the colonization of the Coptic Orthodox Church and community. The missionaries supplemented their educational work with social services that were readily accepted by a community that had suffered centuries of material deprivation as well as political and social injustice. Protestant missionaries also set up the first Sunday Schools in Egypt, which they called Sabbath Schools.

Nevertheless, the missionaries' attempts to convert significant numbers of Egyptians to Protestantism failed. Despite their sufferings and persecutions, the Copts largely resisted conversion, as did the Muslim masses. That said, the missionaries' attempts did stir the Copts and awakened in them a spirit of inquiry and an impulse to reform. The missionaries were fellow Christians who spoke Arabic and worked hard to spread the gospel. Lieder and his schools had an effect, for example, on the curriculum of the Great Coptic School later established by Kyrillos IV. That school employed at least one former student of a mission school, and Lieder, who lived close by the seminary, may have visited frequently.

* * *

Neither of the two leaders of Egypt who succeeded Muḥammad 'Alī—'Abbās I, who reigned 1848–54, followed by Sa'īd I (1854–63)—continued down the path chosen by Muḥammad 'Alī. On the contrary, 'Abbās chose to consolidate by closing down many of the schools his predecessor had established, particularly the military ones, and opening in 1849 a single large school for elite students. This Madrasat al-Mafrūzah ("school for the chosen") combined into one institution a primary, a preparatory, and a military school. Muḥammad 'Alī's naval and infantry schools, which had fallen into a state of disorganization, were shut down. In 1851 'Abbās did away with the school of languages and accountancy, transferring most of its work to the new preparatory school at the Madrasat al-Mafrūzah. He retained the successful engineering school, which had more than two hundred students, and the medical school with more than one hundred and twenty. Fortunately,

'Abbās did not stand in the way of educational reform in the Coptic Church and in 1854 supported the accession of Kyrillos IV to the papal throne.

For his part Khedive Sa'īd I cared little for education, purportedly saying that an ignorant nation was easier to govern than an educated one. He has been described by some historians as careless, impetuous, extravagant, and unstable. During his reign public education regressed. The notable exceptions were the private civil schools set up by Pope Kyrillos IV, and some of the mission schools.

The mammoth task of educational and social reform among the Copts was indeed left to the enterprising and enlightened Pope Kyrillos IV, later dubbed the "father of reform." He concentrated his efforts on educating the priests and deacons; establishing Coptic schools, including some for girls; and founding a printing press to encourage reading and writing among the faithful. These reforms were not propagated systematically according to some manifesto or agenda, but rather promoted in response to the degraded state into which the Copts, and especially their clergy, had sunk, and as a result of Kyrillos' observations of the activities and achievements of Western missionaries.

To rescue his community from decline, Kyrillos IV first turned his attention to the clergy of Cairo and its environs. He understood that the Church, if it were to move into the modern age, needed an enlightened leadership of bishops and priests to serve as role models for the community. Only then could they lead the way by teaching the faith and raising the community's moral standards.

Toward this end, he established and personally supervised mandatory weekly classes for priests in theology and religious readings. Kyrillos also cared for the young deacons, from whose ranks priests were recruited. He provided them with suitable clothing, found the best cantors to educate them in the hymns of the Church, and helped educate them in the Coptic language and Orthodox doctrine.

Kyrillos' most important legacy was the establishment of the Great Coptic School, located next to the patriarchal Cathedral of St Mark that he had built in the al-Azbakiyyah district of Cairo. Founded in 1853, the school officially opened its doors in 1855 as an elementary school, to which secondary education was later added. The first Coptic school to function on sound pedagogical lines, it employed both local and foreign teachers and taught European languages alongside Arabic and Coptic. This school was to form a generation of lay elites before missionary and state schools made formal education widely available to the Copts. One of its graduates would be Habib Girgis.

Kyrillos also established three other schools: one for boys, in the mostly Coptic suburb of Harit al-Saq'in, and two for girls. These girls' schools, among the first of their kind in Egypt, were an important development in Coptic social reform. Having come to appreciate the importance of education for women partly as a result of observing the work of Western missionaries, Kyrillos instructed the principals of the girls' schools to visit Coptic families and urge them to enroll their daughters. Although the schools met with resistance from some quarters, for the first time in the history of modern Egypt significant attention was being paid to female education.

Kyrillos' reforms certainly encountered a hostile reception from the cantors and teachers who worked in the traditional *kuttāb* system of elementary schools. They feared losing their jobs and livelihoods, although Kyrillos appeased them somewhat by granting them nominal positions in his new schools.

Kyrillos' schools were funded by land endowed to the patriarchate by Khedive Sa'īd, who was impressed by Kyrillos' achievements. His schools taught the Coptic language for the first time in centuries, a matter of particular symbolic importance to the Coptic community's sense of Egyptian identity. The schools employed modern pedagogical methods and even attracted Muslim students. The boys' schools produced some particularly fine graduates, many of whom went on to play significant roles in the life of the Church and in wider Egyptian society. This higher level of education enabled many Copts to assume positions in the transport and postal services, banks, and other new institutions that were emerging as a result of Egypt's increasing engagement with Europe.

Kyrillos IV foresaw that publishing would be an important means of disseminating knowledge in Egypt. In 1859 he purchased a printing press from Austria and had it installed as the first non-government press in Egypt. When the machine arrived at the train station, Kyrillos organized a great celebration and a procession led by clergy and deacons that carried the

Pope Demetrius II of Alexandria (1862–70) who resisted the incursions of the American missionaries particularly in Upper Egypt. (Wikipedia Commons, https://commons.wikimedia.org/wiki/File:Pope_Demetrius_II.jpg. Accessed January 31, 2017.)

press from the station to the Patriarchate. Kyrillos said that if he had been in Cairo at the time he would have danced in front of the press, just as David the prophet had danced before the Ark of the Covenant—so strong was his conviction that printing could transform the lives of his parishioners. He sent four Copts to the government press offices to learn the art of printing and publishing, but unfortunately the press was not put into action until after his death.

Although these achievements of Kyrillos were significant, the Copts still suffered under Sa'īd's rule. Any attempt at reform, in particular, was met with governmental resistance. Kyrillos attempted to negotiate with Sa'īd to enable the Copts to progress in the bureaucracy, to participate in local councils, and to attain positions of command in the army. He also asked that Copts be allowed to enroll in the military, engineering, and medical schools. Sa'īd remained aloof until Kyrillos' sudden death at the age of just forty-five (some say he was assassinated by poisoning), when these matters were dropped.

Kyrillos IV awakened the Church from its slumber and lit a flame in the hearts of its clergy and people. But his death meant the elimination of the driving force behind the reform movement. It remained to be seen whether the Church would take up the challenge that Kyrillos had extended, or revert to its previous lethargy.

* * *

From this time onward, both the Church and the cause of Coptic educational reform suffered significant setbacks. Under Pope Demetrius II (1862–70), inactivity again became the norm. Demetrius was elected more on the basis of his piety than out of a desire for reform; his main preoccupation was resisting the incursions of the American missionaries. He was accused of burning foreign Bibles, having missionaries beaten by government soldiers, excommunicating Copts thought to have Protestant sympathies, and imprisoning or threatening anyone of whom he disapproved. Historians disagree over whether Demetrius' aim was to resist reform outright or simply to regain control over the reform process by eliminating missionary influence in the Coptic communities. His patriarchal bull of 1867 warned his flock sternly against sending children to the Western mission schools in Asyūṭ.

> There are to be found two things which are displeasing, nay exceedingly grievous, and depressing, and heart-rending. The first of these is the reception by some of you of the doctrines of those opposers who follow the Protestants, sometimes by receiving and reading their books, and sometimes by hearkening to their words, and being made to doubt by them and follow them. The second, that it has not sufficed that the adults have looked upon these poisons, but with your own hands you have cast your little ones into their deadly snares, since one gives over his boy to their school, and another his daughter unto them, that they may cause them to drink from their childhood the milk of error. . . . Therefore, O my children! My heart is not at peace, nor are my joys full since the fullness of joy is, that I hear, as said the Apostle John, that my children walk in the truth, not in doubts and corrupting confusions.[6]

Demetrius II encouraged his flock in Upper Egypt to send its children to a new Coptic school that he established for the purpose of protecting them from proselytism. He threatened his parishioners with excommunication if they sent their children to the missionary schools. While this approach may appear harsh, he believed that this question threatened the very community and its identity. Unfortunately, the quality of education at the new

[6]His Holiness Pope Demetrius II, "Patriarchal Bull, Issued by the Patriarch of the Copts Against Protestantism," trans. Gulian Lansing, *The Evangelical Repository and United Presbyterian Review* 6.6 (1867): 353–58 (see Appendix 4 in the present volume for full text).

Hegumen Fīlūthā'us (Philotheos) Ibrāhīm Baghdādī (1837–1904). Baghdādī travelled throughout Egypt, delivering powerful sermons to the Copts on the richness of their Orthodox faith and heritage. (Girgis, The Coptic Orthodox Seminary.*)*

Coptic school was far lower than that of the missionary schools to which some Copts had been attracted.

It was during the papacy of Demetrius II that Father Fīlūthā'us (Philotheos) Ibrāhīm Baghdādī (1837–1904), dean of St Mark's Cathedral and the man who would have a powerful influence on the young Habib Girgis, became well known for powerful sermons and public expositions that could last for up to three hours. Traveling throughout Egypt, he organized a Coptic version of the revival meeting. In 1883, for instance, he led forty-five days and nights of religious celebration in Asyūṭ, where the churches were filled to overflowing. Baghdādī strengthened Coptic conviction by revealing to the people the richness of their own faith and a heritage far surpassing anything offered by the Western churches.

Egyptian public opinion changed dramatically during the reign of Khedive Ismā'īl I (1867–69), as modern education once again flourished across the nation. Ismā'īl reactivated the education bureaucracy and began to establish primary and secondary schools. He reorganized the military as a permanent force of men who were compelled to live together as a distinct community perpetually in training, even when not involved in any conflict. A similar level of discipline and regulation was implemented in the government schools, leading to a regime of confinement, surveillance, and constraint of the students. Students were supervised at all times, required to wear uniforms, and follow rules controlling every aspect of their daily lives: discipline, physical fitness, curriculum, exams, clothing, rations, teaching staff, administration, and inspections.

In 1867 the government decreed the end of the *kuttābs* and forced their integration into the modern school system. At the same time it formally recognized education at the Coptic schools set up by Kyrillos IV, permitting students to take public examinations on a par with government school students. These reforms were among the many innovations of the new minister of education, ʿAlī Mubārak (1823–1893). Educated in France, Mubārak was a powerful and highly accomplished bureaucrat, engineer, historian, and teacher who formally centralized Egyptian education and organized it into three levels: elementary, secondary, and higher. He set up the education ministry to operate from a palace on Darb al-Gamamiz, in the center of the nation's recently reconstructed capital, and located the new government preparatory and engineering schools nearby. He then opened schools of administration and languages, surveying and accounting, ancient Egyptian language, and drawing, followed by an infirmary, a royal library, an amphitheater for public lectures and exams, and a teacher training school. Placing schools at the center of the city heralded a new politics of the modern state. If the educational goal of his predecessor, Muḥammad ʿAlī, had been to produce a professional and loyal army, Mubārak's aim was to mold the individual citizen. New laws governed every aspect of school life down to the student uniforms, classroom layout, and furniture; learning had suddenly become an active and extensive concern of the state.

ʿAlī Mubārak (1823–1893), Minister of Education - who formally centralized Egyptian education. (Wikipedia Commons, https://en.wikipedia.org/w/index.php?title=File:Ali_Mubarak.jpg. Accessed January 31, 2017.)

Girgis in his turn would seek to reform religious education by centralizing, standardizing, and imposing Western ideals of industry, discipline, and order. Girgis' hub was not to be a palace, however, but the Coptic seminary. Here he would not only train future priests, monks, and cantors but also manage massive Sunday School and youth club movements, send preachers into villages across Egypt, and publish and distribute religious texts, including his own influential periodical *The Vine*. Indeed, during Girgis' long tenure as dean, the Coptic Orthodox Seminary would become the center from which emanated all theological and religious education in the Coptic Orthodox Church.

Evangelical missionaries continued their role in the establishment of modern education in Egypt (and elsewhere in the colonized world). During the reign of Muḥammad ʻAlī, some 10,000 Europeans lived in Egypt. By 1865 the figure exceeded 80,000. This strong Western presence meant that Cairo and Alexandria felt very much like European cities. In the mid-nineteenth century, schools sponsored by French missionaries (and, later, by British, German, and American missionary groups) were erected alongside non-denominational schools sponsored by French citizens residing in Egypt. Minority schools were also run by the Greek, Jewish, and Armenian communities. The Jewish schools were of a particularly high caliber, producing graduates who would later take up posts in government service. The number of such schools grew from fifty-nine in 1863 to 146 in 1878, catering to 12,539 students.

Khedive Ismāʻīl's notable achievements across Egypt would eventually lead the nation into massive financial debt, resulting in Britain increasing its control over the country. In 1881, the British controller-general in Egypt cut spending on education by eliminating fellowships and increasing tuition fees. Now only the upper class could afford a modern education; the controller-general's view was that education should be a private rather than a governmental responsibility. By 1892, seventy-three percent of students were paying all their own expenses. While such cost-cutting was ostensibly imposed to help restore Egypt's financial stability, the British may have had another motive: they were nervous that modern education might give rise to a nationalist, anti-British elite that would threaten British rule, as would happen in India.

Accordingly, in the years after Muḥammad 'Alī, schools emphasized rote learning. Any attempt to cultivate intelligence, sensitivity, or political awareness among students was ruthlessly quashed. As Egypt came to be largely governed by Britain, teaching was delivered in English, a language to which most students had no exposure outside the classroom. Teachers were not properly trained and made little effort to make the learning experience a fruitful one. Rather, they insisted on obedience, discipline, and memorization of the curriculum. It is important to note that education in Egypt did not become a discretely defined process, with set instructions and self-discipline, until the nineteenth century. Before this time there was no distinct location nor institution dedicated to teaching, nor a body of adults for whom teaching was a profession, and no word for "education" in the Arabic language. The *kuttāb* system offered a relatively informal way to convey basic knowledge to the community and lacked a tightly organized educational system and bureaucracy.

The inspectors and organizers of the new education system began to write books and manuals for purpose of explaining the new practices. One such example, written in 1872 by Rifā'a al-Ṭahṭāwī, an Egyptian writer, teacher, and translator, was entitled *al-Murshid al-amīn lil-banāt wa-al-banīn* [A Guidebook for Boys and Girls] and explained the need for the new educational practices "in terms of human nature."

During the papacy of Kyrillos V (1874–1927—the longest reigning Coptic pope), Coptic schools continued to operate with papal support. After the departure of Demetrius II, a group of Copts lobbied for the formation of a Lay Community Council (*Majlis millī*). Chaired by the pope and composed of twelve members, both laity and clergy, plus twelve elected adjuncts, its role was to work toward communal reform and proper administration of the community's needs.

At first Kyrillos V worked closely with the new Lay Community Council, establishing a girls' school and a short-lived Clerical School. On the whole, however, his long papacy (Kyrillos lived well into his nineties) was a turbulent one, characterized by struggles with the laity over reform. It was during this tumultuous period that Habib Girgis was born, educated, and began his educational and social reforms.

As relations between the pope and the Lay Community Council deteriorated, clergymen began to feel threatened by lay involvement in church affairs. They convinced the pope that the council was illegitimate, and that he alone possessed absolute power. This led to a severe clash between Kyrillos V and the council, whose members insisted that the board had the right to deal with civil and financial matters. By maintaining this line, however, the council succeeded only in confirming the clergy's charges, eventually alienating the pope himself. The previous harmony was replaced by outright confrontation, which led in turn to the abandonment of all efforts at reform, including the closure of the Clerical School that had been only recently founded. The situation worsened when Protestant missionaries encouraged the laity to disobey papal authority. As matters disintegrated further, the pope was banished by khedivial decree to al-Bārāmūs Monastery on September 1, 1892. Following lengthy negotiations between the bishops and the council, another khedivial decree, issued on January 30, 1893, returned Kyrillos V to his see. On February 4 the pope, accompanied by a special government envoy, returned to Cairo in a triumphal procession, cheered by huge numbers of Muslims and Christians. Churches were repaired, new ones built, and the Clerical School reopened in 1893, with Habib Girgis among the first students to enroll.

But total harmony was not yet restored. Kyrillos believed that the lay reformers were being supported by Protestant missionaries, and hence constituted a threat to the Church and its doctrines. The reformers, on the other hand, wanted well-educated clergy who could guide the Coptic community and enable the Copts to assume their rightful place in the nation. A further khedivial decree in 1893 invested Kyrillos V with complete authority and dissolved the Lay Community Council, replacing it with a committee of four to assist the pope in running the affairs of the community. In 1896 Kyrillos issued an encyclical enjoining the clergy to teach and preach, perform religious services, administer communion, console the bereaved, and show charity to the needy. In another encyclical in 1899, he established three new schools for the education of monks and a school for the laity.

In 1898 the Holy Synod issued a decree on the necessity of providing Christian education to schoolchildren. This subject was not included in the public school curriculum, nor were there teachers with the requisite biblical and ecclesiastical knowledge, so the Holy Synod decided to fill this void. The Synod's aims were to accustom children and youth to attending church; teach them religious tenets and the truths of the Bible; stress the importance of sanctifying Sunday; familiarize them with virtues and sublime morals; prepare them to be useful members of their nation; teach them personal hygiene, such as keeping their clothing clean and taking care of their health; instill in them a spirit of nationalism; and motivate them to serve their community.

In 1903 the government published its first textbook on education. It began by defining *tarbiya* [education] as the discipline and exercise of individuals for the sake of coordinating them to perform as a unit, "putting them in readiness and strengthening them to perform their function as required, in the most efficient manner. There is no way to educate and strengthen something, except by training and drilling it in the performance of its function, until it can accomplish it with smoothness, speed, and precision."[7] This publication marked the emergence of a political power that sought to use education to benefit the state rather than the individual.

Also in 1903, Pope Kyrillos sponsored the founding of a technical college at Bulaq. Around this time several Coptic schools were established by the laity through the various Coptic societies. The Tawfiq Coptic Society in al-Fajjālah district founded a technical college in 1904, while al-Jami'yyah al-Khayriyyah al-Kubra at al-Azbakiyyah and the Tawfiq Society at Zahir opened schools for girls. The same Tawfiq Coptic Society established a secondary girls' college in 'Abbasiyyah in 1911, along with schools in Alexandria, Tanta, al-Fayyūm, and other cities along the Nile Valley. In 1908, Egypt's first tertiary educational institution was established, albeit on a small scale.

For his part, Girgis wanted Christian religion to be taught in every school in Egypt, and at both elementary and secondary levels. The government, however, prohibited the subject from being taught during regular school hours and refused to pay the salaries of religion teachers. In the end, Girgis persuaded Christian teachers of secular subjects to take on the extra duty of teaching religion. This battle in the schools continues even today.

[7]Quoted in Mitchell, *Colonising Egypt*, 85

In 1908, the Egyptian minister of education responded positively to the request of Pope Kyrillos V to have religion taught in public schools by deciding to include Christianity as a core subject for all Coptic students in the elementary schools. (Muslim students were already being instructed in their religious tenets.) The minister stated in his decree: "We wish the Copts, who are our partners in this nation, to know the principles of their doctrines and to have a good grasp of the tenets of their faith. As those who have no religion cannot be trusted and are not loyal."[8]

In 1908 and again in 1912, the Lay Community Council, which had been re-established in 1906, saw its powers curtailed through a series of reforms. The pope became solely responsible for appointing his clerical deputy to the council; along with four monastic abbots, the pope also administered the *awqaf* (charitable land endowments). The council's membership was reduced to a total of twelve: eight laymen elected by general suffrage and four clerics nominated by the pope. Furthermore, the council's responsibility for personal status cases (marriage, divorce, alimony) was eventually transferred to the civil courts, and the council stripped it of its control over Coptic schools and all benevolent societies. These, too, were placed under the jurisdiction of government authorities. For twelve years these amendments were resisted by the laity until they were abolished by parliament, the original constitution remaining in force.

In 1913 a law passed that made elementary education compulsory throughout the Ottoman Empire. Starting in 1919, the Copts began to join Egypt's political movement for independence and became involved in the nationalist Wafd party. But even after Egypt gained independence in 1922, British influence continued. Of the numerous social and economic matters requiring attention, education was the only one given its own clause in the new nation's constitution, namely, Article 19, which provided for compulsory and free elementary education. Nevertheless, there remained a dualism in the educational system. Elementary schools that led to secondary and higher education continued to operate on a fee basis, whereas elementary schools that provided a terminal education for the masses were free. In 1925, secondary education generally consisted of six years of study (later

[8]Ṭal'at Dhikrī Mīnā, *Ḥabīb Jirjis wa-turāthih al-ta'līmī* [Habib Girgis and His Educational Legacy] (Cairo: Maṭba'at Madāris al-Aḥḥad, 1993), 61.

reduced to five) on a half-day basis. The aim was to attract as many children as possible by reducing costs and enabling rural children to continue to work alongside their parents in the fields. The first three years covered general subjects, followed by two years of specialization in either mathematics and science, or social studies and literature. A student who excelled might spend another year concentrating in mathematics, science, or literature, concluding with a final examination. The curriculum was later modified to allow students to commence specialized study at an earlier age. Regardless of these revisions, however, Egypt's system of secondary education remained largely medieval in approach, with the main emphasis placed on preparation for the dreaded final examination and the memorization of large quantities of unrelated factual data.

Egypt's university system was similar in nature. In 1925, the first Egyptian university was established, absorbing the tertiary college that had been founded in 1908. However, even as secondary and tertiary educational institutions expanded rapidly, serious problems such as unemployment increased.

Until 1934 Christian education in the government schools was limited to elementary level students. Pope Yu'annis XIX complained to the minister of education, who agreed to offer Christian education at all levels in the government schools. Habib Girgis wrote the curricula for the preparatory, primary, and secondary levels, titled *al-Mabādi' al-Masīḥiyah al-Urthūdhuksiyah* [Orthodox Christian Principles].

During this period, even the Coptic schools were not providing sufficient religious education. That same year, Hegumen Ṣalīb Mīkhā'īl, the senior priest at St Mark's Cathedral, complained to the pope and the Lay Community Council that the schools were not fulfilling their duty in this regard. He admonished the council:

> What is the benefit to the Church or to the Coptic community, then, of having schools, if they do not strengthen moral values? What is the benefit of filling the children's minds with various teachings, if we forget to educate their souls religiously? This is like the person who wears new clothes on a dirty body, or like the house that is built with bricks that are not cemented together and hence quickly collapses. So, how many

> young men and women fall in an atmosphere of darkness and are sunk in a pit of corruption because of not being religiously instructed?[9]

Other problems included inconsistencies in curricula between school sectors. It was not until 1951 that a unified curriculum was adopted, but even then it was impossible to implement nationwide because of limited resources. Elementary schools were under-resourced and could not teach students a second language, although this was a prerequisite for secondary education. By 1952, the inadequacies of Egypt's educational system had contributed significantly to the fragmentation of society. There were differences between the elite and the masses, between town and country, and between graduates of the religious system and those of the the secular schools.

Many of the obstacles to reform in the Coptic Church, the education system, and the Coptic community in general can be traced back to the strained relationship between clergy and the laity. As Girgis put it,

> If the leaders [the clergy] are weak, then how will they lead troops more advanced than them in education and knowledge? That resulted in misunderstandings between the two ranks—the clergy and the laity. The effect of this was the weakness of the ranks, and such an obstacle stood in the path of advancement and reform, since neither rank understood the other.[10]

The main area of conflict had to do with authority, power, and control of finances. It was also clear that the educated laity had a leaning toward the West, a disposition supported by the Lay Community Council but strongly opposed by the Holy Synod of the Coptic Church. Girgis identified seven main obstacles to reform in the Coptic Church: alienation between the laity and the clergy; criticism, slander, and tarnishing of the clergy's reputation; the clergy's belief that the laity had encroached upon their rights; conflict between monks and laity; the false belief among the laity that money was

[9]Ṣalīb Mīkhā'īl to Lay Community Council, December 1, 1934, Patriarchal Archives, 4–1.62–63/33.

[10]Habib Girgis, *al-Wasā'il al-'amaliyah lil-iṣlāḥāt al-Qibṭiyah* [The Practical Means Toward Coptic Reform: Hopes and Dreams], 2nd ed. (Cairo: Dār Madāris al-Aḥḥad al-Qibṭiyah, 1993), 10.

being amassed in the monasteries (in fact, they were very poor at the time); misunderstandings concerning differing viewpoints; and negligence on the part of many among the laity in meeting their obligations toward the Church.

These circumstances form the background to the life of Habib Girgis. It was an explosive era replete with struggles between the Coptic hierarchy and laity. Government interference in Church administration created further tension, although such interference served ultimately as a catalyst that kept the reform process moving forward. The hidden agenda of the foreign missionaries, who sided with the laity against the hierarchy, made the situation worse. At the same time, it must be understood that the laity was reacting to widespread corruption among the clergy. In the long run, it was the laity who succeeded in reforming the Church.

CHAPTER THREE

From its Milk One May Drink and Learn: The Sunday School Movement

Our hearts overflow with deep thanks to God, who has counted us trustworthy, and has made us servants in the field of Sunday School; but as time passes, we feel greater responsibility toward every child and youth throughout the See of St Mark. For the fields are white for harvest and we are in need of laborers.[1]

—Habib Girgis

THE ESTABLISHMENT AND SUCCESS of the Sunday School movement, which flourishes even today in the Coptic Orthodox Church, are attributable largely to the work of Habib Girgis. While still a student at the Coptic Orthodox Seminary in Cairo, Girgis realized that children were the key to the revival of the Church. Not only had generations of young Copts been deprived of a sound education in their faith, but they were the most vulnerable to conversion to competing religions. Girgis' community was mired in illiteracy, ignorance, and apathy. He decided to attack this problem head on and, as in the case of most of his conquests, he chose education as his weapon. He began informally by gathering local children on Sundays at the various churches and societies in Cairo, beginning with the Church of the Virgin Mary in the middle-class suburb of al-Fajjālah. He taught these young people about the Bible, the Coptic rites, church history, and the lives of Egyptian saints and martyrs.

Since the mid-nineteenth century, Western missions in Egypt had been running Sabbath Schools to attract and teach youthful converts from other faiths.[2] The American Presbyterian Mission was the first, followed by

[1]Habib Girgis to teachers of Coptic Sunday Schools, June 25, 1949, Patriarchal Archives 4–1.385/30, Sunday School Grants, Part 1.

[2]The principal secondary sources for this chapter include Charles Casey Starbuck, "A General View of Missions, 2d ser, pt 2: Egypt," *Andover Review* (Boston, MA) 11.65

other Protestant denominations and the Roman Catholics. In 1870, there were 236 Sabbath School pupils, a number that increased to 658 in 1875, 1,494 in 1880, and then, in a huge leap, to 4,438 in 1887. The majority of these pupils were Copts, a fact that troubled the Coptic Church hierarchy. They felt threatened by the development of a religious educational activity imposed by foreigners and taking place right in front of them, but they had little ability or means to react. These Sabbath Schools used methods specially designed to appeal to children, such as distributing attractive religious pictures, reading from illustrated books, and teaching tenets of the faith through the dynamic question-and-answer method known as catechism. In order to compete with these Sabbath Schools, Girgis decided to emulate them. He wrote a Coptic catechism, which was published in a series of four books in 1898,[3] and the popularity of his classes continued to grow.

At this time the Coptic hierarchy was starting to take action in the field, and no doubt this inspired Girgis in his work. In 1898 the Holy Synod issued its decree on the necessity of Christian education for schoolchildren, and the following year Pope Kyrillos V acknowledged the Church's responsibility to provide Christian education to the young. Then, in 1903, the third decree was issued from the Holy Synod on four major concerns that had a strong bearing on Girgis' work. The first was the imperative to implant Christian education among Coptic children from a young age, and to spread rigorous religious values among the Copts so that they would live upright lives to benefit themselves, their families, and the nation as a whole. The

(May 1, 1889): 529–39; Paul D. Sedra, "John Lieder and His Mission in Egypt: The Evangelical Ethos at Work among Nineteenth-century Copts," *The Journal of Religious History* 28.3 (October 2004): 219–39; G. Roper, *Arabic Printing in Malta 1825–1845: Its History and Its Place in the Development of Print Culture in the Arab Middle East* (Durham: University of Durham Press, 1988); Sana' Hasan, *Christians Versus Muslims in Modern Egypt: The Century-Long Struggle for Coptic Equality* (Oxford: Oxford University Press, 2003); Ṭal'at Dhikrī Mīnā, *Ḥabīb Jirjis wa-turāthih al-ta'līmī* [Habib Girgis and His Educational Legacy] (Cairo: Maṭba'at Madāris al-Aḥḥad, 1993); Ṣalīb Sūryāl, "Tārīkh Madāris al-Aḥḥad al-Qibṭiyah al-Urthūdhuksiyah bi-al-Jīzah" [The History of Coptic Orthodox Sunday Schools in Giza], (Giza: Kanīsat Mār Murqus, unpublished manuscript, n.d.); John L. Elias, *A History of Christian Education: Protestant, Catholic, and Orthodox Perspectives* (Malabar, FL: Krieger Pub. Co., 2002).

[3]Habib Girgis, *Kitāb khilāṣat al-uṣūl al-īmāniyah fī mu'taqadāt al-Kanīsah al-Qibṭiyah al-Urthūdhuksiyah* [The Doctrines of the Coptic Orthodox Faith: A Foundational Synopsis] (question-and-answer catechesim), Grades 1–4, 3 vols. (Cairo: Maṭba'at al-Tawfīq, 1898).

second concern advocated religious education in Coptic schools and the rearing of Coptic Orthodox children through attendance at Sunday liturgies and other general worship services. Third, attention was given to the compulsory teaching of Coptic history and faith in all Coptic schools and in the *kuttāb* system. Fourth, lessons were to be based on Coptic Orthodox principles, and school books to be approved by a religious education committee based at the Patriarchate. All teachers and students at Coptic schools were obliged to attend weekly church services, while the parents of Coptic children enrolled in state schools were obliged to take their sons and daughters to church regularly.

Meanwhile, the Sunday School system had been blossoming. In November 1907 Pope Kyrillos V issued a comprehensive letter to the pastors and teachers of Sunday Schools, stressing the importance of children's education. It included advice and counsel on the care and righteous upbringing of children, who constituted the "nation of tomorrow" and the congregation of the future Church. Girgis took this as further encouragement. Realizing that the hierarchy of the Church at its highest levels now gave priority to the religious education of the young, he took full advantage of the opportunities this brought.

Pope Kyrillos V, probably acting on a suggestion offered to him by Girgis during one of their regular weekly discussions, decided in 1918 to form a general committee to oversee the religious education offered to state school students on Fridays and to Coptic school students on Sundays. The committee had ten members, including Girgis, and was headquartered at the seminary. Branches were set up throughout Egypt, including Alexandria, Damanhūr, West Birmā, Manṣūrah, al-Fayyūm, Manfalūṭ, Asyūṭ, Sūhāj, Armant, Bibā, Abū Qurqāṣ, Minyā, Mallāwī, Naqqādah, and Bahjūrah. As Girgis later recalled,

> In the year 1918, Hegumen Salāmah Manṣūr and Yūsuf Afandī Iskandar Jurays considered the establishment of a society, to be named Jam'iyyat al-Ṭifl Yasū' [The Society of the Child Jesus], and they requested that I join them in that society. And so I suggested to them the project of Sunday Schools which I had previously prepared. But they objected to the name, and so we changed it to Injīl al-Aḥḥad lil-Madāris [The Sunday

> Gospel for Schools]. And when the work succeeded, I reverted to the original name of Sunday Schools. Shortly afterward, a general committee was established: it was called al-Lajnah al-ʻĀmmah li-Madāris al-Aḥḥad al-Qibṭiyah al-Urthūdhuksiyah [The Coptic Orthodox General Committee of Sunday Schools].[4]

Basing the formative work of the Sunday Schools at the seminary was a strategic move on Girgis' part. The seminary was the heart of education in the Church, the place where future Coptic leaders—priests, deacons, and lay leaders—were formed. It thus became an ideal laboratory where Girgis could test his ideas and theories on the faculty and students. The seminary's intellectual environment fostered the publications and research needed to develop sound pedagogical methods, textbooks, and curricula, setting the right tone for this vital work of educating the young.

Educational materials introduced by the Western missionaries, such as religious pictures and illustrated books, became central to Girgis' method. The Americans and other Protestant missionaries in the second half of the nineteenth century were supplied with books and tracts by the CMS Press in Malta. As early as the 1820s these were being given free to schoolchildren in Cairo, who received them eagerly. Titles distributed in Egypt by the Malta press included *Scripture Stories, Watts' Catechism, The Bible Catechism*, and *Companion to the Bible*. No printed Coptic Orthodox educational resources for children existed at Girgis' time, so he may have drawn upon this foreign material when writing his catechism for grades 1 to 4, published in 1899 as *The Doctrines of the Coptic Orthodox Faith: A Foundational Synopsis*. There is ample evidence to prove that Girgis heavily utilized literature from abroad in his teaching, though he made sure he adapted this material to suit the Orthodox faith.

As defined by Girgis, the aims of Sunday Schools (later set out in the Sunday School constitution of 1949, known as *The Fundamental Law for Coptic Orthodox Sunday Schools and the Coptic Youth League in the See of St Mark*)[5] included encouraging children to keep Sunday as a holy day, to

[4]Girgis, *The Coptic Orthodox Seminary*, 134–35.

[5]Habib Girgis, *al-Qānūn al-asāsī li-madāris al-Aḥḥad al-Qibṭiyah al-Urthūdhuksiyah wa-Jāmiʻat al-Shabāb al-Qibṭī bi-al-Kirāzah al-Murqusiyah* [The Fundamental Law for Coptic Orthodox Sunday Schools and the Coptic Youth League in the See of St Mark]

attend the Liturgy, and to receive Holy Communion (on Sunday in Coptic schools, and Friday in government schools). The appointment of monitors to watch over the activities of the students shows the application of some aspects of the Lancastrian model of education, which will be discussed further in Chapter 4. Teaching the students Scripture and virtues, and implanting in them a spirit of nationalism and community service, were also part of Girgis' vision. Girls were to be taught, too, but separately from boys.

> As for the ministry to girls after the age of ten, they are to be cared for by women [who would conduct their meetings] at different times than the meetings for boys. The male Sunday School teachers and the members of the Coptic Youth League are not to interfere [in] or oversee [the ministry to girls]. Women are to set suitable activities, separate from those of the Coptic Youth League, and the Higher Committee is to set up a special organization to supervise and direct the ministry of young females.[6]

Girgis began moving in an expansive way to ensure that religious education spread beyond Cairo to every church and society in Egypt, and even into Sudan and Ethiopia. Branches of the Sunday School movement were established in each Egyptian parish and its surrounding villages and towns, all under the leadership of the local parish priest. This governance arrangement was a significant asset to the movement since it meant that Sunday Schools were an activity the priests controlled, rather than one that challenged their authority. Because the Sunday School movement was not led by the better-educated, urban non-clerics, it was not perceived as a threat by the priests. At each church a Sunday School was established while in each city a Coptic Youth League was set up. The league had branches in every church and brought members together on a regular basis to discuss general strategies.

The Coptic Youth League officially commenced in 1918 and continued to evolve until its final structure in 1948. The earliest extant *Fundamental Law for Coptic Orthodox Sunday Schools and the Coptic Youth League in*

(Cairo: al Lajnah al 'Ulyā al Markaziyah li-Madāris al Aḥḥad al Qibṭiyah al Urthūdhuksiyah wa-Jāmi'at al Shabāb al Qibṭī bi-al Kirāzah al Murqusiyah [The Central Committee for Coptic Orthodox Sunday Schools and the Coptic Youth League in the See of St Mark], June 1949).

[6]Ibid., 16.

Some female Sunday School students, Cairo, class of 1927–28, with His Excellency Yusuf Suleiman Pasha (deputy of the Lay Community Council or Maglis Milli), Erian Bik Jirjis (director of Coptic schools) and some members of the General Committee of Sunday Schools. (Girgis, The Coptic Orthodox Seminary.*)*

the See of St Mark is dated June 1949. However, the text refers to a previous constitution, which to our knowledge has not been preserved. The 1949 constitution details the Sunday Schools' and Youth League's purpose, administration, committees, branches, affiliations, finances, female ministries, and general matters.

The strong links between the Sunday School movement's headquarters and branches helped to entrench a uniform educational philosophy across the country. The organization was reformed in 1927 and the committee enlarged to twenty members, including Girgis as general secretary. All those who worked with Girgis were volunteers; initiatives and projects were made possible by donations and the support of the various charitable societies that played such an essential role in Church reform. The Sunday Schools established branches in provinces all over Egypt that grew into centers of spiritual activity, with prayer groups, classes, and meetings for every grade. It was not unusual for Sunday School classes to be initiated even before a church had its own priest.

Sunday School students (class of 1927–28) with His Excellency Yusuf Suleiman Pasha (deputy of the Lay Community Council or Maglis Milli) (to the right of Habib Girgis), the Honorable Kamel Bik Ibrāhīm (general president of Sunday Schools) (third to the right of Habib Girgis), Erian Bik Girgis (director of Coptic Schools) (second to the right of Habib Girgis), Habib Girgis, and members of the General Committee of Sunday Schools. (Girgis, The Coptic Orthodox Seminary.*)*

Habib Girgis took this work extremely seriously. He considered every child his own and cared deeply about his or her salvation. He saw how the influence of Western missionaries and other internal and external pressures posed a real threat to the Coptic community—a threat that could be withstood only through the religious education of the community and the training of its leaders at the seminary. He strove to bring unity to the Sunday School movement and among its teachers by visiting every branch and holding meetings to exchange ideas. Although many Sunday School teachers and students came from modest backgrounds, some eventually moved into the Church hierarchy, becoming monks, priests, bishops, and even popes.

Girgis was recognized for his efforts at a 1924 celebration organized by the Sunday School Committee in Asyūṭ. The function took place on January 4, with the great Coptic Church in Asyūṭ overflowing with men, women, and students. One of the Sunday School leaders and a prominent lawyer, Mr Tādrus Afandī Iqlādiyūs, gave an address in which he praised Habib Girgis:

The Zaqa Ziq Coptic Sunday School, 1938, with Habib Girgis (general secretary of Sunday Schools), Dr Abd al-Massih Bik Jirjis, Fahmi Effendi Jirjis, and the members of the Zaqa Ziq committee. (Girgis, The Coptic Orthodox Seminary.*)*

> I extend sincere thanks to the pious man, Mr Habib Afandī Girgis, the dean of the Theological College in Cairo and the general secretary of Sunday Schools in Egypt, for his great toil and dedication to Sunday Schools, and for preparing such beneficial religious lessons for these schools. We pray and hope that God will not deny the Church of such role models, who are highly profitable, hard working, and diligent.[7]

As Girgis' work in the field of Sunday Schools continued to flourish over the next decade, another celebration took place on March 29, 1935, in the Coptic cathedral. It was attended by the pope, who ordained 260 deacons[8] drawn from the ranks of the Sunday School students. A year later, on March 27, 1936, the pope ordained another seventy-four deacons. By 1938 there were eighty-five Sunday School branches in Cairo and the provinces, three in Sudan, and one in Ethiopia. Altogether, there were 10,000

[7]Habib Girgis, ed., "Madāris al-Aḥḥad al-Qibṭiyah al-Urthūdhuksiyah bi-Asyūṭ" [Report on Sunday Schools in Asyūṭ], *al-Karmah* [The Vine] 10.2 (1924): 86.

[8]The term "deacon" is used loosely in the modern Coptic era to identify all the ranks of the diaconate: psaltos, reader, sub-deacon, and deacon.

The Society of the Sons of the Coptic Orthodox Church—Cairo, with Pope Yu'annis XIX, December 19, 1921. (Church of the Virgin Mary el-Mu'allaqa, Cairo, courtesy of Nash'at Nisīm Ṣubḥī.)

students of various ages attending Sunday Schools across Egypt, and 1,000 in Ethiopia. Girgis printed 9,000 four-page lessons each month for the older students and 6,000 religious pictures (with a simple description of the lesson on the back) for the younger ones. He approved a library for Sunday Schools at Giza that served as a hub for communicating with Sunday Schools in both Upper and Lower Egypt (outside of Cairo and Alexandria). Giza was given responsibility to follow up with the other branches and supply them with publications and whatever was necessary for their spiritual needs. Lesson notebooks from some of the branches were sent to Giza to be corrected and returned each month.

The Sunday School movement grew rapidly, becoming especially powerful in the period between 1935 and 1942. "Wherever [Habib Girgis] preached he ended his sermon with an urgent call to provide religious

President and members of the General Committee of Sunday Schools with Pope Yu'annis (John) XIX, honorary president of Sunday Schools, c. mid-1930s. Seated on His Holiness' right are Kamel Bik Ibrahim (general president), Habib Girgis (general secretary), and Fawzi Effendi Jirjis. Seated on his left are Assad Bik Morqos (vice-president), Gawargy Bik Ibrahim (secretary), and Bishara Effendi Bastawros. Photograph by Aziz Tadrus, probably a student of the seminary. (Girgis, The Coptic Orthodox Seminary.*)*

education for the children and youth in that place."[9] By the 1940s several of the Sunday Schools in Cairo were of great repute, each excelling in a particular area. For example, Jazīrat Badrān was known for its intellectuality and the branch of St Anthony in Shubrā for its spirituality, while the branch at Giza was recognized as being more socially aware. Members of the Giza branch often travelled to the villages with notebooks (*nuta ruḥiya*) in which the children could record their spiritual practices during the week.

These centers greatly influenced Coptic education and the growth of the Church throughout Egypt. However, the degree of specialization brought occasional disagreements. The social activists of the Giza school, for example, did not always see eye to eye with the Jazīrat Badrān branch, whose critical intellect they considered too innovative for the Church. The members

[9]Wolfram Reiss, *Erneuerung in der Koptisch-Orthodoxen Kirche: Die Geschichte der Koptisch-Orthodoxen Sonntagsschulbewegung und die Aufnahme ihrer Reformansätze in den Erneuerungsbewegungen der Koptisch-Orthodoxen Kirche der Gegenwart*, Studien zur orientalischen Kirchengeschichte (Hamburg: LIT Verlag, 1998), 54.

of the St Anthony branch, referred to as the "spiritual revivalists," sought to revitalize the Church through a return to spiritual roots that had been neglected for centuries. A primary concern of the revivalists was the revival of the Coptic language and the propagation of the life stories of Egyptian saints and martyrs, both of which were aspects of education championed by Habib Girgis. In the end, it was this return to the Church's spiritual roots that turned the Sunday School movement into more than an imitation of missionary Sabbath Schools. The study of the lives of the ancient Church Fathers, the rediscovery of old hymns by Raghib Muftah, and the revival of the Coptic language all helped give the movement an indigenous vitality.

Raghib Muftah (1898–2001), who rediscovered ancient hymns and revived the Coptic language. (http://st-takla.org/Gallery/Saints-and-Figures/10-Reh/Ragheb-Moftah/Dr-Ragheb-Moftah-Passport-1968.html. Accessed January 31, 2017.)

Girgis led and participated in two important conferences for Sunday School teachers, one held in 1941 and the second in 1949. The first of their kind in the Coptic Church, these conferences served both as an opportunity to further the spiritual growth of the teachers and as a forum to foster collaboration by discussing planning, organization, and teaching methods. The first conference, which took place in November 1941, was attended by more than 350 teachers representing fifty Sunday Schools in Cairo. Girgis opened the proceedings by reading a letter of blessing from Pope Yu'annis XIX. Participants at this conference decided that a department for the training of Sunday School teachers should be established at the seminary, with a special system and program for three years of study. Nobody could be accredited to teach Sunday School without this qualification. Those living in remote areas might study by correspondence, marking the first time that distance education had been offered in Egypt. Girgis always tried to devise new methods of reaching out to his teachers; in endeavoring to make education accessible to all, he was well ahead of his time.

Habib Girgis' ivory letter openers. (St Mark Coptic Orthodox Cultural Center, Dayr al-Anbā Ruways; photograph by Hani Gadoun.)

By the mid-1940s the Sunday School movement was well established throughout Egypt. It was highly regarded not only in Church and religious circles, but also in government circles and by Egyptian society as a whole. As a result, the Ministry of Social Affairs wrote to Habib Girgis in 1945 to request that the Sunday Schools be officially registered as an organization. Girgis perceived this as a bid for government control over Church institutions. He responded by stating that the Sunday School movement was not a social organization but rather a religious educational one, headed by the Pope of Alexandria and overseen financially by the Lay Community Council. Girgis explained that the Lay Community Council was responsible for assigning the Sunday School budgets and releasing funds donated by churches, bishops, and laypeople. He insisted that Sunday Schools did not provide any social services; their mission was limited to religious teaching among the Copts. Girgis concluded by arguing that just as the state did not interfere in the affairs of the Church, it should not interfere in the running of Sunday Schools, remarking that this principle applied to all churches around the world. The Ministry of Social Affairs backed down from its request.

Despite the success of the movement, there were problems. In March 1948, Pope Yusāb II expressed disappointment to Girgis over an apparent lack of organization.

> We have observed that Sunday Schools are in dire need of great care and strong supervision, along with a unified administration, so that they may become an effective power for the good of the Church and its revival. Thus, we have seen it fit to suggest that you meet with those whom you choose to become a higher committee under our leadership. [This is] to

> examine all that is required for the care of these schools, which are our only guarantee of building upon the foundation [of Sunday Schools] a strong generation of faith, deeply rooted in Orthodox doctrine and sound principles. We await your opinions and decisions concerning this matter.[10]

The pope also wrote to priests in Cairo whose churches did not yet have Sunday Schools, directing them to open one.

In response to the pope's criticism, Girgis implemented a new committee structure and administrative system. The Higher Central Committee for Sunday Schools and the Coptic Youth League in the See of St Mark was established to oversee the whole enterprise. Under this main committee sat two boards: a general committee and an executive board. By 1949, members of the general committee numbered thirty-six. They were required to reside in Cairo, to have experience in Sunday Schools and youth affairs, and to be at least twenty-one years of age and of the Coptic Orthodox confession. The executive board comprised fifteen members chosen from the general committee. The work of the Higher Central Committee was divided into three main areas: administrative (secretarial work and the system of ministry according to the *Fundamental Law*); educational (pedagogy, the preparation of educational programs and publications, and the spiritual nourishment of Sunday School teachers); and financial.

As well as these committees, the system included diocesan administrative branches under the supervision of the local metropolitan or bishop. Each branch had a diocesan priest, two archons (lay members of the Church considered leaders of the community because of years of service), and four local Sunday School and Coptic Youth League coordinators. From among these, a secretary and treasurer were chosen. Branches were required to hold monthly meetings, to oversee all religious education work in the diocese, and to implement the decrees and directives of the Higher Central Committee.

The second element of Girgis' response to Pope Yusāb's stern letter was a suite of detailed forms and reports prepared for use in the administration of Sunday Schools. These were to be completed regularly by every

[10]Habib Girgis "Madāris al-Aḥḥad ta'mal" [Sunday School Performs], *Majallat Madāris al-Aḥḥad* [Sunday School Magazine] 2.2 (1948): 38.

Sunday School teacher and coordinator, then checked and signed by the parish priest. On one such form Girgis placed this scriptural verse in the header as a reminder to educators: "Be faithful until death, and I will give you the crown of life" (Rev 2.10).[11] Adding a spiritual touch even to prosaic administrative forms was a hallmark of Girgis' work. He wanted educators to remember at all times the ultimate goal of their work: their own eternal life, and that of the students they served.

Girgis sought to complete a census of the Coptic community in Egypt and Sudan. The new forms accordingly requested information on the number of teachers, classes, and students, as well as the day, time, and place where classes were held. They requested details on the weekly meetings of teachers for the purpose of prayer, spiritual edification, biblical studies, and the discussion of teaching methods. All this information was to be sent to the assistant general director of the Coptic Sunday Schools in the See of St Mark.

Additionally, attendance forms were to be completed by Sunday School coordinators three times a year. These forms requested information on attendance at Sunday School, the Liturgy, and Holy Communion, along with the number of students visited in their homes. Another form, also required every four months, asked the coordinator to evaluate the teachers. It sought information on how often they received Holy Communion, the number of days of fasting, Bible chapters read, spiritual practices maintained, liturgies attended, and lessons prepared, as well as the number of teaching sessions held in urban and rural areas. There was also a place for comments by the coordinator.

The information from these and many other forms was eventually collated into a comprehensive annual report on the state of the Sunday School movement and subsequently presented to the pope, the Holy Synod, priests, the Lay Community Council, and the Coptic community at large, allowing them to gauge the progress (or lack thereof) of the movement. In a cover letter dated July 22, 1948, Girgis instructed the Sunday School coordinators on how to complete the forms. Each was to be filled out in triplicate: the original was kept at the local Sunday School branch; the blue copy was sent to the local metropolitan, and the yellow copy to the Higher Central Committee of

[11]Habib Girgis, several blank statistical reports for the Coptic Sunday Schools and related documents, July 22, 1948, Patriarchal Archives 4–1.75/30, Sunday School Grants, Part 1.

Sunday Schools, which in turn presented it to the pope. The process was to be completed within a week of the end of the four-month period. Along with the form, a detailed report was to be sent to the Higher Central Committee of Sunday Schools and to the metropolitan. This report covered all activities of the branch such as homework, innovative visual aids, trips, celebrations, gifts and the occasion on which they were presented, visits to surrounding rural areas or general activities organized within the city such as church services, congregational home visits, social work offices, and classes for the working classes and the illiterate. It asked for the names of new teachers and of those who had been absent, along with the reason for their absence, and for a discussion of any difficulties or problems encountered and how they were overcome, along with the type of assistance required if the problems remained. Three copies of any local publication were to be provided.

After completing the report, the coordinator was to discuss the results with the teachers under his or her supervision, highlight any deficiencies, and soliciting prayers for the development of the ministry. The report was presented to the parish priest with a request for his signature, prayers, blessings, and support for the ministry and the Sunday School.

These administrative systems represented a type of technology of power similar to the secular schooling system under ʻAlī Mubārak, which in turn relied heavily on the highly regimented Lancastrian system of education discussed in Chapter 4. In fact, Girgis' administrative system for Sunday Schools and the Coptic Youth League was even more complicated than the brief summary presented here. It was idealistic, tedious, and unachievable, particularly given the unfolding political situation in the Coptic Church that led, after Habib Girgis' death, to the deposition of Pope Yusāb II. How could all this information be communicated? How many hours would have been necessary to meet Girgis' intricate and detailed requirements? It seems that Girgis built an administrative bureaucracy that would have hindered rather than helped the implementation of religious education. How could he expect each parish, Coptic Youth League, and branch, with the limited resources at their disposal, to apply his system uniformly? Moreover, there is no evidence that training was presented to any of these branches or committees about how to run the system.

Today, the Patriarchal Archives beneath St Mark's Cathedral in Cairo house a treasure trove of documents pertaining to the work of Habib Girgis—over 7,000 pages including correspondence to and from Girgis, reports on the Sunday School movement and the seminary, various budgets, curricula, and many of the standard forms just described. Girgis believed that a well-structured administrative system was necessary in order to educate, and he gave great attention to implementing such a system for the Sunday School movement and the Coptic Youth League. We can only conclude that Pope Yusāb's letter of criticism caused Girgis to go to extremes in order to meet his demands, without properly considering how the system would actually be implemented. While Girgis' idealism is admirable, in a practical sense it was untenable: it was naïve of him to believe that such a complex administrative system could be implemented, particularly given the Church's state of turmoil at the time.

In 1949 a second conference of Sunday Schools, focusing on the role of Sunday Schools in forming the Christian personality, took place. As with the first conference, Pope Yusāb II sent a letter of blessing.

> We value the mission of the Sunday School movement, especially the certainty of its aptitude. We acknowledge that it has a lofty role which aims to build the upcoming generation on upright religious principles, that they may be adorned with godliness and become strong pillars upon which the bright glory of this Church will be founded—the Church that has a luminous history and noble legacy.[12]

By then Habib Girgis had written three series of curricula for Sunday Schools, published in 1898–99, 1937, and 1947–48. The first comprised four volumes entitled *Kitāb khilāṣat al-uṣūl al-īmāniyah fī mu'taqadāt al-Kanīsah al-Qibṭiyah al-Urthūdhuksiyah* [The Doctrines of the Coptic Orthodox Faith: A Foundational Synopsis], and was designed for elementary levels one to four. The first volume was a question-and-answer catechesim simplified for that age group, while the other three covered basic Christian definitions, the sacraments, the believer's duties toward the Church and the clergy, and other Christian duties and virtues. At the end were verses for rote learning by the students, plus educational guidelines for the teacher. This

[12]Mīnā, *Habib Girgis and His Educational Legacy*, 46.

series was also used in Coptic and private schools, and in 1913 the Ministry of Education decreed its adoption by Coptic students in government schools.

In 1937 Girgis wrote his second curriculum, another four-volume series for use at the elementary level titled *al-Mabādi' al-Masīḥiyah al-Urthūdhuksiyah lil-madāris al-ibtidā'iyah* [Christian Orthodox Principles for Elementary Schools] (Grades 1–4). This curriculum consisted of lessons on the Old and New Testaments and Church history. In the first two levels, Girgis moved from illustrated religious stories of the Old Testament to Christian teaching in the New Testament, introducing theological concepts such as incarnation, redemption, and the three hypostases. The curriculum then moved to practical implementation of the religious stories. In 1948, Girgis discussed the various stages of the development of the Sunday School curriculum.

> Coptic Sunday Schools, in their modern revival, have undergone many stages to achieve what they desire for the advancement of their curricula and the methods of teaching the children of the Church, while entreating from the heart that the Lord of the Church would establish them as a strong and righteous generation, and return the Church to its former glory. In the first stages of the establishment of Coptic Sunday Schools from 1918 onward, there was just one general curriculum for all students, which was based on the Gospel reading of the Liturgy. Then it progressed by using the curriculum that was developed by the Theological College for primary and secondary schools. Around 1935, it was decided that separate curricula for Sunday Schools for each age group would be prepared. These curricula, however, were not printed or prepared for publication until 1939, and from that time Sunday Schools attempted to improve their curricula. These curricula continued to develop, and were trialed in years to follow. Particular Sunday Schools in the cities and the provinces began to try systems specific to them.[13]

[13]General Central Committee of Sunday Schools and the Coptic Youth League, *al-Manhaj al-'ām li-madāris al-Aḥḥad al-Qibṭiyah al-Urthūdhuksiyah bi-al-Kirāzah al-Murqusiyah* [The General Curriculum for Coptic Orthodox Sunday Schools at the See of St Mark] (January 1, 1948), in Sūryāl, "Tārīkh Madāris al-Aḥḥad al-Qibṭiyah al-Urthūdhuksiyah bi-al-Jīzah" [The History of Coptic Orthodox Sunday Schools in Giza], vol. 4, section 10, appendix 2, 4.

In developing the 1948 curriculum, the General Central Committee first assessed the success and failure of various types of curricula, seeking to establish a unified curriculum that would standardize the programs, lessons, pictures, and strategies circulated in Sunday Schools throughout the See of St Mark. The purpose of a unified curriculum was to maintain a spirit of unity in the Church, safeguard consistency of teaching, and preserve doctrines and traditions so that the schools might carry out their mission in the most perfect form for the glory of the Savior and the ministry of his Church. The unified curriculum was based on books written by Girgis, with the addition of lessons centered on the weekly liturgical readings and an explanation of biblical readings. These four-page lessons helped connect the children to the Liturgy and rites of worship. City branches implemented this curriculum in 1947 as a trial in preparation for the issuing of the permanent *General Curriculum*. At the request of the committee, branches sent in suggestions along with the results of their trials, all of which were used to refine the final version published in 1948. In this way the new curriculum would promote the spirit of stabilization even as it served to improve the mission of Sunday Schools.

While working on the *General Curriculum*, Girgis took into account both the content of lessons and suitable spiritual practices, providing teachers with useful information on the stages of human development and pedagogical data to help them in teaching each age level effectively. Girgis' experience and readings over the many decades of his career enabled him to write an elaborate and detailed program for religious education in the Church as a whole, catering specifically to children, youth, the working class, and those in rural areas. It also included a fifty-two-week curriculum for the spiritual edification and pedagogical development of teachers. Further, Girgis prepared support materials for teachers that were published and distributed in the six volumes of the *Educational Studies for Teachers of Coptic Orthodox Sunday Schools*.[14]

[14]Habib Girgis, *al-Dirāsāt al-Tarbawiyah li-madāris al-Aḥḥad al-Qibṭiyah al-Urthūdhuksiyah* [Educational Studies for Teachers of Coptic Orthodox Sunday Schools], 6 vols. (Cairo: al-Lajnah al-ʻulyā li-Madāris al-Aḥḥad wa-Jāmiʻat al-Shabāb al-Qibṭī, 1947). Volumes 5 and 6 were located in the Patriarchal Archives.

In their entirety, these volumes address teachers of children from infancy until thirteen years of age, describing how lessons should be prepared on a solid pedagogical and psychological foundation. As such, the books tell us much about Girgis' educational philosophy and pedagogical views. Volume six, for example, targets children aged ten to thirteen and is divided into four sections. The first outlines the most important characteristics of children of this age group; the second discusses methods of teaching them; the third describes the most important skills that teachers need for effective teaching; and the fourth has questions for reviewing the material presented. Girgis notes that children aged ten to thirteen dislike interacting with younger children, and that from age eleven on they begin to develop rapidly. He also states that any principle that crystalizes in a child's mind at this age will remain with him or her for a long time. For this reason such children should be immersed in an atmosphere conducive to correct thinking, so that they might become self-reliant and able to make sound judgments. Girgis continues by citing a further twenty characteristics of children in this age group. His ideas draw upon the Christian message and Coptic heritage, as well as Western models of education. He advocates a holistic view of child development:

> Teaching is neither the dictation of advice, nor of orders, nor of instruction; rather it is the participation between the teacher [and the child] in a common spirit for knowledge. Therefore, it is the teacher's duty not to dictate information or to hand out absolute orders to these children in their care, but they should provide them with the opportunity to discover everything on their own, and offer sufficient assistance to enable them to make these discoveries. Among the aims of this important theory of education are 1) to ensure that the child lives a virtuous life from an early age and to go beyond stating mere facts about how to live it thereafter; 2) to ensure that activity gives rise to vigor; 3) to combine research with pleasure and happiness; and to reap and harvest the results to deepen the effects of research on life; and 4) to ensure that the pleasure and happiness of the children ignite their inner desire [for knowledge] rather than mere facts provided for memorization.[15]

[15]Ibid., vol. 6, 8.

Such pedagogical views stem from those of nineteenth-century German educator Friedrich Froebel, dubbed "the inventor of kindergarten," who championed child-centered education. Like Froebel, Girgis wanted children to see themselves as part of the unity of the world and encouraged teachers to help youngsters develop self-determination and freedom. Girgis also insisted that teachers inspire children to meet their own needs and establish their own identities. We know that Girgis was aware of Froebel's work, for he mentioned him in his writings. This example gives us a glimpse into how Girgis drew upon the theories of Western thinkers and educators to give Coptic Sunday School teachers a modern educational philosophy, crystallized in Arabic, that they could implement in their classes—if they heeded his advice.

Habib Girgis was familiar with various strategies for religious education, including debates, catechism, self-directed learning, pantomime, storytelling, excursions, handicrafts, and self-directed research or projects. Poetry and hymnology also played an important role. Girgis believed that he could teach the central beliefs of the Coptic faith to children through hymns that he wrote himself. He also favored the use of hymns because they were part of the Orthodox tradition that he strived to preserve. For example, the hymnology of the "Midnight Praise" of the Coptic Church defends the Orthodox teaching that St Mary is the Mother of God (Theotokos)—a belief that Nestorius denied in the Third Ecumenical Council of Ephesus in AD 431, and for which he was excommunicated. Thus, in Girgis' hymn books we find hymns containing various teachings concerning the saints, the sacraments, the Trinity, the incarnation of the Logos, the virtues, and the Ten Commandments, as well as hymns particular to St Mary, the apostles, fasting, the creed, Church history and even Sunday School, to name but a few.

Habib Girgis' use of hymnology served two purposes: it was educational, and it helped preserve Coptic musical heritage. In his book *A Key to the Tunes for Orthodox Hymns*,[16] Girgis lists the Coptic melodies to which he set his hymn texts. Each text could be sung to a number of different melodies, according to the season of the liturgical calendar. This meant that the hymns were versatile and mostly timeless, since the words could be

[16]Girgis, *Muftāḥ al-anghām lil-tarānīm al-Urthūdhuksiyah* [A Key to the Tunes for Orthodox Hymns] (Cairo: s.n., n.d.).

sung repeatedly throughout each year. Girgis understood that unless he used Coptic music, rather than the Western church music then being introduced to Egypt by Catholic and Protestant missionaries, much of the Coptic musical heritage and tradition would be lost.

In addition to producing well-organized curricula, Habib Girgis also prepared meticulous and thorough budgets for Sunday Schools and the Coptic Youth League. His budget in the report for the activities of the Higher Central Committee for Sunday Schools for the period of July 1948 to March 1949 offers one example,[17] and reveals vital information about the progress of the Sunday School movement. The first section records the income from and expenditures for the various publications: religious pictures, curricula, adult lessons, pedagogical volumes for teachers, statistical forms, books, administrative forms, spiritual pamphlets, attendance cards, letters with return slips for parents, teacher registration applications, monthly report forms for teachers, and family report forms. Girgis lists each publication with the number of copies printed, sold, or freely distributed; the cost of printing; the profit made; and the number of remaining undistributed copies. Overall, a total of EGP891 was spent on printing while EGP674 was generated by sales, resulting in a shortfall of EGP217.

The second section is a report on the main budget and final financial account for the year. On the income side, EGP245 is brought forward from the previous year, to which is added EGP200 from the Lay Community Council for the current period; EGP563 from the printing of pictures; EGP17 from curricula; EGP80 from general lessons for adults; EGP1.6 from educational studies; and EGP1.5 from miscellaneous publications for a total of EGP1119.

Expenditures appear as follows: EGP100 for the printer; EGP715 for religious pictures; EGP56 for curricula; EGP92 for general lessons for adults; EGP22 for educational studies; EGP6 for miscellaneous publications; EGP42 for printing plates, periodical letters, and advertisements; EGP35 for general excursions; EGP19 for correspondence and communication with the branches; EGP16 for complimentary publications; and EGP15 for miscellaneous expenses, also totaling EGP1119.

[17]Higher Committee of Coptic Sunday Schools, Report, May 1949, Patriarchal Archives 4–1.218–227, 400–409/30, Sunday School Grants, Part 1.

The final section is a detailed forecast for the year from April 1, 1949 to March 31, 1950. In it, Girgis predicts that it will be possible to execute the projects described within this budget. This document reveals Girgis' ambition, zeal, and passion for the goals that he wanted to achieve for the Sunday School movement. The variety and volume of the publications listed demonstrate his precision in attempting to care for every family, youth, and child. Many of Girgis' letters to the Lay Community Council request funds for the varied requirements of the Sunday School movement. Because of his determination and persistence, he was granted two budget increases in a relatively short time, going from EGP80 to EGP200 in July 1948 and then to EGP500 in February 1949.

According to this budget, Girgis spent approximately seven times the average annual salary of a teacher at the seminary on the Sunday School movement during the period in question. However, even this significant amount was insufficient for Girgis to fulfill all of his desires for the movement's continued growth. Despite the increases granted by the Lay Community Council, Girgis was forced to delay some projects because of lack of funds.

It appears that the report of the work of the Higher Committee of Sunday Schools for 1948–49 was a means for Girgis to respond to Pope Yusāb's critical letter of March 1948. Girgis was attempting to convince the pope that the Higher Central Committee was fulfilling its function by showing him that Sunday Schools were now better organized, and therefore successful. He provided figures to highlight the strength of the movement and demonstrate how the Sunday Schools were structured. He reported that there were two types of Sunday School branches: central branches serving the cities and the villages immediately surrounding them, and individual branches concerned with ministry in towns only. The fifty central branches had 900 classes, while their 400 associated villages had 400 classes. There were 200 individual branches with 800 classes. The total number of classes in all of Egypt, Sudan, and al-Wāḥāt (an oasis about 230 miles from Cairo, located in the Giza governorate) was 2,100. The number of children aged between five and twelve years was 43,000, with an average of twenty students per class, while the number of teachers and teaching assistants was 2,500. This meant that there was an average of thirty teachers in each central branch, and five in each individual branch. The fact that Habib Girgis was able to present such detailed figures indicated to the pope that an organized system was now in place.

Girgis attempted to formulate and implement a comprehensive system for Sunday Schools that cared for every aspect of the child: physical, spiritual, intellectual, and social. In other words, he wanted to care for the whole person. This concern extended to wanting to know the reason for any absenteeism from Sunday School. He formulated and printed letters that Sunday School teachers were asked to send to parents, with a perforated section that was to be returned to the teacher explaining the child's absence. The purpose of these letters was twofold: first, to demonstrate to parents that the Church deeply cared for their child and his or her welfare, and second, to inform the teacher about any problems that needed attention, perhaps by raising the matter with a clergyman who might help resolve it. Typical problems included an illness or death in the family, unemployment of the main breadwinner, financial hardship, or marital conflict. Girgis also printed church cards for children to bring to liturgies so that their attendance could be recorded; at Sunday School each child received a stamp for attendance. Finally, Girgis prepared cards of encouragement and awarded prizes for those children who were achieving and striving in spiritual matters, and were regular attendees at Church.

Today, such a regulatory system might seem too intrusive into the lives of children and families, and would probably meet resistance from some parents. But Girgis viewed it as a means to cultivate self-control and spiritual discipline, and to ensure that those who did not attend Sunday School regularly would still participate in the most important activities of religious education. He feared that children without a solid foundation in Coptic Orthodox faith, tradition, and history were more vulnerable to losing their Coptic identity as they grew up, and would thus be more easily attracted by Western missionaries, or even to Islam. This is why Girgis emphasized the teaching not only of doctrine, but also of history, Coptic language, and hymnology, and why he encouraged regular participation in liturgical services, the partaking of Holy Communion, and study of the Scriptures. The result was an integrated and modern approach to religious education.

However, under Girgis' system it was not enough to care for the child alone. It was also essential to nurture and develop the teacher from both a spiritual and educational perspective. This concern is apparent from his spiritual publications, which were printed periodically throughout the entire year and mainly describe the spiritual experiences of the lives of the saints. In the 1948–49 report, he notes that he printed 5,000 such publications, and that 3,200 were distributed. Through pedagogical publications, Girgis strove to raise the educational standard of Sunday Schools, and to increase teacher skills in lesson preparation and delivery. It was also his goal to make teachers accountable on a periodical basis by asking them to record aspects of their spiritual lives and to report on what was happening in their classrooms.

Habib Girgis' efforts in the ministry of Sunday Schools were crowned when, in April 1948, he was appointed editor-in-chief of the well-known publication *Majallat Madāris al-Aḥḥad* (Sunday School Magazine: Religious, Educational, Social), which had been founded the previous year. This magazine was produced chiefly as a means for the Coptic community to disseminate information about the progress and activities of the Sunday School movement, with a target audience of clergy, parents, and Sunday School teachers. Once Girgis took it on, the magazine acquired a new vitality. He invited many of his students to contribute, including Idwār Binyāmīn, Dr Hinrī al-Khūlī, Naẓīr Jayyid (later Pope Shenouda III), Wahīb 'Aṭā-Allāh, Dr Sulaymān Nasīm, Wilyam Sulaymān, Labīb Rāghib, Zakariyā Ibrāhīm, Nasīm Mijallī, Dr Najīb Zakī, Dr Rāghib 'Abd al-Nūr, Wilyam al-Khūlī, Ṣūfī Buqṭur, and other outstanding writers, teachers, and researchers such as Dr 'Azīz Sūryāl 'Aṭiyah, Īrīs Ḥabīb al-Miṣrī, and Murād Wahbah.

Girgis considered Christ's teachings to be central to the magazine, and the magazine essential for sharing Christ's teachings with the community. He wrote:

> The mission of Sunday School is to deliver the teachings of our Lord, God, and Savior Jesus Christ to every person. The front cover [of this magazine] expresses this mission. In it we see the Lord, to whom glory is due, standing upon the cross which Sunday School has adopted as its emblem; a shelter under which a family lives—a man, his wife, his son,

Habib Girgis, "Ghilāf al-sanah al-thāniyah" [The Cover of the Second Year],
Majallat Madāris al-Aḥḥad *[Sunday School Magazine] 2.1 (1948): 40.*

> and daughter. These look to him, seeking him. He points to this emblem saying, "This cross will carry me to you."[18]

The magazine under Girgis' direction included a variety of articles for Sunday School teachers and parents. These might discuss how to manage a troublesome child in the classroom; how to conduct prayer meetings and their effect on the ministry; moral education; or how to encourage children to practice at home what they had learned at Sunday School, as the following piece by Girgis demonstrates:

> A student, who was twelve years of age, came to Sunday School for the first time. The lesson was about prayer, and the teacher explained a sample of this prayer. When the young boy went home, at the family meeting in the evening, he brought out the Holy Bible, opened it, and surprised the family by telling them that he would read a chapter aloud, and that they would afterward pray "Our Father, Who art in heaven." The entire family submitted to this young boy, and in this way, the family began, for the first time, to practice family prayer.
>
> This deed should have been carried out by the father, but the student of Sunday School accomplished what the father neglected to do. O father, will you reclaim your status as the priest of the family? If you do not wish to do so, or are incapable of such, then we have a humble request: we beseech you not to stand in the way of your son, but allow him to live in freedom in the bosom of his God.[19]

Thus the *Sunday School Magazine* emerged as the embodiment and expression of the modern role of the Coptic Church. It was the pioneer for a spiritual movement that God placed in the heart of the Coptic Church in the twentieth century. Its greatest benefits were the development of educational work at Sunday School fostering cooperation between its adult members and the youth of the Church.

* * *

[18]Habib Girgis, "Ghilāf al-sanah al-thāniyah" [The Cover of the Second Year], *Majallat Madāris al-Aḥḥad* [Sunday School Magazine] 2.1 (1948): 40.

[19]Habib Girgis, "Ilayka ayyuhā al-Wālid" [To You, O Father], *Majallat Madāris al-Aḥḥad* [Sunday School Magazine] 2.2 (1948): 21.

The Sunday School movement represented a decisive moment in the reform movement of lay Copts that would change the course and mindset of the entire Coptic community. At the same time it also marked a new stage in the long contest for power between the laity and the popes. Wahīb 'Aṭā'-Allāh, in describing Habib Girgis' spiritual virtues that led to the success of the mission of Sunday Schools, declared:

> Habib Girgis did not only believe in Sunday School but loved it abundantly and was utterly faithful to it. And he loved each one of us individually and knew us by name, as our Savior said of the good shepherd, "He calls his own sheep by name." We felt his love toward us through the signs of happiness and joy which appeared on his countenance every time he met with us. He genuinely expressed his feelings of yearning and compassion toward us if a period had passed in which we did not meet with him. He asked about those who were absent, would send for them, and would often visit them himself. And when he spoke to us, it was with compassion and love; and if, occasionally, he felt harshness in his own tone, he would lighten the discussion with a pleasant smile, a gentle word or a gracious apology. Among the indications of his love for Sunday School was that it was never absent from his thoughts, even in the days of his old age. He would think of it even when he was in need of rest and calmness. In the hours of his final sickness also, he would ask about everyone who was involved in Sunday Schools. He asked about individuals, the conferences, the pictures, and the lessons. And he asked about those who were involved in Sunday Schools either closely or from afar. The physician would order him to be quiet and remain silent, but despite this, whenever he saw one of us he would speak to us with great concern. Guests were instructed only to give him joyful and happy news to bring enjoyment to him in these remaining few days. And he was truly happy and would lift up his pure hands in thanks to [God] and pray for Sunday Schools and those working therein; and he would proclaim that his hopes and those of the Church rested in it. I will never forget what he conveyed to me once after I had told him a series of good news: "You have brought joy to me and refreshed my soul, and you have reassured

me; I desire to hear such news. May God bless the work and may his name be glorified."[20]

Despite the many early obstacles, Girgis' efforts ultimately brought success to the Sunday School movement. The handful of Sunday Schools that he had set up at the outset of his mission at the turn of the twentieth century had, by the end of his life, grown to more than 650 branches offering 2,100 classes across all of Egypt, Sudan, and al-Wāḥāt, with 43,000 children being educated by 2,500 teachers and assistants.[21] In 1948 he wrote:

> These days, we are no longer in need to write about the importance of Sunday School to the Church. Its practical effects in the lives of the children and the teachers have become manifest. Its spirit and principles have nourished homes immensely. Fathers and mothers have felt its value in the lives of their children. Parents have loved it, for it has also influenced their lives in an indirect way; children have imparted the message of life to their parents.
>
> The time in which we exerted every effort to convince our fathers, the bishops and priests, of the importance of Sunday Schools has passed. Now, not only do we see them encouraging it, but requesting its expansion in all the cities and villages in their dioceses. Every priest desires to have a Sunday School in his parish. Sunday Schools did not reach this stage except after the clergymen trusted in it when it proved itself to be one of the members of the Church. It is, in fact, among its most important members. Being in the bosom of the Church allows it to develop and thrive, and from its milk one can drink and learn. One may grasp its laws and traditions and remain firm.[22]

[20]Wahīb 'Aṭā'-Allāh, "Kalimat Madāris al-Aḥḥad fī ḥaflat al-Ta'bīn" [The Sunday Schools' Speech at the Commemoration Celebration], *Majallat Madāris al-Aḥḥad* [Sunday School Magazine] 5.9–10 (November–December 1951): 26–33, at 30–31.

[21]Higher Committee of Coptic Sunday Schools, Report, May 1949, Patriarchal Archives 4–1.218–227, 400–409/30, Sunday School Grants, Part 1.

[22]Girgis, "Madāris al-Aḥḥad ta'mal" [Sunday School Performs], 37.

CHAPTER FOUR

The Duty of the Heart: The Coptic Orthodox Seminary

FROM HIS EARLY YEARS Habib Girgis held a firm conviction that the Coptic Church was in dire need of a seminary. This conviction was inspired by the Scriptures. In his history of the Coptic Orthodox Seminary, he recalls: "Hence, these religious schools were established and were called in the Old Testament the schools of the prophets, and the first to establish them was the Prophet Samuel. In the New Testament, these are the theological schools and colleges that the apostles instructed to be established, as is the consensus among historians."[1] In reflecting on the early Church, Girgis reminisced about the glories of the Catechetical School of Alexandria, said to have been founded by St Mark himself, and its enormous influence on the Christian world. But he also pondered the long centuries that followed, characterizing them as "the age of darkness, stagnation, and backwardness."[2]

In reality, that age was neither as dark nor as bleak as Girgis maintained; many learned Coptic figures and popes played significant roles in the life of the Church over the centuries.[3] But Girgis wanted to impress upon his readers the importance of the theological reforms that he had begun and to encourage them to support that fundamental ministry, which he hoped would lead to a better future for the Copts. And, as Buṭrus Pasha Ghālī reminded the Copts, a training school for priests was of fundamental importance: "Be concerned with the Clerical School before any other institution, for if all your Coptic schools close down, you can find an alternative to them in the other schools. But if you do not have the Clerical School, where will you

[1]Girgis, *The Coptic Orthodox Seminary*, 5.

[2]Ibid., 7–9.

[3]Principal secondary sources for this chapter include Sharkey, *American Evangelicals in Egypt; Sedra, From Mission to Modernity*; Robert F. Taft, *Beyond East and West: Problems in Liturgical Understanding* (Rome: Edizioni Orientalia Christiana, 2001); Sedra, "John Lieder and His Mission in Egypt"; Mitchell, *Colonising Egypt*.

Buṭrus Ghālī Pasha (1846–1910), who from 1908 to 1910 served as Egypt's first and only Coptic prime minister. (http://media.almasryalyoum.com/News/Large//2011/02/19/4886/btrs_bsh_gly_.jpg. Accessed January 31, 2017.)

train your pastors [*fa-Ayn Tu'allimūn Ru'ātakum* فاين تعلمون رعاتكم]?"[4] Girgis would later quote these words on several occasions.

In 1843, the Church Missionary Society (CMS) established in Cairo a seminary that it referred to as the "Coptic Institution," for the purpose of training Copts for ordination as Orthodox priests. There are conflicting views on the true motivations of the CMS in setting up the seminary. Some scholars believe that the CMS did not aspire to convert Copts to Protestantism, but wanted to keep the Coptic Orthodox Church institutionally intact as the national church of Egypt. Others have argued that the CMS was attempting to subtly infiltrate the Coptic community and infuse it with an evangelical ethos. And, indeed, there is significant evidence supporting the latter interpretation. For instance, CMS journals and correspondence sent back to England portrayed the Copts as an ignorant race that used an archaic dead language and needed to be saved. At its seminary, the CMS missionaries tried to teach a "functional" Christianity, which encouraged candidates for the Coptic priesthood to abandon their supposedly superstitious idolatry and fasting practices in favor of a "practical" approach. The seminary eventually failed when the Copts became suspicious of its aims, and it closed its doors in 1848.

Consequently, the need for a Clerical School run by the Copts themselves became even more pressing, but several decades were to pass before a solid foundation was laid. The first attempt was the opening of a clerical college on January 13, 1875, during the papacy of Kyrillos V. This institution

[4]Quoted in Girgis, *The Coptic Orthodox Seminary*, 23.

was enthusiastically hailed as a new incarnation of the ancient Catechetical School of Alexandria. However, few of the students—all monks from the monasteries—applied themselves to their studies, and the seminary survived only a few months.

By the end of the nineteenth century, the Coptic Church urgently needed a seminary for the formation of priests. Girgis commented:

> Since religious service was among the most esteemed services [to the Church], and its position was the highest, this required, therefore, that pastors [*al-ru'āh* الرعاة] be sufficiently prepared in the [Orthodox] faith. They needed to be especially cared for and to be chosen from among those with excellent qualifications, from the sons of the community generally. [Various] efforts and finances are also required for the sake of these pastors, who will lead the community to the place of safety, and for the benefit hoped for.[5]

Girgis could not imagine a priest serving without the education necessary to equip him for such an important role. He understood how impossible it would be for any person to be employed in a profession or trade without proper training—how much more important was this for a priest, who was responsible for people's souls? He wrote:

> But the Church cannot present to us true leaders, counselors, and reformers unless her leaders and pastors are specially trained to practice their lofty and critical roles. Who can be compared to them except those with similar critical positions in life? An engineer cannot take on this role without proper training in the faculty of engineering. The physician cannot be trusted over people's bodies and souls unless he receives both theoretical and practical education in his faculty. The situation is similar also for a judge, lawyer, teacher, farmer, and mechanic, as well as others who are comparable. . . . Hence, a religious pastor is not exempt from this, since a pastor worthy of this title and worthy to be responsible for souls needs to be educated in religious and secular subjects. But it is more important that [the priest] perfect the sacraments and characteristics of his profession than any of those other professions, so that he may fulfill his obligations

[5]Ibid., 7–9.

Celebration of the ordination of Hegumen Yusuf Hanna, a graduate of the Coptic Orthodox Seminary, c. 1925. The new priest is seated in the center, with Habib Girgis on his right, surrounded by faculty, students, and visitors. (Girgis, The Coptic Orthodox Seminary.*)*

and carry out his burdens. In this way, he may transcend to a most eminent relationship with the eternal souls [he cares for].[6]

Girgis argued, idealistically perhaps, that progressive Christian nations chose their pastors from those with the highest level of education, electing only the most advanced intellectuals and scholars—those who were both widely experienced and well read—to carry out their vocation as the servants of God and his representatives on earth.

That a priest, pastor, or preacher should, like every other professional, have appropriate training and qualifications might have been taken for granted in other churches, but that had not been the case for the Copts for many centuries before Girgis was born. Indeed, according to Girgis, in the second half of the nineteenth century there was only one priest in all of Egypt who was both capable of preaching and well versed in the Orthodox faith: Hegumen Fīlūthā'us (Philotheos) Ibrāhīm Baghdādī (1837–1904).

[6]Habib Girgis, "al-Madrasah al-Iklīrīkiyah: Māḍīhā wa-ḥāḍirhā wa-mustaqbalahā" [The Clerical School: Its Past, Present and Future], *al-Karmah* [The Vine] 9.9 (November 1923): 463–65, at 464.

Baghdādī, well known for his powerful sermons on the Orthodox faith, travelled throughout Egypt to teach Copts the richness of their heritage and beliefs. Girgis called him "the only man proficient in the faith in that age . . . the only preacher that the pulpits anticipated from the farthest end of the country to the other; there was no other in the whole denomination."[7] Baghdādī had a great influence on Girgis, becoming his mentor and eventually helping to shape the man Girgis would become. Girgis later described their relationship:

> The relationship between him and me was [so] strengthened in that short period that he even entrusted me with the teaching of the subject of religion to the first year classes, from what he saw of my inclination toward religious research. This is what consolidated my relationship with him and allowed me to frequently visit him all the days of his life, and so I benefited from him immensely and was guided extensively by his skills and knowledge.[8]

This historical background underscores the importance of the dedication ceremony that took place on November 29, 1893, a date widely considered to be the official opening of the Coptic Orthodox Seminary in Cairo. Girgis considered the seminary to be the greatest success of Kyrillos V: "The great pope had many influences and his pure life is filled with glorious works, such as the establishment of churches and schools; however, we do not exaggerate if we say that his establishment of the Seminary School was the precious pearl in the glory of his crown, and the seminary continues to be proud that it was the planting of his blessed hands."[9]

When the seminary opened, it had no teacher of religion or theology. The first dean, Yūsuf Manqariyūs, would simply choose some religious books and hand them out to the students to read aloud in front of him. The students complained repeatedly to the pope and to the Lay Community Council about the lack of proper theological instruction, but to no avail. This bizarre situation continued for four years and led many students to leave the seminary. There was one attempt to rectify the situation: on January 13, 1896,

[7] Girgis, *The Coptic Orthodox Seminary*, 17.
[8] Ibid., 18.
[9] Girgis, "The Clerical School," 468.

Yūsuf Bik Manqariyūs, the former dean of the seminary. (Girgis, The Coptic Orthodox Seminary.*)*

the Lay Community Council appointed the elderly Hegumen Baghdādī to teach at the seminary. Sadly, however, he lasted only two weeks, collapsing in class because of old age and illness and never returning. Following this disappointment, the Tawfīq Coptic Society (founded in 1891 with the aim of establishing high-caliber schools, a public library, and a printing press) proposed two candidates to teach religion at the seminary: ʻAyyād Marzūq and Tādrus Ḥannā. Both were of Protestant background, and therefore rejected by the seminary for fear that they might infuse the students with non-Orthodox teachings. In February 1897 Yūḥannā Bik Bākhūm was appointed, only to be replaced in November by Father Yūsuf Ḥabashī, who was in his sixties. Ḥabashī had spent the first part of his life in Rome and was fluent in Italian and French, but weak in Arabic and Orthodox doctrine. His lessons, delivered in his inadequate Arabic, were copied word for word from foreign books on the principles of Christian teaching.

Subjects taught at the seminary in its early years were civil history and geography, taught by the dean, Yūsuf Manqariyūs; Coptic language, taught by Iqlādiyūs Labīb; English language, taught by Mīkhā'īl ʻAbd al-Sayyid (the founder of *al-Waṭan* newspaper); mathematics, taught by Mīkhā'īl ʻAffat; Church hymnology, taught by cantor Mīkhā'īl Jirjis; and Arabic language, taught by several graduates from al-Azhar University and the Sciences Center for Arabic and Islamic Studies. Most of the teachers were brought in from the Great Coptic School, located nearby.

Habib Girgis was one of twelve graduates of the Great Coptic School who were chosen to be part of the first class of forty students to enter the seminary. Many of his cohort dropped out because of lack of interest or academic ability, but Girgis was a bright scholar who was appointed by special decree to teach religion on a temporary basis during his final year. He graduated shortly thereafter (the first student to do so) and, on May 8, 1898, having shown great potential and success as an instructor, he was promptly appointed to a full-time position, teaching theology and homiletics.

Girgis compared the relationship between the seminary and the Coptic community to that between the heart and the body: "For as the duty of the heart is to pump blood to the organs of the body, accordingly, from this spring, the spirit of teaching, guidance, and the transmission of the good news of salvation, will spread among people."[10] The mission of the seminary was twofold: to teach Orthodox theology and doctrine, and to form priests and preachers who would enlighten members of the Coptic community, both young and old.

Preaching was also important to the project of revitalizing Coptic culture and identity in the broader sense. Over many centuries, the Coptic language had slowly withered away in favor of Egyptian Arabic. By Girgis' time, only a meager number spoke Coptic fluently, and among these only a few were literate in the language. Reawakening a love for the Coptic language became part of the seminary's mission, and an important step toward reclaiming Coptic identity. Girgis wrote:

> A long time had passed over the Coptic language while it was abandoned, subdued, and shut off from speech and circulation among the Coptic community. The first to show affection toward the Coptic language and rescue it, loosen its bonds, and bring it to life, was the Clerical School, which revived it and breathed from its spirit into it and worked toward its promulgation among individuals, families, and the entire community.[11]

The seminary's first lecturer in the Coptic language was the scholar Iqlādiyūs Bik Labīb, who went on to publish the most comprehensive Coptic-Arabic dictionary of its day. Labīb taught the language to his own family, and encouraged his students to learn all aspects of it, including its grammar and literature.

[10]Habib Girgis, "al-Madrasah al-Iklīrīkiyah" [The Clerical School], *al-Karmah* [The Vine] 6.7 (1912): 305–8, at 307–8.

[11]Girgis, *The Coptic Orthodox Seminary*, 145.

Iqlādiyūs Bik Labīb, the seminary's first lecturer in the Coptic language. (Girgis, The Coptic Orthodox Seminary.*)*

The first statutes for the seminary were formulated by Yūḥannā Bik Bākhūm, a member of the Lay Community Council and the director and inspector of Coptic schools. Dated July 25, 1893, these statutes, or bylaws, were relatively simple. They prescribed a five-year period of study and listed the subjects to be taught. All were taught by foreigners with the exception of theology, which was to be taught from the third year of the course onwards by a capable Orthodox priest. Students were to be between twenty and twenty-five years of age when they started at the seminary, although under special circumstances candidates up to the age of thirty would be accepted. (In practice, during these early years of the seminary, students as young as sixteen were accepted.) The pope was to admit candidates to the seminary after they had passed an examination in the principles of faith and the Coptic language. Additionally, a library was established, and the administration of the seminary was placed under the authority of the Coptic schools. Bākhūm also stated that he would prepare a separate document to further address the seminary's administrative practices. (This document has not been located.)

Despite their simplicity, Bākhūm's statutes were not easy to put into practice. No proper administrative systems existed to organize the affairs of the seminary, and as a result its work was haphazard. Girgis, while still a teacher at the seminary and well before he was appointed dean in 1918, formulated a more comprehensive and detailed set of statutes consisting of fifteen chapters and eighty-three articles. These, along with bylaws for the cantors' school and bylaws for preachers, set out a far more ambitious mission. They were approved by Pope Kyrillos on September 9, 1911, and, after some alterations, accepted by the Holy Synod and published in *The Vine* in 1912.

Yūḥannā Bik Bākhūm with his son Fahīm and grandson. (Girgis, The Coptic Orthodox Seminary.*)*

In formulating his statutes, Girgis probably borrowed from Western models, adapting them to suit an Orthodox setting. Certainly, he came into contact with many foreigners who visited the seminary. He later recalled being embarrassed in those early years by the shabby state of the buildings and the unpleasant appearance of the students, apologizing for them whenever American and English religious dignitaries visited. He actively sought out examples of curricula from theological colleges in Greece, Rome, England, and America—whether Orthodox, Catholic, or Protestant—and translated them into Arabic, from which he and his colleagues designed the curriculum for the seminary in Cairo.

Under the new statutes, the direction of the seminary, its theological education, and the appointment of graduates to parishes were all placed under the direct control of the pope or his delegate. Curriculum and pedagogy were the responsibility of the seminary's board, which consisted of the dean, the teachers of religion and the Coptic language, and appointees of the pope. The board oversaw all aspects of the seminary while the dean was responsible for internal affairs (in his absence, a deputy would be appointed). The dean met with the faculty each month, and at other times if necessary, to discuss the students' academic progress and the administrative needs of the seminary. Finally, minutes were recorded and signed by the dean and the faculty staff.

Faculty members were expected to attend all meetings designated by the dean, and they were prohibited from calling meetings in his absence unless he delegated a deputy in his place. Interestingly, the faculty was forbidden

Two seals bearing the name of Habib Girgis, probably used when signing official documents. Red ink was the norm, and can still be seen on many of the archival documents. (St Mark Coptic Orthodox Cultural Center, Dayr al-Anbā Ruways; photograph by Hani Gadoun.)

from participating in even the smallest demonstrations that concerned internal issues at the seminary, or from colluding with students in such incidents. Any complaint from the faculty was to be brought to the attention of the board.

The 1912 statutes covered numerous administrative matters. All students were required to live at the seminary, sleeping in dormitories or large rooms; only with special permission could a student lodge outside the seminary. Class sizes were capped at twenty-five students. Admission requirements included passing an entrance exam, presenting three letters of recommendation, including one from the student's diocesan bishop, a minimum age (in practice) of sixteen years, and at least four years of elementary school education. Each applicant had to undergo a medical examination and be physically fit, without blemish or physical deformity. He had to nominate a sponsor—an individual who would vouch for his character, his commitment to completing his studies, and his willingness to be employed wherever the need arose and to continue in religious ministry. This sponsorship was, in effect, an enforceable contract: if the student deviated from these terms, his sponsor was liable to pay EGP15 for each year spent at the seminary.

Girgis enshrined in the statutes numerous highly detailed disciplinary rules; almost nothing was left to the discretion of the staff or students. His specifications covering religious obligations, for instance, included the exact hour and minute that morning prayers began (7:40 a.m.). These prayers were to be attended by the students, the seminary's monitor or regulator, as well as the faculty teaching in the morning session, and should last no longer than twenty minutes. They included a daily Bible chapter followed by a contemplation offered by a different student each day—all to be completed quietly and with devotion.

Imposing such strict rules upon seminary students may seem strange to us today, but we must remember that Girgis was unable, at first, to attract older students. Most of those attending in 1912 had enrolled as teenagers, some as young as sixteen.

Girgis' requirements for students to partake of Holy Communion were surprisingly low by today's standards. After preparing themselves by confessing to the seminary's priest, they were obliged to attend on only three occasions each year: the first Sunday of the academic year, Covenant Thursday during Pascha Week, and one week before the end of the academic year. (After 1931, when Girgis built a church on the grounds, liturgies were conducted more regularly at the seminary.) At that time most Copts only partook of the Eucharist on special occasions, such as the major feasts and fasts. In 1884, one scholar noted, "Communicants now are very few, and for the most part children. They walk round and round the altar, and continue receiving until all the wafer is consumed."[12] One early twentieth-century visitor to Egypt observed a priest inviting a great congregation to communicate, but his efforts were almost in vain. Men would crowd around to see the performance of the holy mysteries, but did not prepare themselves to participate by fasting and confession. Even pious Copts communicated only about once a year, during Lent, although confession was ordered at least twice a year. Before the reign of Pope Kyrillos VI (1959–71), who is said to have celebrated mass every day for more than thirty years, daily mass was largely unknown among the Copts, even in monasteries. Few laypersons received communion more than once a year. Girgis encouraged the laity,

[12]Alfred Joshua Butler, *The Ancient Coptic Churches of Egypt* (Oxford: Clarendon Press, 1884), 291.

both young and old, to attend and partake of the Eucharist more frequently, for he saw the importance of the Liturgy as an educational tool and a way for Copts to define their identity. Evidence of this emphasis is found on the forms that Girgis required Sunday School teachers to complete, where the frequency of communion had to be noted. His instructions in *General Visitations to the Village*, written in the 1940s, also emphasized communion.

The 1912 statutes for the seminary also specified matters of hygiene; forbade students from smoking; prohibited graffiti on walls, doors, and desks; and prevented students from gathering for protests either inside or outside the seminary (students who did protest were expelled immediately). They were not to join any society whatsoever, or contact, comment to, or serve as representatives of newspapers. They were required to seek the permission of a member of faculty if they wished to write in religious or humanities journals.

Today, such strict controls over every aspect of the lives of young people would be characterized as censorship. However, Girgis faced many obstacles in his reform efforts and wished to protect the reputation of the seminary by avoiding negative publicity. If, for example, students leaked information to the newspapers about the poor condition of the seminary building, or about illness caused by inadequate nutrition or hygiene, future students might have been discouraged from enrolling, and the seminary's standing in the Coptic community damaged. Girgis was trying, with limited resources and through many pleadings and disputes with the Lay Community Council and the Patriarchate Church Council (the administrative body that oversaw the day-to-day operation of the Church as a whole), to raise the academic level and physical infrastructure of the seminary.

Girgis' statutes even prescribed the students' clothing. Each student was to have two linen suits: one for Sundays, feast days, and formal occasions, and the other for everyday wear. Later, Girgis requested that students wear a uniform similar to that worn by priests. Students ate common meals in the seminary's dining room, during which Scripture or another spiritual book was read aloud by the students in turn. Girgis adopted this monastic tradition for the edification of his pupils, thereby using meals for spiritual reflection rather than as wasted time when the mind could wander.

The statutes also covered the lives of priests and teachers beyond the confines of the seminary. For example, the board could transfer a preacher from one place to another according to need and circumstance. Preachers were required to prepare for the board an annual report on their ministry. Parish priests could allow only graduates of the seminary to preach in their parishes, and they had to obtain written permission from the pope. The seminary kept a record of qualified preachers and each year announced the names of the new graduate preachers, along with their places of ministry. These rules served two purposes: they ensured that those who preached were trained and formed at the seminary and preached according to the Coptic faith, and they prevented followers of other religious denominations from infiltrating Coptic parishes and teaching views not in accordance with Coptic Orthodox theology. Such measures gave the Coptic community a layer of protection by ensuring that those who preached came from a reliable source, approved by the pope himself.

One chapter of the seminary's 1912 statutes was dedicated to the curriculum. It set forth the subjects to be studied without specifying which were to be taught in which years of the program; such details would be posted on a notice board. The fields to be covered were broad and varied. They included religion and theology; education; legal studies; Coptic, Arabic, and English language; and liturgical hymnology.

The theological subjects included theoretical theology; Church doctrine, rites, exegesis (critical explanation or interpretation of a biblical text), and homiletics; Church history, in particular, that of the Coptic Church; patristic texts; Christian archaeology and international archaeological sites that proved the authenticity of the Bible; the rights and obligations of pastors, pastoral care, and Church canons. The educational subjects included principles of arithmetic, geometry, algebra, astronomy, natural science, chemistry, zoology, botany, physiology, geology, philosophy, logic, the history of philosophy, philosophical ideologies, intellectual philosophy, moral philosophy, civil history (particularly Egyptian history), the history of the nations of the Torah, the principles of political economy, and the principles of health sciences. Legal studies included principles of general law, personal status laws, and administration and council laws. Students learned Church hymnology specific to the deacons' responses in the three liturgies

His Grace Bishop Kyrellos, Metropolitan of Ethiopia; seated on his left is Bishop Butros of Ethiopia, on the day of the ordination of students as deacons, c. 1935. Habib Girgis is also seated in the front row. (Girgis, The Coptic Orthodox Seminary.*)*

and liturgical rubrics. Finally, physical education was mandated in order to train and strengthen the body.

It is unimaginable that such a vast number of subjects could have been taught in any depth. The seminary struggled to find competent teachers who were qualified in their fields, and many had to be replaced as the seminary progressed. In 1912, when Girgis wrote this program, he had not yet sent for the curricula of theological colleges abroad. It is possible that this first curriculum drew upon ideas gleaned from Catholic missionaries, or from the Evangelical Theological Seminary founded by Presbyterian missionaries in Cairo in 1843. It is imaginable that the subjects that were secular in nature were of particular importance to those students who joined the seminary as teenagers and did not have the opportunity to study such material at school.

Study in the seminary was for a period of up to five years. The course was divided into two streams: weaker students completed only two years, while the more capable scholars continued for a further three years at a more advanced level. Two articles in Chapter 5 of the statutes dealt with the seminary's monitors, a subject of particular significance since it revealed Girgis' pedagogical philosophy.

Article 15: Two or more monitors are to be appointed for the college, according to the needs of the college. They are to be elected from among the most excellent students, or from those who are highly regarded with respect to their virtue, manners, circumspect life, and great zeal. They are to monitor the students during the times of physical activities, when they leave the college for physical activities or when travelling to churches, at meal times, and at sleeping times. Each of them is to inform the dean of their observations. They are to monitor the servants and pass by their sleeping quarters to observe their organization, as well as inspect the kitchen before the placing of the food on the table, requesting that those who do not maintain cleanliness be disciplined.

Article 16: The monitor is to observe the attendance of the students and their meetings, morning and evenings at the set times, as well as to report absentees to the dean of the seminary, along with the reasons for their absence; also, those who are late in attending at the set times and the measure of their lateness, and to record all of this in a book dedicated for this purpose.[13]

This system of students supervising fellow students was based on the Lancastrian system, part of a teaching method developed by Joseph Lancaster (1778–1838), a Quaker educator of the poor in London. Lancaster's own schooling had been rudimentary: attendance at two Dame schools (modest private elementary schools, usually run by women in their own homes) where he learned to read, followed by a stint at a school run by a former army officer, where he learned military discipline. He subsequently gathered together poor children in his area and taught them to read. As student numbers increased but funds remained scarce, Lancaster chose some of the older students to monitor and teach the younger ones. This developed into a formal system in which a head monitor supervised the other monitors, thus making it possible to provide a basic education to large numbers of poor children while employing only the minimum number of paid teachers.

Lancaster's use of monitors in schools was not new; it was also the approach used by the Scottish Episcopalian priest and educationalist

[13]Habib Girgis, "Qānūn al-Madrasah al-Iklīrīkiyah al-Qibṭiyah al-Urthūdhuksiyah" [Statutes of the Coptic Orthodox Clerical School], *al-Karmah* [The Vine] 6.7 (1912): 308–28, at 310–11.

Joseph Lancaster (1778–1838), who introduced the monitorial system of education into Egypt. (https://en.wikipedia.org/wiki/Joseph_Lancaster. Accessed January 31, 2017.)

Andrew Bell (1753–1832). However, in Lancaster's system of collaborative teaching the monitors helped maintain discipline by meting out punishments, including the use of cages and pillories, as well as rewards (rank badges, orders of merit, and prizes). The system was highly regimented: huge classrooms of up to a thousand pupils were divided into benches of eight or ten, each bench under the supervision of a student monitor. Every segment of time was controlled, as was the movement of each group of students through the different tasks. Students stood while being taught (this was thought to be better for health) and sat down only during writing exercises. Because of financial constraints, a limited curriculum of arithmetic, writing, and reading was taught. Monitors' duties also included ensuring the hygiene, order, and development of each boy in the class. Lancaster selected and trained the brighter students as future teachers who would spread his system.

The British and Foreign School Society (BFSS) spread Lancaster's monitorial system throughout the British Isles and abroad. When in 1825 Reverend John Lieder of the Church Missionary Society arrived in Egypt, he established a school based on Lancaster's system. Part of his aim was to introduce evangelical notions of industry, discipline, and order to Egypt. This went beyond religious conversion to the point of cultural colonization by imposing a European way of life and controlling the individual's use of space and time. To some extent Lieder succeeded in his aims, for his model was adopted in Egypt by both Coptic and Muslim educators as a way to inculcate these values in their students.

The CMS Press in Malta began publishing mission materials in 1825 in several languages, including Arabic, and distributed them across the mission stations in the Mediterranean region. An 1831 manual for instructing elementary school students set out the goal of conveying not only certain

Habib Girgis in his office as dean of the Coptic Orthodox Seminary. Behind him hangs a photograph of Girgis with Pope Kyrillos V; to the right hangs a portrait of the previous dean, Yūsuf Manqariyūs. (St Mark Coptic Orthodox Cultural Center, Dayr al-Anbā Ruways.)

values but also a particular frame of mind. On the subject of reading the Bible, for instance, the manual stated: "It becomes an object of the highest importance that the pupil should not only understand the meaning of what is read, but be so far interested in its communications as to regard them with reverence, and habitually to apply them to his own conduct and conscience."[14] Other earlier tracts outlining the Lancastrian system in Arabic were also circulated widely in the nineteenth century. Such manuals would have been readily available to Girgis when he was developing the curriculum and pedagogical approach of the seminary.

The Lancastrian system appealed not only to Egypt's educators but also to its state administrators, The latter believed that if they could coerce their citizens into institutions such as the army or schools, where space and time

[14]British Foreign School Society, *Manual of the System of Primary Instruction, Pursued in the Model Schools of the British and Foreign School Society* (London: Longman and Company, 1831), 25.

Habib Girgis in his office at the Coptic Orthodox Seminary in Mahmashah, c. 1940s. The room survives to this day, as part of the school at the Virgin Mary Church. (St Mark Coptic Orthodox Cultural Center, Dayr al-Anbā Ruways.)

were controlled closely, they could drill into them an awareness of industry and discipline. In 1847 Muḥammad ʿAlī decreed the establishment in Cairo of eight schools based on the Lancastrian system. These were called *makatib al-milla* (national schools) to distinguish them from military establishments, and there were plans to build them throughout the country. Pope Kyrillos IV also became a supporter of Lieder's methods, implementing them at the Great Coptic School.

Girgis promulgated Lancaster's regimented learning methods both at the seminary and in his Sunday School program. He required teachers and students to memorize parts of Scripture along with other important religious teachings, such as the Nicene-Constantinopolitan Creed. While Girgis' statutes do not mention monitors *teaching* other students, only supervising them, it is conceivable that the brighter and more knowledgeable students were required to instruct their peers, particularly in the early days of the seminary when there were few or no teachers of theology. As mentioned, Girgis himself, as a final-year student, had taught religion to his peers at the seminary.

Habib Girgis, early in his career as dean of the Coptic Orthodox Seminary. The desk is now preserved in the St Mark Coptic Orthodox Cultural Center, Dayr al-Anbā Ruways. (St Mark Coptic Orthodox Cultural Center, Dayr al-Anbā Ruways.)

The governance structure of the seminary evolved over several decades. In September 1913, the Holy Synod announced the appointment of a board to administer the seminary, comprising the Very Reverend Father Ḥannā Shinūdah (president), Yūsuf Bik Manqariyūs (dean), Iqlādiyūs Bik Labīb (Coptic language teacher), Habib Girgis (theology lecturer), and the Very Reverend Father Sīdārūs Ghālī (supervisor). But Girgis saw little value in this body, arguing that it did no more than oversee student affairs; it did nothing to improve or develop the seminary, either financially or academically. Because of inactivity and a lack of administrative expertise, this board was disbanded after several meetings.

When Girgis became dean in 1918, he inherited an institution with virtually no organizational structure, vision, or sense of direction. The curriculum was inadequate in many ways, particularly with regard to religious and theological education—the very purpose for which the seminary had been established. Financial constraints led to friction between Girgis and the Lay Community Council, and Girgis felt stymied in his efforts to improve the seminary's infrastructure, increase faculty salaries, meet daily running expenses, and much more.

Girgis, ever resourceful, devised plans to overcome each obstacle that he met along the path. His progress was sometimes bright and at other times

Habib Girgis at his desk at the Coptic Orthodox Seminary. The artefacts on the desk are now preserved at the St Mark Coptic Orthodox Cultural Center, Dayr al-Anbā Ruways. (St Mark Coptic Orthodox Cultural Center, Dayr al-Anbā Ruways.)

full of thorns and pain, but his goal for the seminary was always clear: he wanted it to render an important service to the Church and the community by preparing young men for the priesthood. He also wished to educate those with a monastic vocation, for some of them would eventually become bishops, members of the Holy Synod, and leaders of the Church. Indeed, one such student, Naẓīr Jayyid (b. 1923), would become Pope Shenouda III, the 117th Pope of Alexandria and Patriarch of the See of St Mark, who reigned from 1971 until his death in 2012.

Girgis also wanted to raise to international levels the standards of the seminary's administration, the quality of its faculty and curriculum, and the standards of the student body. He knew that the seminary needed a high-quality library full of useful resources, and he aimed to upgrade the buildings in order to support those aspirations. He wanted the seminary to be able to offer other exceptional degrees in addition to those in theology. He forbade the staff to take up work outside the seminary, so that they could concentrate on their reading, research, acquisition of knowledge, and teaching. He encouraged his more advanced students to write books, publish in *The Vine* and other suitable journals, translate educational materials, and present research papers.

Another important goal was teaching the students to preach. Girgis, a brilliant and convincing preacher, in 1916 delivered an important lecture on the subject at the Coptic Orthodox Society of Faith: *The History of Preaching and Its Importance in the Christian Church Generally, and the Coptic Church Specifically*.[15] The society printed the sermon and sold it to the public, with the proceeds donated by Girgis to the Society. So that seminarians would serve the wider community while gaining firsthand experience at preaching, Girgis eventually sent more than a hundred students to preach in parishes throughout Cairo and in several governorates and dioceses elsewhere in Egypt. In this way education was not dispensed within an ivory tower, but became integral to the life of the community. Girgis remarked:

Dean Habib Girgis at the Coptic Orthodox Seminary, dressed elegantly and wearing a tarboush (fez), which was very popular during his lifetime. (St Mark Coptic Orthodox Cultural Center, Dayr al-Anbā Ruways.)

> This light [of preaching] had a great effect, for the Clerical School filled the churches with preaching and counseling. It used the pulpits for the word of God after they had remained empty with no preachers for a long time. . . . As for now, the seminary has graduated those who have loved the pulpits, shaken them, and enlivened preaching, and hence benefited the people as well as spread the doctrine. They abundantly filled the remote districts with their preaching and knowledge, after the

[15]Habib Girgis, *Tārīkh al-wa'ẓ wa-ahammiyatih fī al-Kanīsah al-Masīḥiyah 'umūman wa-al-Qibṭiyah khuṣūṣan* [The History of Preaching and Its Importance in the Christian Church Generally, and the Coptic Church Specifically] (Cairo: Jam'iyat al-Īmān al-Qibṭiyah al-Urthūdhuksiyah, 1916).

community had been deprived of knowing their faith, and thus led them to the word of salvation.[16]

As dean of the seminary, Girgis had his work cut out for him. He took on a monumental list of reforms under dire circumstances, embracing a task that might have discouraged the most formidable and talented of educators. He was fully aware of the immense responsibility placed on his shoulders, later recalling:

> In truth, I felt my weakness in front of this precious trust with which His Holiness the Pope entrusted me. I also felt my weakness in front of this heavy and exhausting burden. What encouraged me is that I am a son of this school and one of the most loving and enthusiastic [individuals] toward it, and the one most desiring to see its renaissance and progress. So, I have borne the burden willingly while remembering the Lord's saying, "For power is made perfect in weakness" [2 Cor 12.9]. I consecrated my life for its service, sacrificing every effort in serving the Church and the seminary. I relied on God, who said to his servant Paul, "My grace is sufficient for you" [2 Cor 12.9], and on the support of the great pope and the loyal sons of the community.[17]

Girgis described his love for the seminary and his zeal for educational and theological reform in strong metaphorical language, likening it to the "shedding of blood," "putting one's life and spirit at its service," and "the kindling of fire and hope in one's heart."[18] He concluded:

> I felt a voice calling me from the depth of my heart. . . . My soul is ignited, moving to rise up to the duty toward the seminary, for which God created me—for I was created for its sake. Hence, I did not rest for one instant, nor did I become tepid for one second; nor did I slacken from working for its progress. This was an inner voice and call, a desired hope, a deep love, and a definite desire.[19]

[16]Girgis, *The Coptic Orthodox Seminary*, 145.
[17]Ibid., 30.
[18]Ibid.
[19]Ibid., 30–31.

When he first took up the post of dean in 1918, Girgis was dissatisfied with the curriculum, arguing that it lacked social studies, philosophical subjects, and languages, all of which were essential for training priests. His ambitious curriculum of 1912 still had not yet been fully implemented. Now he decided it was time to introduce logic, philosophy, education, psychology, and the Hebrew and Greek languages, with special attention to the study of English and Arabic.

On January 17, 1919, a new board for the seminary was announced by papal decree. Kyrillos V explained that the board's role was "to be concerned with its [the seminary's] business, and do all that is good toward safeguarding its prosperity."[20] That board consisted of some of the most prominent Copts of the day: the Very Reverend Father Buṭrus 'Abd al-Mālik, president of the Lay Community Council and the Great Church of St Mark, was its president, while members included the Very Reverend Father Sīdārūs Ghālī, Marcus Pasha Simaika, Bāsṭawrūs Bik Ṣalīb, and Habib Girgis. However this body was no more successful than the one instituted in 1913. According to Girgis it met several times, but its decisions were not put into action, so it ceased to meet and was dissolved. The main reason for this failure was that the reforms envisaged by Girgis required a great deal of funding. This subject became the basis of an almost daily power struggle between Girgis and the Lay Community Council.

Girgis never lacked enthusiasm and ambition for the seminary, but his optimism was sometimes soured by the financial constraints constantly imposed by the Lay Community Council. Two events led to the council's desire to exert this type of control. The first occurred before Girgis became dean, but he certainly would have been aware of the circumstances. This was the struggle between Kyrillos V and the council for control over the Coptic Church's financial and administrative affairs, which led to the banishment of the pope to his desert monastery for five months in 1892–93. Despite the fact that the pope was the head of the council, the laity colluded with the khedive to have the pope banished. Although this exile was relatively short in duration, its repercussions continued for some time, damaging the Coptic community and severely reducing the income of the Patriarchate.

[20]Ibid., 54.

The problem continued to worsen because of bad financial administration at the Patriarchate between 1893 and 1912.

In his 1938 history of the seminary, Girgis reiterated what Yūsuf Manqariyūs, his predecessor as dean, had stated in an earlier publication, *A History of the Coptic People in the Last Twenty Years from 1893 to 1912*: the financial hardships afflicting the Patriarchate after the events of 1892 were caused by expenditure exceeding income, particularly in the schools. The educational standards of the missionary schools had easily surpassed the Coptic ones. As a result the Patriarchate, in trying to catch up, had expended more money with no corresponding increase in income. Ultimately the Coptic schools could not compete, and the Patriarchate's budgetary situation was badly affected by these efforts.

The second event that affected the Church finances was World War I. When Girgis began his tenure as dean in 1918, the Patriarchate's treasury had already suffered from wartime exigencies, which in turn had detrimental effects on the seminary. Fortunately, Girgis was an energetic and successful fundraiser. He attracted donations of EGP243 to assist the cantors in 1919; in 1923, he collected EGP1,915 for the seminary buildings, plus EGP54 during the Golden Jubilee celebrations for Kyrillos V in November of that year. Kyrillos V himself donated EGP713 in 1923, while in 1926 EGP550 was bequeathed by Bitrū Fara'awn, a Copt who had lived next door to the seminary. In total, Girgis managed to raise close to EGP3,500, which was a substantial amount at that time. He was an eloquent preacher, and his fundraising success reflects how convincing he could be in persuading Copts of the importance of the seminary. The threat of losing their identity drove many Coptic notables and others in the community to support the cause of the seminary as a place to train future leaders.

Nevertheless, funding still fell short. The Lay Community Council controlled various religious endowments (*awqāf*) that it could have drawn upon to enable Girgis to achieve at least part of his goals for the seminary, but chose not to. Rather, the council asserted its authority and control through the allocation and withholding of funds. Never did Girgis have funding secured for several years in advance so that he could plan confidently for the long-term development and growth of the seminary. To make matters even more difficult, personal agendas and interpersonal dynamics hindered the advancement of the seminary. For instance, during a visit to the seminary near the end of his papacy, Kyrillos V was told by Marcus Simaika Pasha, deputy of the Lay Community Council: "I confess to Your Holiness, that, because of the [constraints of the] budget, we were resisting this work."[21] The pope was taken by surprise, for he had not been told that there was resistance from that quarter. Friction between Kyrillos V and the council over authority and finances led to the laity often sidelining the pope and making its decisions independently. At times the council even acted in direct opposition to his instructions. In one such instance Kyrillos V directed a certain amount to be paid to the seminary, but the council transferred only half that figure. The lay council members saw themselves as the learned, knowledgeable elite of the Coptic community and hence entitled to overturn or defy the decisions of their spiritual leader. This tension between the pope and the council continued to be an obstacle to the educational reform that Girgis envisaged for the Coptic community and caused him much grief over the years, despite the fact that Kyrillos V held Girgis in great affection and supported his educational mission.

Marcus Simaika Pasha (1864–1944), a prominent member of the Lay Community Council, who resisted much of Girgis' work at the Coptic Orthodox Seminary. (https://upload.wikimedia.org/wikipedia/en/3/3d/Marcus_Simaika_Pasha_1864-1944.jpg. Accessed January 31, 2017.)

Another obstacle to improving the seminary was the lack of student entrance requirements. Girgis' statutes of 1912 required only that candidates be at least sixteen years of age and have completed their fourth year of elementary schooling. Such poorly educated boys often struggled with theological studies and, as a result, the curriculum remained elementary at best.

[21]Ibid., 52.

Most students did not enroll for the purpose of studying religion, but rather to be ordained priests. The nominal length of study was five years, but most students remained for only two or three before returning to their towns to be ordained. Those who desired more knowledge might remain for four years, but the ostensible five-year course was not put into practice. Girgis aimed to raise the prerequisites for admission while convincing students of the value of a theological education and the significance of the instructive role they were to play in the Coptic community.

As well as attending formal lessons on preaching during the school term, students were required to gather after hours with the teacher of homiletics. They were expected to preach daily, initially on the premises and in later years at the seminary's church. Students in their two final years were to preach in the churches of Cairo and surrounding regions during Lent and on Sundays. In January 1938, students were sent to preach in fifty-seven areas including seven districts in Cairo, nine in the diocese of Giza, fifteen in Qalyūbiyah, nine in Munūfiyah, fourteen in Daqahliyah, and three in al-Sharqiyah. A month later the number of areas covered had grown to sixty-six. Each preacher was to provide a weekly report detailing the district, the title of his sermon, the main points taught, and the number of males and females in attendance, along with any other salient observations.

After graduation, students needed a license from the Lay Community Council if they were to preach in the churches. Their application had to include a statement from the seminary certifying that they had successfully completed their studies. In this way the Lay Community Council maintained control over who was preaching, preventing non-Orthodox teachings from infiltrating Coptic Orthodox pulpits.

* * *

At the time of Girgis' appointment as dean, the administrative body that oversaw the day-to-day operations of the Coptic Church was the Patriarchate Church Council. Since the boards appointed to run the seminary had failed, the Church Council itself supervised the seminary directly from 1913 to 1926. In 1925 the seminary presented to the council two reports based on an outline written by Girgis two years earlier, in which he highlighted five areas that required attention if the standards of the seminary were to be

Habib Girgis and faculty and students of the Coptic Orthodox Seminary, with His Eminence Metropolitan Kyrellos, metropolitan of Ethiopia, and Bishop Butros of Ethiopia, c. 1931. (Girgis, The Coptic Orthodox Seminary.*)*

raised to an acceptable level. The first need was for proper infrastructure, especially buildings, furniture, and stationery; second, that the seminary should become a full-time boarding school; third, that enrolling students must have completed their secondary education; fourth, that the number of qualified faculty be increased; and, finally, that graduates be guaranteed a career.

Girgis had observed a wide disparity in the prior levels of educational attainment between students from rural and urban areas. For this reason he had, in 1912, divided the seminary's program into two levels: intermediate and advanced. By 1925 his thinking had developed further. He now proposed that students with only an elementary education (primarily those from rural areas) be accepted at the intermediate level and expected to complete a five-year course, rather than the previously mandated three years. These students would study the humanities, Coptic language, religious subjects, and Church rites. After graduating they could preach or serve as priests in rural areas only, or teach religion at an elementary school. Anyone with higher ambitions would be required to enter the advanced level of the seminary for further training.

The advanced level would accept only students who had completed their secondary (high school) education and received the so-called baccalaureate.

First-year advanced level students of the Coptic Orthodox Seminary, with Habib Girgis, c. 1930s. (Girgis, The Coptic Orthodox Seminary.*)*

To attract such students, the seminary would pay them a monthly stipend of at least EGP2. They would study for four years, rather than the original two, taking on higher theological studies as set out by Girgis in 1925. Upon graduation, these students could work as preachers in urban areas, with a monthly salary of at least EGP12; when ordained as priests, this would increase to at least EGP15.[22] Girgis argued that such salaries were necessary to attract intelligent young men to the seminary and the ministry. These provisions would guarantee their futures and limit clerical ordinations to graduates of the seminary.

Girgis' distinction between the levels of education required of a preacher—defined as an unordained layman with some level of theological education who preaches in local parishes on Sundays and other occasions—and an ordained priest, along with where each could serve, reflects his views on the relative level of educational attainment between urban and rural Coptic communities. In his booklet *General Visitations to the Village*, he notes the high level of illiteracy in rural areas, attributable to the low levels of

[22]Girgis did not state the period covered by these proposed salary payments, but we can assume he was referring to a monthly salary.

Second-year (probably advanced level) students of the Coptic Orthodox Seminary, with Habib Girgis, c. 1930s. (Girgis, The Coptic Orthodox Seminary.*)*

education and extreme poverty in the villages. These poor villages had been fertile ground for Western missionaries since the latter arrived in Egypt in the nineteenth century. Girgis' idea of sending the less-educated preachers and priests to rural regions seems unwise, as they would have had difficulty competing with well-educated missionaries from England and the United States. In fact, these rural areas needed the best clergy, capable of raising the spiritual, doctrinal, and educational level of the villagers. (Nevertheless, unordained preachers, some with no academic theological qualifications, continue to serve in the Coptic Orthodox Church today.) In Girgis' time the more affluent Coptic preachers and priests probably preferred staying in the big cities, where their names were recognized and remuneration was higher, over going to a remote village under difficult conditions, and where the pay was far lower.

Girgis' 1925 report further suggested dividing the seminary into several departments: one for the intermediate and one for the advanced seminarians who were boarding; one for recently ordained priests who had not completed their studies and were required to take two lessons per day, two or three days per week; a department for the education of monks; one for affiliated students who studied part-time in the evenings, because of their work commitments, and also served as Sunday School teachers; and a translations and publications department, which would employ those students who excelled in languages to translate religious books. This department would also publish other religious materials and booklets, whether from the patristic writings or from contemporary works.

But Girgis' plans were not taken up. Instead, the Patriarchate Church Council created yet another committee in October 1926 to investigate the seminary's existing academic and administrative systems and put forward a plan to organize it as a higher education provider. Again, the committee was made up of prominent community members: His Eminence Metropolitan Lukās of Manfalūṭ and Abnūb (president), Habib Girgis, Dr Jurjī Bik Sūbhī (a professor at the Egyptian University), Kāmil Afandī Jirjis (a lecturer at the Higher Institute for Teachers), Dr Jundī Wāṣif (a dentist), and Da'ūd Afandī Ghālī. Its task was not an easy one, particularly as it was required to complete its work within two months. The committee was instructed to

> investigate the curricula, the current system of education and the level of the current students, as well as to put in place a plan to raise the level of the Clerical School to the highest one possible, while keeping in mind the local situation. It is first to indicate the temporary remedy, either with respect to the current students or faculty staff; and then to indicate how long it would take to move from the current system to the future one. It is to indicate how this gradual change will come about with respect to the curricula, the guidelines for accepting new students, or in the appointment of faculty staff. It is also to present the final curricula that would be used once the Clerical School has reached that highest level.[23]

The committee met several times before delivering in February 1927 a report based largely on Girgis' suggestions, and a budget for the forthcoming school year. The report acknowledged the seminary's financial difficulties and the economic crisis that the country was facing, asking only for what was considered to be essential, fundamental, and practical. Acknowledging Girgis' "great endeavors" in developing the seminary religiously, spiritually, and academically, the committee sought the support of the Patri-

[23]Ibid., 58–9.

First-year intermediate level students of the Coptic Orthodox Seminary, with Habib Girgis, c. 1930s. (Girgis, The Coptic Orthodox Seminary.*)*

archate Church Council, the Lay Community Council, and the pope to raise standards even further.

Among the 1927 report's recommendations was a change of name, from the Clerical School (*al-Madrasah al-iklīrīkiyah*, المدرسة الاكليريكية) to the Coptic Orthodox Seminary (*Kulliyat al-lāhūt al-Qibṭiyah*, كلية اللاهوت القبطية). This rebranding was intended to give the institution a new outlook and sense of prestige, and to convey the impression of a higher-caliber educational establishment. But the name change came to fruition only in 1946, although the other change proposed in 1927—to upgrade Girgis' role from principal (*al-mudīr* المدير) to dean (*al-nāẓir* الناظر)—was accepted.

The committee wanted all faculty to be appropriately qualified, both academically and spiritually, with preference given to Clerical School graduates who had completed the higher-level course. This would entail transferring some unqualified faculty members to other schools. The committee also proposed two academic streams. The first was study at the intermediate level for five years; a graduate of that level could then skip the first year of the higher level and complete a further three years. Prerequisite for the intermediate level was an elementary school certificate; to enter the higher level a student had to have completed senior high school. In both streams there were boarders, who were being prepared for religious ministry, along

Faculty of the Coptic Orthodox Seminary, c. mid-1930s. FROM LEFT, SEATED: *Marc Baruck (English), Shenuda Effendi Abd al-Sayyid (Coptic), Hegumen Ibrahim Attiya (theology), Habib Girgis (dean), Father Constantine Musa (students' primary supervisor and confessor), Yassa Effendi Abd al-Massih (Greek), and Boctor Effendi Shehata (Biblical exposition).* FROM LEFT, STANDING: *Cantor Mikhail Jirjis (Church hymnology), Edward Effendi Yustus (Church history), Manqariyus Effendi Awadallah (doctrinal theology), Boulos Effendi Bassili (boarding supervisor), Aziz Effendi Tadrus (Coptic), Kamel Effendi Matta (Biblical studies) and Cantor Labib Mikhail (Church hymns). Photograph by Aziz Tadrus, probably a student of the seminary. (Girgis,* The Coptic Orthodox Seminary.*)*

with new priests and monks wanting to improve their theological education. Evening classes were proposed for those unable to study full time. A translation department was suggested, to overcome the scarcity of religious and theological books published in Arabic. Girgis had begun to import books and pamphlets, mostly in French and English, that needed to be translated into Arabic for the benefit of clerical students and the Coptic community more widely.

The report also stressed the importance of having qualified lecturers, preferably chosen from among the higher-level graduates of the seminary or from those holding higher diplomas from other schools, colleges, or universities. The low salaries paid to local faculty affected their morale, and gave them little incentive to improve their academic standards. Girgis

Third-year (probably advanced level) students of the Coptic Orthodox Seminary, with Habib Girgis, c. 1930s. (Girgis, The Coptic Orthodox Seminary.*)*

understood their predicament and made repeated requests for increased pay, to no avail. He wrote bitterly to the Patriarchate Church Council: "I have said that the moral state of the teachers is unacceptable, and their spirits are low with pain, and overburdened with hardships. How can a teacher work while his mind is disturbed and his soul is in pain and in a miserable state?"[24] Being poorly paid, the existing lecturers showed little desire to develop their knowledge and skills, nor did they exert themselves to strive for academic excellence among their students. To attract well-qualified and ambitious staff, the committee recommended salaries between EGP20 and EGP30 per month. Current salaries were about one-quarter of this, equivalent to those of elementary school teachers or those teaching in the *kuttāb* system. Twelve teachers were needed; the budget for 1927–28 requested a salary allocation of EGP2,880—an average of EGP240 per annum per teacher. The dean's salary was to be increased to EGP600 per year, out of a total proposed budget of EGP9,610.

Even at the most basic level, the students faced hardships. The report proposed raising the meals budget almost fourfold, from a dismal EGP500 per year for 120 students to EGP1,875. Such requests for more generous allocations for food were ignored, year after year. A full decade later, in 1937, Girgis wrote:

> I see the student at the beginning of the academic year in good health, strong and vibrant, and yet, shortly afterwards, signs of emaciation and weakness begin to appear, because of the lack of proper nutrition. This is to be expected in a student who is exhausted from studying many subjects while not receiving sufficient nutrition. This is an extremely vital

[24]Habib Girgis to the Patriarchate Church Council, February 21, 1929, Patriarchal Archives 4–6.2–4/33.

matter for the success of the seminary, and so I hope it can be treated with care, since the right mind exists within a healthy body.[25]

The 1927 budget also addressed the physical infrastructure of the seminary and the need for expansion to accommodate the growing number of students. It proposed building a church, sporting facilities, and a lounge. A dean's residence on the premises was requested, to allow Girgis to oversee the work of the seminary more easily and remain in close contact with the students. Part of the proposed budget was allocated for student uniforms, and EGP200 for new books for the library. Additionally, it included spending on secretarial and medical staff; other ancillary staff such as cooks and gardeners; building maintenance; printing and stationery; newspaper advertisements; and EGP1,000 for translation and publication.

The report that was presented alongside this budget emphasized that the seminary was "the spinal cord of the Coptic Church and the measure of its revival and refinement,"[26] and argued that the proposed new system would raise standards to a level suited to modern developments and circumstances. Despite all this work by a committee that the Patriarchate Church Council had expressly appointed, there was no immediate response. Girgis followed up with a letter to the council on May 31, 1927, after the academic year had ended, seeking a response so that improvements could begin at the start of the new academic year. Almost two months later, he received a hasty and brief reply requesting a report on the last academic year before the committee could look into the new curriculum.

Both Girgis and the committee must have been deeply frustrated by this apparent lack of interest from the very body that had demanded such a thorough inquiry and imposed such a stringent deadline. The reasons for the Patriarchate Church Council's ambivalence are unclear. The most likely explanation is a lack of finances to implement the recommendations, although the council may also have been trying to exert its authority over the seminary.

[25]Habib Girgis, Theological College budget for 1937–38 (1937), Patriarchal Archives 4–6.154–5/8.

[26]Committee of the Coptic Orthodox Seminary, Report to the Patriarchate Church Council, February 11, 1927, Patriarchal Archives 4–6.191/2, Theological College Restorations & Repairs, Part 1.

Rare photographs of Habib Girgis (on the left) relaxing: enjoying some refreshments at the Pyramids of Giza with Najīb Fulayfil, Na'īmah Najīb Fulayfil (seated next to Girgis), and Marc Baruck (at the front right), the English teacher at the Clerical School who owned a chalet near the Pyramids. Monday 25 September 1939. The Fulaayfil family lived in the same apartment block with the Girgis family, and the two families had a very close relationship. (Private collection, courtesy of Emad Asad—Helwan, Egypt.)

However, Girgis did make some needed additions to the curriculum during the 1927–28 academic year: geography lessons, plus translation from English into Arabic. Among the teachers was a Frenchman named Marc Baruck, who taught English; it is possible that Girgis asked Baruck to bring back theological books from Europe on his many trips there. Girgis also added the subjects of education and the Ethiopian language, with the latter taught by an Ethiopian since students from that country had begun to attend the seminary. Ethiopia was still under the full care of the Coptic Church (a situation that continued until the Ethiopian Church gained autocephalous

Habib Girgis with Najīb Fulayfil and Najīb's daughters, (from the left) Su'ād, Na'īmah and Nādiyah. The photo seems to have been taken at the Fulayfil chalet near the Pyramids. (St Mark Coptic Orthodox Cultural Center, Dayr al-Anbā Ruways.)

Habib Girgis with Najīb Fulayfil and Najīb's daughters, (from the left) Su'ād, Nādiyah and Na'īmah. The photo seems to have been taken at the Fulayfil chalet near the Pyramids. (St Mark Coptic Orthodox Cultural Center, Dayr al-Anbā Ruways.)

status in 1959), and the relationship between the two churches was very strong. Indeed, Emperor Haile Selassie I asked Pope Yu'annis XIX to select a new archbishop for Ethiopia, and accordingly Archbishop Qerelos was appointed the 111th Archbishop of Ethiopia in 1929. In early 1930, Girgis accompanied Pope Yu'annis on a significant trip to Ethiopia, subsequently dedicating an entire issue of *The Vine* to a report on the festivities and the warm welcome that had been extended to the patriarch. Relations between the Egyptian and Ethiopian churches did not turn sour until after the Italian occupation of Ethiopia in 1935.

Habib Girgis lived in a world—and, most notably, a Coptic community—that was profoundly political and nationalistic. This nationalism is reflected in projects such as the push to establish a Coptic Museum in Cairo at the turn of the twentieth century. Girgis' focus on teaching the Coptic language was part of a wider effort to create a religious community connected

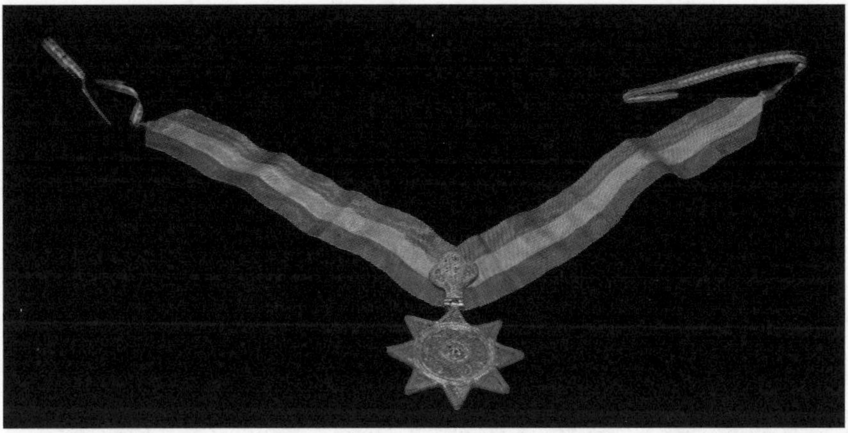

A pendant of the Ethiopian star, the highest-ranking decoration in the Ethiopian order of Commander. This was presented to Habib Girgis in 1925 by the Emperor of Ethiopia. (St Mark Coptic Orthodox Cultural Center, Dayr al-Anbā Ruways; photograph by Hani Gadoun.)

by a sacred language and written script. He was not only training the next generation of leaders of the Coptic Orthodox Church but at the same time creating a generation of self-identifying Copts who could communicate using what Westerners labeled some a "dead" language.

This, however, was not Girgis' only motive. He was also aiming to mold a generation of Egyptian nationalists. Copts played an important role in the revival of the classical Arabic language and the spread of Arab nationalism around this time. Girgis employed Muslim sheikhs from the venerable al-Azhar University to teach Arabic at the seminary, and, in 1927–28, added another subject to the curriculum: "national education" (*tarbiyah waṭaniyah*, تربية وطنية). Girgis was part of the small, liberal intelligentsia, the product of increasing literacy and the spread of print media, who fostered such nationalism. Nation-building, by then the norm across the world, had already become a policy of the relatively new state of Egypt. This policy blended popular and official nationalisms and depended upon the educational system as an important tool to instill those values in the young. National identity and political consciousness were virtually inseparable. Nationalist leaders deliberately deployed civil educational systems to teach courses modeled on official nationalisms. This modern style of education espoused by Girgis—and embodied in his plans for the seminary, even

Fourth-year (probably advanced level) students of the Coptic Orthodox Seminary, with Habib Girgis, c. 1930s. (Girgis, The Coptic Orthodox Seminary.*)*

though it was a private religious organization—was a central factor in his identity-building ethos.

Nevertheless, Girgis was adamant that the Church not become politically partisan. Students at the seminary were not permitted to participate in activities such as demonstrations, nor to publish in magazines without prior approval. Neither the Sunday School movement nor the Coptic Youth League was permitted to become involved in political parties or sectarian matters.

Girgis appointed foreign lecturers to teach subjects for which no qualified Coptic teachers could be found. For instance, in October 1928 he announced that the seminary's "elite group of instructors of theology, the humanities and law" had been joined by the honorable Mr John Leonard Wilson, who held a higher degree in theology from Oxford University, to teach philosophy of religion. This was a surprising move, given Kyrillos V's previous refusal to permit two non-Coptic lecturers to teach theology, but might be explained by the fact that the appointment took place during a vacancy of the papal throne. Pope Yu'annis XIX was not to begin his incumbency until December 16, 1928, and Wilson signed his contract on October 1. In his letter of application, Wilson stated: "I respect the doctrines and creeds of the Coptic Church and will undertake not to attempt to confute such doctrines

Dr Isrā'īl Wulfinsūn, lecturer of Hebrew language at the seminary. (Girgis, The Coptic Orthodox Seminary.*)*

Māyir Dahhān, adjunct professor of Hebrew language at the seminary. (Girgis, The Coptic Orthodox Seminary.*)*

Ḥāmid Mutawallī al-Khawlī, lecturer of Arabic language at the seminary. (Girgis, The Coptic Orthodox Seminary.*)*

or to establish any other in any way."[27] He was granted the generous salary of EGP40 per month (more than twice the wage of the local faculty members) for an initial one-year contract. Girgis understood that appointing a highly credentialed scholar from Oxford would help raise both academic standards and the prestige of the seminary. While he did not allow non-Orthodox doctrine to be taught to his students, Girgis looked beyond dogma to the other benefits that such a scholar could bring.

He also employed foreign teachers of French, English, and Greek while appointing rabbis to teach Hebrew and imams to teach Arabic. Meanwhile, there were great arguments over whether or not to send some students to study at an Anglican seminary in Britain. This had been suggested by several members of the Lay Community Council, but after lengthy discussion the proposal was rejected by the Holy Synod, in yet another example of the existing tensions over authority and power between the laity and Church hierarchy.

Throughout most of Girgis' career, students were accepted into the seminary with little prior education; many had not even finished elementary

[27] John Leonard Wilson to Ibrahim Takla Bey, September 3, 1928, Patriarchal Archives 10–10.10/28.

school. The Patriarchate Church Council preferred to admit only high school graduates, but this proved very difficult to achieve in practice. In 1928, Girgis wrote to the Patriarchate Church Council:

> The decree of the council stated that no student is to be accepted at the Clerical School unless he has either his certificate of competence [*al-kafā'ah*, الكفاءة, equivalent to Year 11] or the secondary baccalaureate [*bakālūriyā*, بكالوريا , equivalent to Year 12]. We have now twenty-four students who have presented themselves to join and there are no students who have the certificate of competence. Five of them dropped out in Year 11, fourteen have their primary school certificate, and the remainder have not completed their primary education.[28]

At least some of the students were teenagers attending the seminary out of necessity rather than a love of theology. A case in point was a priest who, in 1930, pleaded with Pope Yu'annis XIX to accept his son into the seminary because he could not afford to send him to a secondary school after he had completed his elementary education. The pope requested that Girgis accept the boy. This was far from the caliber of students that Girgis envisaged: young men who were well qualified, eager to study theology, and desirous of spending the rest of their lives serving the Church.

During the 1930s the curriculum continued to evolve. Although the names of subjects remained largely unchanged, Girgis regularly updated their content to keep up to date with advancements in education that he characterized as "the educational renaissance, which we witness in our beloved country in our present time."[29] He divided the subjects into nine categories, clearly setting out the years in which each subject was to be taught, the number of lectures for each, and the grading system for assessment. Staff salaries, however, remained disappointingly low. In 1937–38, for example, the teacher of religion in the cantors' school was earning only EGP5.5 per month; the other teachers probably earned similarly small amounts.

In May 1942, Girgis outlined a further refinement of the curriculum of the seminary. Along with adding Semitic languages, French, and social

[28]Habib Girgis to the Patriarchate Church Council, October 12, 1928, Patriarchal Archives 4–6.7–8/21.

[29]Girgis, *The Coptic Orthodox Seminary*, 93.

Fifth-year (probably advanced level) students of the Coptic Orthodox Seminary, with Habib Girgis, c. 1940. (Girgis, The Coptic Orthodox Seminary.*)*

studies, he restructured the seminary by dividing it into nine streams. There would now be only one level for the main course of study, which was primarily for those aspiring to the priesthood, requiring four years to complete. The Sunday School teachers' course would require three years of part-time study, comprising two lessons per week. The clerical course, for ordained priests, would also be part-time over a three-year period, but with six lessons per week, into which Girgis proposed introducing the subject of comparative theology. He described this innovation as the teaching of the "points of difference between the doctrines of the Coptic Church and the doctrines of the other churches, proving the correctness of Orthodox doctrine."[30] Unfortunately the 1942 plan only partially came to fruition because of a lack of funding.

Another largely unrealized ambition at this time was Girgis' proposal to set up a branch of study for monks that would enhance the main program of study with further subjects such as monastic teachings, politics, and social studies. This was considered important because it was from among the monastic ranks that bishops were ordained, and these extra subjects would be useful for bishops in dealing with government officials, and in

[30]Habib Girgis, memorandum to the director and members of the Churches Committee, May 11, 1942, Patriarchal Archives 4–6.2–9/45.

various other aspects of their ministry. Girgis also proposed a branch for Ethiopian studies, seeking to educate the seminary's Ethiopian students so that they could better serve their own people. A branch for studying the Coptic language and its various dialects was another part of Girgis' vision, a proposal of particular importance since part of his desire was to maintain and strengthen Coptic identity.

Three years after this reorganization, in March 1945, Girgis' final development of the seminary's curriculum was decreed. Henceforth, the seminary would accept only students who had completed their secondary education, and the intermediate level of study would be abolished. After a transitional period the prescribed years of study would be reduced to three, starting in October 1946.

In 1944 Girgis had established the Coptic Teachers' School,, located at the seminary. Its two-year course concentrated on training teachers in pedagogical skills, with the purpose of equipping Coptic teachers to deliver Christian religious instruction in public elementary and secondary schools, or to teach all subjects in Coptic elementary schools. The curriculum covered Christian religion and Orthodox doctrine, education and the history of education, educational techniques, and special methods of teaching various subjects, as well as school health and physiology. The teaching of Christian religion in Egypt's public school system had been approved in 1908, a development in which Girgis had played a significant role. But such teaching was not yet taking place in the Coptic schools, a matter on which Girgis sent many letters to the Patriarchate Church Council and the Lay Community Council between 1925 and 1934. Girgis was confident that having trained Coptic teachers educating elementary school-aged children in their compulsory subjects, as well as schooling them in Christian beliefs, would provide them with a solid Christian formation.

In 1946 Girgis introduced further part-time study in the evenings for university graduates who were employed and yet still desired to serve as volunteers in their own parishes. Many leaders of Sunday Schools from Cairo and Giza enrolled in the seminary at that time, although women were not admitted until October 1959, nearly eight years after Girgis' death. Sadly, however, the Lay Community Council ordered the closure of this new graduate seminary during Girgis' last illness.

The curriculum was at a more developed stage than it had ever been, with distinct fields of study and the precise content of each subject now documented in greater detail. For instance, the curriculum in the field of Old Testament studies comprised, in essence, study of the ancient Hebrew language in which the books of the Old Testament had been written. The student would progress in the language from the Book of Genesis through to the Book of Isaiah. He would learn the principles of writing, reading, and translation, as well as methods of studying the Old Testament, the geography of the regions where the books were written, and the history of its peoples from Israel's beginning until the birth of Christ. The main personalities of those times were studied, as well as contemporaneous archeological discoveries.

The seminary still struggled to find qualified Coptic Orthodox faculty members to teach such subjects, eventually conceding that if no suitable Coptic teacher could be found, a theological teacher might be recruited from another (preferably Orthodox) denomination. The depressingly low pay rates were still in place: even in 1948, the average teacher was earning around EGP12 per month. Girgis, as dean, was paid just over EGP40, while the cantor Mīkhā'īl Jirjis was earning less than EGP4 for teaching liturgical hymnology. There was also the continuing dilemma over whether or not to send students abroad to gain higher qualifications in Western seminaries and universities. Girgis struggled with this predicament throughout his career. In November 1945 the committee suggested that some of the seminary's brighter graduates be sent abroad to study Hebrew and Greek, in order that they might, upon their return, replace the foreign faculty members.

It was also decided at this time to form an administrative committee for the seminary, consisting of three metropolitans chosen by the Holy Synod, three members of the organizing committee, the dean, and two members of the faculty. Its role would be to examine every nomination to the priesthood from across Egypt and present its recommendations to the pope for his approval. Any ordination carried out in defiance of that system would be considered void. This move would bring an unprecedented degree of centralization to the Church and greater authority for the pope. Girgis wished only to ensure that those who had earned their qualifications at the seminary would be ordained to the priesthood, and no one else. Whether this goal was achievable is open to question; the decree was followed to a great extent during the papacy of Kyrillos VI, but less closely under subsequent popes.

There are similarities between Girgis' various curricula and several others that were recently found in the Patriarchal Archives. Michel Marie Jullien (1827–1911), a French Jesuit missionary, established Egypt's first Coptic Catholic seminary in Ṭahṭā in 1899. A curriculum from around 1939 includes guidelines for the admission of students, who had to present a letter of recommendation from their pastor or bishop as part of their application, just as Girgis required of his candidates. The Catholic curriculum also made it clear that no bishop could ordain a priest unless he had proof that the candidate had completed his theological qualifications, and that the committee responsible for examining proposed candidates had given its approval—again, similar to the system Girgis implemented. Study at the Catholic seminary was for a period of four years, whereas Girgis had reduced study at his seminary to three years, probably because of the lack of qualified faculty. Many of the subjects taught at the Catholic seminary were similar to those Girgis had brought in. The Catholics placed such an emphasis on philosophy that they had a specialized college for the subject, with a period of study lasting two years. Girgis likewise specified several philosophy subjects. The Catholics spread their curriculum over four years, during which time each field of study would develop from year to year, whereas the curriculum at the Coptic Orthodox Seminary was simpler. In 1945, it was unclear how the curriculum progressed over the three-year period.

Also found recently in the Patriarchal Archives was a four-year curriculum for training priests, prepared in the mid-1940s by the Reverend E. G. Parry for Kelham Anglican Theological College in England. Girgis had access to these documents when preparing some of his curricula, and the similarities are clear. For instance, logic and psychology were to be taught in the first year of the four-year program at Kelham, while part of the fourth-year course concentrated on a priest's pastoral work. Girgis adopted both in his curriculum. There were contrasts, of course: Kelham emphasized the history of the Reformation, while understandably the same emphasis was not given to the subject at Girgis' seminary, although comparative theology was taught. Both curricula placed great importance on preparing sermons. At Kelham the focus was more on the planning and writing of the sermon, whereas Girgis concentrated on the practice of preaching in the parishes. Girgis' emphasis on physical activity and sports was borrowed from Kelham. He had already mentioned it in his statutes of 1912, and now he wrote to the Patriarchate Church Council, requesting that a physical education teacher be appointed to deliver four lessons per week.

Dr I. F. al-Minyāwī, a member of the Lay Community Council, in 1946 corresponded with Bishop Llewellyn Gwynne of All Saints' Anglican Cathedral in Cairo about the possibility of an Anglican lecturer teaching at the Coptic Orthodox Seminary, with Coptic students to be sent in turn to study theology at Anglican theological colleges. Gwynne was willing to help raise the level of the Coptic Orthodox Seminary: "It is of great interest to me to know that the Coptic Church is considering putting their seminary for the training of clergy, on a sound and practical basis. I need hardly say that the Church of England will do her best to assist the Ancient Coptic Church in any way possible."[31] It is likely that Girgis obtained material from the Anglican Theological College and had it translated into Arabic for the benefit of his students.

* * *

Throughout its early history, the physical infrastructure of the seminary went through numerous changes of location. The exact site of the initial—and short-lived—Clerical School that opened in 1875 is unknown. The seminary that opened on November 29, 1893, was located for its first year in a house in the Cairo suburb of al-Fajjālah owned by the al-Muḥarraq Monastery. It then moved to the Patriarchal Center (at that time in the suburb of al-Azbakiyyah), taking over three damp rooms on the ground floor near the small church. At various unknown dates it was transferred to Sūq al-Qabīlah, very close to the Patriarchal Center, then moved to Bayt al-Hajīn, in a dilapidated building nearby. In 1904 the seminary moved to a house in the Cairo suburb of Mahmashah that had been bought for its specific use. It then moved back to the Patriarchal Center, taking over three rooms above the kitchens, for an unknown period before finally settling back in Mahmashah in 1912. Today, the Coptic Orthodox Seminary is located at the site of the ancient church of

[31]Llewellyn Gwynne to Dr I. F. al-Minyāwī, May 17, 1946, Patriarchal Archives 4–6.80/45.

Dayr al-Anbā Ruways, together with St Mark's Coptic Orthodox Cathedral (inaugurated in 1968) and the Patriarchal Center.

No doubt these repeated moves, which were not conducive to any type of education, caused a sense of uncertainty among students and staff, and prompted them to question the seriousness of the Church and the Coptic community about improving the level of theological teaching. That *any* members of the seminary persisted in the face of such adversity only shows their resilience and determination. Girgis himself was a student during some of those early uncertain years, witnessing at first hand the rapid and turbulent changes.

There was initial optimism. Girgis described the first year of the seminary at al-Fajjālah as "resplendent and bright . . . the students were full of hope, had delightful dreams, and an energetic and powerful determination to serve the community after graduation. The students were proud of their association with the seminary and felt happy looking toward a beautiful future, as well as an everlasting life in serving God and the Church."[32] Although those hopes may have been dashed by all the rapid changes that took place, Girgis was resilient. Pope Shenouda III later described his style: "Habib Girgis believed in constructive work. He did not waste his time and effort in criticizing the weakness that was present during his time, but he began to work and build."[33] In 1901 Girgis convinced Khristah Jirjis Jawharah, a wealthy elderly woman who lived next door to his residence, to endow some land to the seminary and to the Coptic Charitable Society (*al-Jam'iyah al-Khayriyah al-Qubṭiyah* الجمعية الخيرية القبطية). She had inherited a great deal of property in Akhmīm (Upper Egypt) from her father, and eventually endowed six acres to the seminary and three to the Charitable Society.

Girgis reached out to his community and discovered that many of its members were willing to support the seminary. This encouraged Girgis and Armāniyūs Bik Ḥannā, a Coptic notable and auditor of the Patriarchal Dīwān (central finance department), in 1901 to collect donations from the community in order to establish a foundation. The two men visited cities across Egypt for this purpose. For three years, Girgis spent every Saturday

[32]Girgis, *The Coptic Orthodox Seminary*, 15.

[33]His Holiness Pope Shenouda III, "Ḥabīb Jirjis: Rā'id al-ta'līm al-Masīḥī" [Habib Girgis: A Pioneer of Christian Education], *Majallat al-Kirāzah* 18.31–32 (September 7, 1990): 1, 7–9, at 1, 9.

and Sunday preaching in different cities and collecting donations, which eventually totaled EGP11,000, and this sum was deposited in the Patriarchate's treasury. From these funds Girgis in 1902 bought the 3,088 square meter mansion in the Cairo suburb of Mahmashah for EGP1,519, intending to house the seminary there rather than constructing a new building. These funds also paid for the construction of an industrial school in Bulāq and for the purchase (at a price of EGP22,800, paid in installments) of 365 acres for the benefit of the two schools.

Armāniyūs Bik Ḥannā, a Coptic notable who was a close friend of Habib Girgis and assisted him in the collection of donations. (Girgis, The Coptic Orthodox Seminary.*)*

Girgis and others hoped that the relocation of the seminary to Mahmashah in 1912 would herald the start of renewed efforts to significantly improve the institution. But the outbreak of the Great War in 1914 brought financial and other hardships, and dreams of reform, renaissance, and progress had to be put aside for the duration. During the war years, Girgis appears to have written nothing about the state of the seminary, and the Patriarchal Archives are also silent until 1917, when the Lay Community Council began discussing the re-formation of affiliated committees.

By 1918, when Girgis was appointed dean, the buildings in Mahmashah had been neglected to the point of imminent collapse, and the furnishings were outdated and dilapidated. There were falling ceilings (including in the Ethiopian bishop's room), broken windows, and skylights that let rain into bedrooms, as well as filthy sleeping quarters for the cantors. Indeed, the facilities were so poor that disease began to spread; some students even fainted during lectures. Their nutrition was poor and the toilets were so badly maintained that sewage overflowed into the corridors, with foul odors reaching the sleeping quarters. Girgis would write repeatedly to the Patriarchate for contractors to be sent out to fix the problems, but the response was always slow and the work apparently shoddy, for the plumbing problems recurred in 1923. The sick were accommodated in the same rooms as the healthy, a situation that brought dire warnings from the physician responsible for Coptic schools, Dr Niqūlā Lūryā Bik, that he would be obliged to inform the Department of Health, a step that might lead to the seminary's closure. Girgis sought financial assistance to set up separate rooms for the sick and a doctor's room for routine checkups. He requested urgent renovations to the filthy bedrooms and bathrooms as well as increases to the meals budget, but to little avail, despite the fact that most of the students came from poor households and depended on the low-quality meals provided at the seminary. In 1919 Dr Bik wrote to Girgis:

> While doing the rounds last Friday at the Clerical School . . . I found that the health condition, especially in the cantors' division and the boarding division, is not pleasing to the soul. On the contrary, I found it worse than what I observed two months ago when I wrote to you requesting speedy necessary improvements; and yet till today nothing has been done. . . . Undoubtedly, His Holiness the honored patriarch would have much pity if he visited the dwellings of these miserable cantors and observed the extreme humidity, the deplorable state of the building, and observed their nutrition that consists of two plain loaves of bread. The matter is not limited only to these cantors, but the facilities of the boarding division have also inherited this problem.[34]

The cantors, many of whom were blind, were chosen largely from among the poor and uneducated of Coptic society. At the seminary they were taught to chant liturgical music so that they could take up their role of leading the congregational responses during liturgical services. Girgis later recalled the cantors' impoverished circumstances:

> They only ate a small amount of food from among what they collected themselves from the homes of charitable people. I personally observed

[34]Lūryā Bik to Habib Girgis, February 17, 1919, Patriarchal Archives 4–6.23–24/2, Theological College Restorations & Repairs, Part 1.

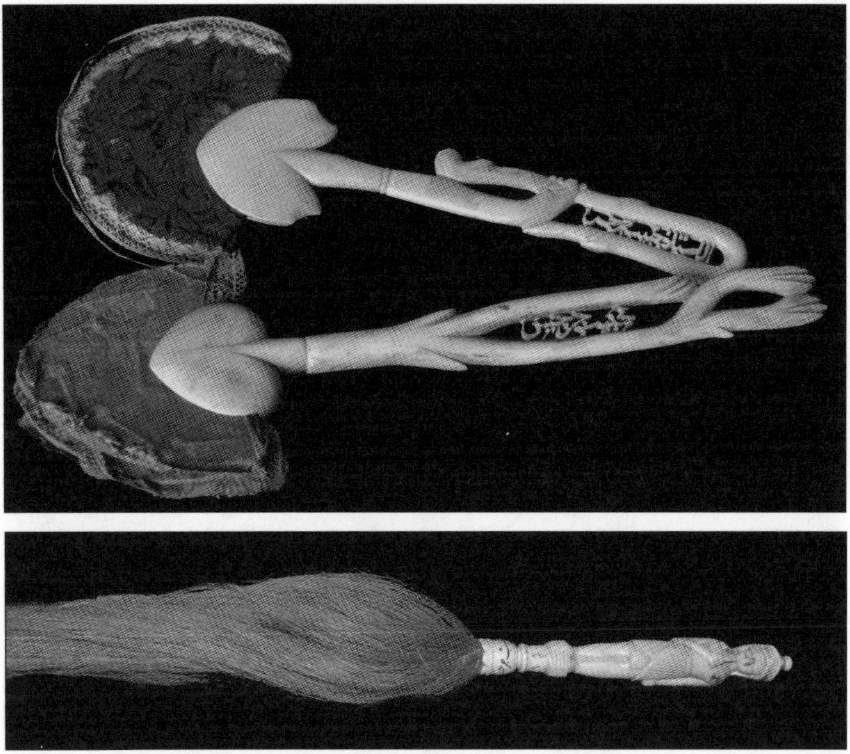

TOP: *Habib Girgis' ivory hand-held fans (the ostrich feathers have fallen off). Girgis' name is carved into the handles.* BOTTOM: *Habib Girgis' ivory and horse hair fly whisk, with his name engraved on it. (St Mark Coptic Orthodox Cultural Center, Dayr al-Anbā Ruways; photographs by Hani Gadoun.)*

some of them sitting in the courtyard of the seminary in the sun, keeping themselves warm through its heat, because of the affliction that they suffered from the cold. They cut the filthy grass from the garden and ate it when hunger struck them. Above all of this, they were crammed in humid sleeping quarters that were originally animal stalls . . . and unhygienic. These rooms were more like mangers for animals than rooms suitable for human use. . . . The miserable scenes that I witnessed with my own eyes every day tore at the very core of my heart, tortured my soul, and disturbed my conscience. I used to write to the office of the Patriarchate requesting the improvement of the state of the miserable cantors, and compassion toward their humanity. However, the financial situation halted the granting of my request, so I headed toward the generous sons

Some of the cantors with goods they produced at the handicrafts factory, c. 1926. (Girgis, The Coptic Orthodox Seminary.*)*

> of the community and I commended the righteous people I knew to send to those cantors all leftover food and any unwanted clothes, and from time to time I collected what was possible to clothe them.[35]

Girgis wanted to help the cantors in a practical way, by teaching them handicrafts such as making bamboo and willow chairs, or weaving baskets and other furnishings. He began to collect funds to buy the necessary tools and equipment for these crafts, and to find community support for the work. But obstacles continued and Girgis was forced to delay the crafts project. Instead, he spent some of the money on clothing and bedding for these poor students, depositing the remainder in the treasury of the Patriarchate. (These funds were subsequently added to the seminary's building fund.) Girgis did eventually succeed in teaching the cantors handicrafts, later opening a factory for that purpose.

By 1922 the seminary buildings, particularly the classrooms and students' sleeping quarters, were manifestly inadequate for use by aspiring priests, preachers, cantors, and teachers. Girgis approached the Patriarchal Dīwān for financial help in renovating the existing buildings and planning for some new ones. He also approached generous Copts who believed in his

[35]Girgis, *The Coptic Orthodox Seminary*, 32.

vision for the seminary and donated accordingly. In this way Girgis raised EGP750 to spend on the seminary's buildings.

Girgis and Armāniyūs Bik Ḥannā decided to collect funds to establish the seminary on five acres owned by the Patriarchate at Dayr al-Anbā Ruways. Ḥannā expanded that project to include an industrial school, orphanage, Coptic Museum, and library. All this work began with the support of the pope and the metropolitans. Indeed, Yu'annis XIX donated EGP500, while Metropolitan Pachomius, abbot of the al-Muḥarraq Monastery, helped raise EGP1,000 in just one day, from the city of Asyūṭ in Upper Egypt. Nevertheless, the relocation and development of the seminary at Dayr al-Anbā Ruways did not take place until 1961, ten years after Girgis' time.

Girgis and Ḥannā were close friends; they and others would meet daily to discuss matters concerning the Coptic community. Girgis credited Ḥannā with raising funds to establish the Coptic Museum, an achievement generally attributed to another member of the Lay Community Council, Marcus Pasha Simaika (1864–1944). Simaika's personal style, sense of self-importance, and close contacts with the Egyptian authorities make it unsurprising that he would elevate his own contribution above anyone else's.

Girgis certainly credited Simaika with succeeding, in 1908, in ensuring the teaching of Christian religion in all public schools. Nevertheless, one senses an unspoken tension between the two men. Simaika came from a prominent family that had served both the Coptic Church and the Egyptian state. Educated at the Great Coptic School, he knew Coptic, Arabic, Greek, English, and French, and had a successful career in the state railways. He was very open to Western influences and the work of missionaries—views diametrically opposing those held by popes Demetrius II, Kyrillos V, and Yu'annis XIX. He vehemently denounced the Coptic clergy as corrupt, ignorant, lazy, and neglectful of their religious duties, accusing them of "selling" justice and enriching their relatives from Church funds. Earlier, he had enthusiastically praised Reverend Lieder's unsuccessful attempt to train Copts as priests. Simaika was one of only two hardliners on the Lay Community Council who in 1893 refused to sign Buṭrus-Ghālī's petition to recall the pope from desert exile. Simaika's attitude was just one example of the obstructions that Girgis faced from the Lay Community Council.

Simaika's prominent position in the Coptic community and his influence among government officials enabled him to convince the minister of education to introduce Christian religion into the public school system. However, a conflict between Simaika and the teachers at the Great Coptic School reveals a certain arrogance. Simaika once entered a classroom and "cross-examined" the teacher on "lessons, regularity, and attendance."[36] Several teachers complained to the headmaster, but Simaika later dismissed the teacher from the headmaster's office.

Girgis envisioned the seminary being housed in a building with several entrances and spacious, well-lit, and properly ventilated rooms. There were to be sleeping quarters, a refectory, study rooms, a library, administrative offices, staff rooms, and rooms for receiving visitors. The amenities should be clean and modern. No doubt Girgis gleaned many of his ideas from the missionary schools that he visited. The renovations required EGP12,000, an impossible sum for Girgis to raise at that time. So he decided to proceed in stages beginning with the lecture rooms, which would cost EGP1,500. He wrote numerous letters and reports to the Patriarchal administration and the deputy, but all his requests were rejected because of budgetary constraints. Eventually, in 1924, he declared that a voice from within had called upon him to complete the renovations regardless of the effort and hardship it would cost him. There was only EGP10 available in the budget, so Girgis came up with a brash solution, which unfortunately brought little success: he arrived early at the annual general meeting of the Lay Community Council (*Majlis millī*) and refused to vacate his seat until the twelve members agreed to pay the EGP1,500 required to complete the renovation of the lecture rooms. Girgis insisted that the council look into the matter that evening, but when the proceedings did not allow him to remain any longer, he left after delivering a fiery address that concluded with these words: "The consequence of all of this is the prevailing ignorance among the ministers of religion, people leaving the Church, and the backwardness and slumber that surround the children of the community."[37] To Girgis' dismay, the EGP10 was increased to only EGP100 that night, and the Lay Community Council

[36]R. Hogan to the headmaster of the Coptic Orthodox School, May 16, 1919, Patriarchal Archives, 4–1.13/18, General Issues.

[37]Girgis, *The Coptic Orthodox Seminary*, 38.

(*Majlis millī*) decreed that these funds should be used to repair the stairwell and bathroom, and to gut the entire building. Of course, this sum was woefully inadequate. Girgis was dismayed, but his resolve and faith remained strong, and he was determined to find a solution to this latest financial crisis.

In September of 1922 a contractor had already begun work on repairing classrooms. The work progressed slowly, and the contractor was reprimanded for using inferior quality materials. In February of that year, a member of the Lay Community Council, Jirjis Bik Anṭūn, wrote at length to one Iskandar Masīḥah, who was working in the Patriarchate's treasury, proposing a total refurbishment and renovation of the seminary's buildings, and enclosing a list of the necessary works. In May, Girgis wrote twice to the deputy of the Patriarchate, requesting that its architect complete, during the school holidays, the necessary drawings for the renovation of the students' dormitories, as well as for building new rooms for the cantors.

> It is sufficient that we spent the whole year, from beginning to end, in severe hardship; and I am unable to describe to you the extent of our suffering, that we, the teachers and the students, have undergone as a consequence of this. I am afraid that this tardiness will delay the work till next year, and the seminary will not be ready for study in September. Moreover, there are many openings in the seminary, and the fence from the direction of the building is very low, which can allow any person from outside to enter. An assault took place at the seminary yesterday by some thieves, who stole some of the students' clothes and took money from them. This has happened many times previously and, in particular, last year during the holidays when the seminary had no students. I am currently very fearful about this matter with regard to the state of the building. Hence, I sincerely hope that you will give attention to the speedy completion of the building.[38]

Girgis hoped that the work, which had begun in September of 1922, would be completed before the beginning of the new school year in September. On June 2, Jirjis Anṭūn wrote again to Iskandar Masīḥah, providing an update on the design stage of the process, asking Masīḥah to provide quotes,

[38]Habib Girgis to the Deputy of the Patriarchate, May 29, 1923, Patriarchal Archives 4–6.123–124/2, Theological College Restorations & Repairs Pt. 1.

and forwarding three pages of basic architectural drawings that outlined the proposed refurbishments, to be carried out according to Girgis' wishes. These plans included a special wing for the pope himself.

Despite letters from the Patriarchate to the contractor, threatening a fine if the work was not completed by the end of June 1923, intrusions and thefts continued into January 1924. The inspector in Shubrā suggested that the seminary hire a guard; Girgis requested approval for this (at a monthly cost of EGP2), along with the raising and repair of the fence. But another weak response from the Lay Community Council and the Patriarchate Church Council finally brought Girgis to the realization that his efforts were to no avail. Having exhausted the proper processes, he decided to bypass both councils and meet directly with Kyrillos V, to explain what had transpired and the seriousness of the situation. To demonstrate the parlous condition of the buildings, Girgis asked the Patriarchate's engineer to examine the retaining walls. The engineer found that they were in danger of collapsing within a week. As a result, the pope ordered that work commence immediately, and that any additional funds required be taken from the Patriarchate's own budget surplus.

Girgis' direct approach to the pope, going over the head of the Lay Community Council, had been a risky move, and he knew it. In case he ran into strife with the council, he made sure that his authority from Kyrillos was in writing. He was anxious not only that he might have destroyed his own relationship with the council by insulting its authority, but also that he might have caused a rift between the council and the pope. When the council heard of what had happened, it sent Jirjis Bik Anṭūn to inspect the work that had been done and write a report. Fortunately for Girgis, who had a good rapport with Anṭūn, the report was sympathetic to Girgis' predicament, expressing approval of the work in progress, and the matter was resolved peacefully. A total of EGP1,500 was spent on the repair of the administrative section and classrooms. In the end, Girgis' decision to go directly to the pope had eclipsed the power of the Lay Community Council and sent a message that its authority was not absolute—ultimately, it too was subject to papal authority.

But Girgis' work was not yet done. The seminary urgently needed other major improvements: construction of a refectory, cantors' school, and church, plus renovation and building of sleeping quarters for the students. The Lay Community Council allocated a paltry EGP130 against Girgis' budget of EGP3,000. But Girgis had learned valuable lessons from the last incident, and decided to seek donations from Copts who supported the seminary's aims. In his letter to these potential benefactors he described the seminary as "the pillar of the Church and its solid support . . . the beginning of the path that leads to true reform."[39] He also explained that the seminary was not a school of the Patriarchate, but an institute that benefited the whole Coptic Church and community, not just those in Cairo. Men from across the land who heard the call to the ministry of priesthood were being trained there, and for this reason assisting and reviving the seminary was among the Copts' most holy obligations. Kyrillos V wrote a letter of support for Girgis' campaign, which eventually succeeded thanks largely to Girgis' persuasive style of writing and extensive network of contacts across Egypt.

Even this was not sufficient for Girgis, whose vision was broader. He embarked upon a third phase of improvements. This part of his grand vision involved expanding the size of the seminary's land and buildings. With the support of Kyrillos V, he purchased four surrounding properties. The initial 657 square meters[40] of vacant land had already been bought in 1920 for EGP263 from Lūsiyah Fara'awn, and funded by the treasury of the Patriarchate. The second and third purchases were paid for by Kyrillos V: land of 713 square meters with a house, bought for EGP713 from the estate of Rizq-Allāh and Mūsá Fara'awn in May 1922, and 330 square meters with a house, bought for EGP550 from the estate of Bitrū Fara'awn in January 1926. The fourth block, 642 square meters plus a house, was purchased for EGP1,200 from Aḥmad Jāmi' in June 1926, using funds provided by the Lay Community Council. In all, these acquisitions increased the land size of the seminary to 5,399 square meters, of which buildings covered 992 square meters.

Girgis continued to overcome prosaic but important practical problems, such as securing an electricity supply. After the extensive renovations and new buildings were completed, Girgis proudly proclaimed: "The seminary had become the bride of Mahmashah, a center of attraction, but it was

[39]Ibid., 42.

[40]Figures have been rounded to the nearest square meter.

View of the Coptic Orthodox Seminary from the direction of Sharābiyah. (Girgis, The Coptic Orthodox Seminary.*)*

lacking electricity to be connected to it."[41] There was no electrical supply to the suburbs of Mahmashah and al-Sharābiyah at that time, and Girgis tried three times, and failed, to have power connected to the seminary. He even signed a petition to the electrical company, along with seventy residents of Mahmashah and al-Sharābiyah, but it was refused. Girgis persevered, taking his friend Tawfīq Bik Ibrāhīm with him to meet the chief engineer at the electricity company, who told Girgis that connecting this region to the electrical network would cost the company EGP400, which it was not prepared to pay. Girgis offered to pay the amount himself, but was refused. He continued to insist, and invited the engineer to visit the seminary and see the beauty of its buildings for himself. On doing so the engineer was impressed, and finally agreed that electricity would be connected at the company's expense. Thus it was through Girgis' efforts that, in October 1925, electricity reached not only the seminary but also the surrounding suburbs.

The expansion of the seminary's landholdings was enormously encouraging to Girgis. However, the seminary still lacked one crucial building: a church. To Girgis, without a church the seminary was merely an academy. A church was not an added luxury, but a building that stood at the very heart of what the seminary stood for, playing a central role in the formation of the students. For similar reasons, Girgis had insisted on having a cantors' school for the study of hymnology. Liturgy and prayer would become the

[41] Ibid., 52.

View of the Coptic Orthodox Seminary from the direction of Mahmashah. (Girgis, The Coptic Orthodox Seminary.*)*

basis of the lives of the students when they left the seminary to follow their vocations. In the church building, they would learn the rubrics of liturgical practice and hymnology, practice preaching, take Holy Communion, and say their daily prayers. Girgis wrote:

> It was inevitable that the seminary would have a church, in order for the students to implement theory into practice, and increase their knowledge of performing the religious rites in the best possible form. When spiritual education [played a very significant role] at the Clerical School, it was compulsory for the students to partake of Holy Communion every now and then, after they had confessed to the priest responsible for them. They [used the church] for morning and evening prayers, and to meet every evening for Bible study, to sing spiritual songs and Church hymns under the guidance and the supervision of the monitor of the boarding school, and to present religious sermons on a daily basis.[42]

Initially Girgis had EGP100 with which to build the church. He paid that amount to a contractor, ʻAṭiyah Afandī Mashriqī, to lay the foundations, followed by a second installment of EGP50. Pope Yu'annis XIX visited the seminary around this time and, impressed that a church was being built,

[42]Ibid., 99.

The church at the Coptic Orthodox Seminary. (Girgis, The Coptic Orthodox Seminary.*)*

personally donated EGP100 and ordered the Dīwān to set aside EGP500. The Lay Community Council, however, reduced the latter amount to EGP250, ostensibly because of financial pressures—another example of the constant tug of war between the pope and lay leaders. Girgis, ever resourceful, resorted to asking his students to collect donations from their hometowns during the summer break. In this way they managed to raise EGP78, which along with what Girgis had raised was given to the contractor to complete the church building. Eventually Pope Yu'annis XIX, along with Metropolitan Kyrillos of Ethiopia and Metropolitan Athanasius of Banī Suwayf, consecrated the church; the pope celebrated the first Liturgy there on Friday, March 6, 1931. About a year later, Yu'annis asked Father Ḥizqiyāl al-Bārāmūsī to supervise the building of a baptistery inside the Church. This suggests that al-Bārāmūsī was the monk-priest responsible for leading liturgical prayers at the seminary, as well as hearing the students' confessions.

Girgis believed that a sound understanding of the sacraments and their theology was essential to his students, and in 1934 he published an important book on the subject: *The Seven Sacraments of the Church*. He also placed great importance on decorating the church building with icons, which he believed would serve to connect his students to the saints; this contact would empower them throughout their lives and teach them the importance of the doctrine of intercession. When there were no funds for the painting of such icons, Girgis personally provided EGP46 for the purpose.

* * *

The seminary's finances continued to fluctuate significantly over the years. For instance, because of renovations and building programs, more was spent in 1927–28 (total budget EGP9,610) than in 1943 (total budget

EGP7,099). Moreover, Girgis earned EGP420 per annum in 1943, well below the EGP600 that had been proposed back in 1927–28. These fluctuations were caused by various factors. For example, in 1927–28, EGP1,000 was allocated for translating foreign books into Arabic. By 1943 this work had been completed, so such a budget line was no longer needed. Regarding his own salary, Girgis probably decided to draw a smaller wage than he was permitted, taking only what was sufficient for his personal needs, in order to save money. The surplus could then be used for the good of the seminary generally. Moreover, he would have received monies from his extensive ministry and preaching.

The church at the Coptic Orthodox Seminary. (Girgis, The Coptic Orthodox Seminary.*)*

Nevertheless, by 1937 Girgis seemed to have lowered his sights somewhat. For some budget items he requested lower sums than he had sought ten years earlier. For instance, Girgis emphasized in 1937 the importance of the library, and requested EGP50 to buy books and journals. The Lay Community Council had reduced that amount year after year until it totaled only EGP5, which Girgis argued was woefully insufficient; he described books as the "only nutrition" for academic institutions. Although the increase he now sought was a tenfold one, it was still only a quarter of the EGP200 library budget requested ten years earlier.

Similarly, in 1937 Girgis asked that a sum of EGP60 previously provided to cover transportation costs of students being sent out to preach in Cairo churches be reinstated. In 1927, an amount of EGP200 had been available for that purpose. Because of the removal of these funds, the preaching ministry had ceased. Also in 1937, Girgis requested a food budget of at least EGP500 per annum for the seminary's 120 students—less than a quarter of the figure he had sought for 1927–28 to feed only 100 students.

Habib Girgis with graduates of the Coptic Orthodox Seminary, 1937. (Girgis, The Coptic Orthodox Seminary.*)*

Girgis wrote in sorrow to the Patriarchate Church Council about its lack of financial support. The following appeal is from 1929, but the sentiments expressed remained true throughout Girgis' career as dean:

> This state has disadvantaged the welfare of the college and the welfare of education, and if this continues the situation will be worse. Who then will carry that responsibility? This, no doubt, is an injustice that no member of the council would accept and, since I have raised this complaint and have not had a response, except that the budget does not allow for more. Why, then, does the budget accommodate all [the Patriarchate's] facilities, yet is restrictive only toward the Clerical School, which is more worthy than any other facility and should be given attention more than any other work?[43]

Girgis took every opportunity to promote the seminary. Every year he would invite the pope, metropolitans, and staff to a great celebration.

[43]Habib Girgis to the Patriarchate Church Council, February 21, 1929, Patriarchal Archives 4–6.2–4/33.

Around 1923 he established an alumni association for graduates, who met regularly and drafted their own bylaws. Its many aims included facilitating communication between graduates and the seminary; establishing a fund to help graduates who were ill or unemployed, by providing educational aid to their children, and other support to their families should they die; and spreading the Coptic language and culture. Thus it supported graduates, helped maintain Coptic identity in the wider community, and delivered practical pastoral care when needed.

Unfortunately, not all graduates found work in the Church. In 1928 one alumnus, Sa'd Rūfā'īl, wrote Girgis a bitter letter:

> As you are aware, I graduated from the college in 1926 and, until now, I have not found work in any city or church. My master the dean, I think that a period of anticipation such as this, whereby a student such as myself, who does not know when this wait will end, and to what extent it will reach, is sufficient to cease one's hope in the Theological College. This college is tantamount to the spirit of the Church, for each student in it imagines that his future is bleak when he sees me. Hence, I request, as an act of mercy toward me and compassion toward the remainder of the students, that you search for the first vacant position for us, that I may not fall into despair, and to grant other students hope.[44]

Graduates complained not only to Girgis, but also to the Lay Community Council and even the pope. Some metropolitans and priests probably resisted accepting these new graduates; perhaps they felt threatened by their higher levels of general and religious education and feared for their own status in their respective communities. They worried that people might compare them adversely to these bright young men, who were full of zeal for their ministry.

Girgis felt the despair of his graduates and repeatedly wrote to the Patriarchate Church Council on the subject. He believed that the success of the seminary depended on the council solving this problem. Yu'annis XIX in turn raised the matter with the Holy Synod in 1930, 1931, and 1938, promoting the ordination of priests only from among the seminary's graduates, and arguing that a financial plan was needed to ensure that those who were

[44]Sa'ad Rūfā'īl to Habib Girgis, March 12, 1928, Patriarchal Archives 4–6.96/8.

ordained remained in their parishes and had sufficient funds for their personal needs. A plan was also needed to change the way these dioceses and parishes viewed the graduates: not as a threat to the status quo or the old guard, but rather as a means for advancing and reforming a community in dire need of reinvigoration, developing it for future generations, and bringing Orthodox education to the forefront.

* * *

Girgis' struggles went beyond those of a pedagogical, administrative, and financial nature. His honor was also thrown into doubt, a development that took a personal toll on him. Around 1932 Father Ḥizqiyāl al-Bārāmūsī, a monk who worked at the seminary, made false allegations against Girgis, sending several letters to the Lay Community Council questioning the dean's means of collecting donations and accusing him of mismanaging funds. Girgis' accuser also questioned the curriculum and some of the subjects taught at the seminary, alleging that they were a waste of time and money. This attack was launched as follows:

> The students of this school are taught Hebrew, Greek, philosophy, logic and psychology, all of which are of no benefit to the Church. These are only supplementary teachings that I hope they would exchange with Coptic language classes, with all its branches, and the Holy Bible with all its contents, as this is what will benefit the Church, and will give the students ample opportunities for the future. But if they are burdened with subjects that the Church will not benefit from, then it is natural that the graduates of the seminary will stand perplexed, having no benefit either to humanity or to the Church.[45]

Girgis responded at length to these allegations on several occasions, defending himself without mentioning the name of the perpetrator.[46] It seems that al-Bārāmūsī felt bitter toward Girgis for some reason; perhaps he was jealous of Girgis' position as dean of the seminary and felt that he,

[45]Ḥizqiyāl al-Bārāmūsī, memorandum to the Lay Community Council, c. 1932–33, Patriarchal Archives 4–6.12/37.

[46]Cf. Doc. No: 4-6.60–67.37 in Appendix 4. In this Girgis explains his work and exonerates himself against such attacks.

as an archpriest, was more worthy of that role than an archdeacon. Possibly he was not paid enough for his duties at the seminary, and this was his way of venting his bitterness. Whatever their cause, al-Bārāmūsī's accusations were very serious and made Girgis out to be a criminal. Ḥizqiyāl al-Bārāmūsī asserted:

> I am honored to raise this detailed memorandum concerning the actions that take place at the Clerical School and the dispersing of funds that have been designated for the education of the students and establishing the support of Orthodox faith and the building of the Church, and spending it on what it was not designated for. But it was embezzled and became a plunder divided among those entrusted with directing its spending.[47]

Those accusations were unjustified. In fact, the documentary evidence shows that Girgis was not materialistic in any way. He used his own money to fund the journal *The Vine* for many years, and funds given to him personally by Kyrillos V were used to purchase a house for the seminary. The classical academic subjects to which al-Bārāmūsī objected were necessary for the formation of any new priest, and Girgis had been wise to introduce them. The study of Hebrew, for example, was essential to understanding the Old Testament, as was Greek for a good grasp of the New Testament, so that students would be able to perform sound exegesis. Girgis believed that students needed to study psychology in order to understand the human psyche and know how to deal with the various types of people they would encounter in their ministry. Girgis' choice of subjects was guided by the latest trends in curricula used in theological colleges at the time, of which he had acquired examples from various countries and denominations, remolding them to suit a Coptic Orthodox institution.

It is true that because Girgis, in his zeal, had prompted a slew of activities and projects during the period in question, much money was being spent. The Church had not seen such vibrant activity in its recent history. Girgis defended all that he had done for the Church and the seminary in several reports and letters to the Lay Community Council, as well as in his book on

[47]Ḥizqiyāl al-Bārāmūsī, memorandum to the Lay Community Council, August 12, 1933, Patriarchal Archives 4–6.7–8/37.

the history of the seminary, in which he outlined exactly where the money collected was spent, and even how his own personal money was deposited into the Patriarchate's treasury for the seminary's use.

* * *

Ultimately, did Girgis achieve his ambitions for the Coptic Orthodox Seminary? Because his work there was central to his mission of reforming the Coptic Church and community, success or failure in that enterprise meant success or failure at broader reform.

The verdict of history is not unanimous. In his 1938 book on the history of the seminary, Girgis observed that in the forty-five years since its opening in 1893, the seminary had produced a total of 320 graduates: two metropolitans, 209 priests, and eighty-seven preachers and teachers (he did not mention the cantors), and acknowledged that twenty-two graduates were still without work. Many of the graduates had served the Church and the community in capacities other than the priesthood, such as by teaching Sunday School, leading youth groups, and joining Coptic societies. Some of these organizations, such as the Tawfīq Coptic Society, are still flourishing today.

Graduates of the seminary had a profound influence on the Coptic Church and community. Nonetheless, later in life, Girgis soberly reflected on the seminary's progress: "The Theological School was established half a century ago. It should have reached, by now, the standard of the finest colleges. Regretfully, however, it did not receive the support needed for its development. Instead, it spent most of its life in wasted struggle, fighting to survive and develop according to the weak means it possessed."[48]

The culmination of Girgis' work at the seminary was its official recognition and accreditation in July 1948 by Egypt's minister of education. The minister recognized a qualification granted by the Coptic Orthodox Seminary as the equivalent of a four-year bachelor's degree.[49] Nevertheless, the seminary never reached the international standards to which Girgis aspired. The prerequisites for admission remained low, as relatively few young Coptic men were interested in studying theology or pursuing a priestly calling, a

[48]Girgis, Practical Means Toward Coptic Reform, 82.

[49]Minister for Education (Higher Education Department) to Coptic Orthodox Patriarchate, Cairo, July 3, 1948, Patriarchal Archives 4–1.22/33.

A diploma awarded by the Coptic Orthodox Seminary. The text is in Coptic and Arabic. (Girgis, The Coptic Orthodox Seminary.*)*

vocation that enjoyed little prestige in the Coptic community. Girgis never achieved his ambition of an educated priesthood, made up solely of men with a proper theological training from his seminary. Indeed, the Coptic Church continues to ordain men with no theological qualifications, although this trend is changing, with more bishops now insisting on theological education for every candidate.

For much of the seminary's history, course content was vague, with no formalized description of what would be taught in each subject. Indeed, it appeared at times that much of the work was done on a piecemeal basis, rather than following a master plan. The library lacked essential academic resources, because of constant funding shortfalls. Most of the faculty was academically weak, and there was a continual struggle to find suitably qualified lecturers. Girgis was forced to call on experts from outside the Coptic community to teach subjects such as Hebrew, English, Arabic, and even philosophy of religion. On this point there was conflict between the Lay Community Council, who wanted to engage teachers from Protestant and other denominations, and the Church hierarchy, who vehemently opposed this view. Girgis was caught between the two: he wanted to attract highly trained scholars from other denominations in order to raise the standard of his school, but at the same time he was concerned about any negativity that might come his way from such a move—in addition, of course, to his wariness of the threat of non-Orthodox teaching affecting the faith of his students. Similarly, while Girgis wanted to raise the professional standards of existing faculty members, there were valid objections to sending them to study abroad as means to improving their qualifications, lest they be overly influenced by Western attitudes.

Girgis also faced personal accusations of impropriety, met with resistance to change from various quarters, and suffered a lack of financial support for improvements and reform, including the dreams he nurtured of significantly expanding and improving the seminary's physical facilities. The seminary was never financially viable and was always struggling to cover its debts.

Girgis claimed success for the seminary while at the same time accusing those who should have been supporting it, i.e., the Coptic laity and clergy, of failing to rally around and work in unison.

> Yes, the Clerical School fulfilled its mission and continues to do so to the full extent . . . it is the only lamp that shines in the gloomy darkness that is the predominance of ignorance. It annihilated much of the ignorance of the ignorant and of blind deviation, as much as possible, according to the means and motives at hand. If you desire more from it, then strengthen those means, increase such motives and do not cut them off so that you do not quench the light of God with your own hands.[50]

There is no doubt that Girgis was successful in making Copts think seriously about reform, and that he instigated a reform process. Thanks to his work in the fields of education, publishing, and preaching, many people were inspired by his vision. He played a crucial role in supporting and encouraging the building of more churches in Cairo, including one in Heliopolis, seven in Shubrā, and two in the outer suburbs of ʻAyn-Shams and Almāzah. Although one can sense through his writings the bitterness he

[50]Girgis, *The Coptic Orthodox Seminary*, 144.

felt at the end of his life because his goals were not fully met, at the same time he hoped for a brighter future—one in which the next generation would carry on his legacy, recognize the central role that his educational reform policies would play in preserving Coptic identity, and assure a successful future for the Coptic community. Girgis' desire was that the Coptic Orthodox Seminary not only graduate priests, preachers, and teachers, but also reformers, in every sense of the word.

A formal portrait of Habib Girgis, c. 1935. (St Mark Coptic Orthodox Cultural Center, Dayr al-Anbā Ruways.)

CHAPTER FIVE

The Orthodox Rock: Taking the Faith to the People

To Habib Girgis, the tenets of the Coptic Orthodox faith were central and immutable, and the inspiration for every aspect of his life's work. In his 1948 book *The Orthodox Rock*, based on lectures he had delivered in Upper Egypt in 1900, Girgis stated: "The apostles and martyrs presented the deposit of faith intact and hence our fathers and grandfathers received it and protected it while shedding their blood. They accepted torture and death, wishing for this faith to reach us without blemish and without decrease or increase."[1] Girgis went on to explain how this presentation of faith was preserved and transmitted, despite the many false teachers and heretics who tried to lead believers from the truth of the gospel. He recalled how the Copts preserved their faith over the centuries, wary of changing even one word of the texts that they had received from the apostles. He paraphrased a common notion of the time: "It was easier to move the Muqaṭṭam Mountain than to move Copts from their faith and doctrine."[2] Girgis went on to demonstrate that

> for the sake of this faith and preserving this holy deposit, the Church stood alone carrying the burden of pain and sufferings during all these centuries. The divisions that took place in the first centuries were due to strange teachings formed by those who loved leadership positions, who in the persecutions they perpetrated were even more hostile than the enemies of Christianity.[3]

[1]Habib Girgis, *al-Ṣakhrah al-Urthūdhuksiyah* [The Orthodox Rock], (Cairo: Dār al-Nashr al Qibṭiyah, 1948), 11–12.

[2]Ibid., 12.

[3]Ibid., 13.

Girgis then reminded his readers of what St John Chrysostom had said of the dangers of such heresies: not only do they lead the individual proclaiming them to eternal damnation, but they also divide the Church and lead other individuals to destruction. Girgis continued his analysis of how the Coptic Church had stood strong throughout the centuries against many attempts at infiltration by un-Orthodox doctrines. It was only in the nineteenth century that Frenchmen were successful in converting some Copts to Catholicism.

> In 1895 the Pope of Rome ordained Father Girgis Maqār, one of the Coptic Catholic monks, along with two other monks, as bishops for their Church in Egypt. The first one, who called himself Cyril II, issued a publication calling our patriarch, bishops, and congregation to join the Church of Rome and accept its leadership and primacy. With the arrogance of youth, he began in his publication to say to us, "Christian faith is based on two principles that are the foundation: Christ Emmanuel and the Pope His Vicar." This strange teaching was not said by a heretic or a heresiarch from the early centuries. So, who is this pope that Cyril Maqār sets as the foundation of faith with Our Lord and Savior, Christ Emmanuel, the Only Divine Head of the Church?[4]

Roman Catholics had a rich legacy of advanced education stretching back many centuries. Being more highly educated, they posed a threat to the Coptic Church—a fact of which Girgis was keenly aware, and one that goes a long way toward explaining his strong language when appraising the work of the Catholics in Egypt. This was Girgis' way of raising awareness among Copts of differences in dogma in order that they not be swept away by the Catholics' superior educational methods, nor attracted by their more advanced schools.[5]

The Copts were always playing catch-up to the organized and advanced work of the Catholic and Protestant missionaries, particularly in the field

[4]Ibid., 15–16.

[5]The principal secondary sources for this chapter include Sana' Hasan, *Christians Versus Muslims in Modern Egypt: The Century-Long Struggle for Coptic Equality* (Oxford: Oxford University Press, 2003); Mitchell, *Colonising Egypt*; Heather J. Sharkey, *American Evangelicals in Egypt: Missionary Encounters in an Age of Empire* (Princeton, NJ: Princeton University Press, 2008).

of education. For generations the Coptic Church had neglected its faithful, especially in Upper Egypt. The lack of educated priests, an insufficient number of churches in the rural regions to administer pastoral care, and the decline of Coptic religious education in general, all gave the Roman Catholics an opportunity to establish a foothold in Egypt. And while their work might well be criticized as proselytism, the centuries of indolence and clerical entitlement in the Coptic Orthodox Church gave them the opportunity to win converts. Girgis understood the situation very well; it was what led him to that series of lectures warning his fellow Copts of the imminent threat facing them. He targeted his lectures particularly at Copts in Upper Egypt, where their numbers were more concentrated. Most of them were farmers who, because of widespread illiteracy and poor education, were easily convinced that Western missionaries could offer them a better future. In presenting that series of lectures, Girgis' aims were twofold. First, he wanted his listeners to recognize the soundness of their Coptic tenets and be wary of Roman Catholic teachings and dogmas. Second, he wanted them to hold firmly to their doctrines and the soundness of their faith. Whether he was successful or not is a matter for debate; he was dealing with a predominantly ignorant audience, drawn from a community that had lacked proper education for several generations.

In *The Orthodox Rock*, Girgis proceeds to analyze each of the doctrinal differences between the Catholic Church and the Coptic Church. The second half of the book takes a similar comparative approach to Protestantism, following a short analysis of the origins of the Protestant Reformation and the role of Martin Luther.

Girgis regarded the West with ambivalence. Strictly Orthodox in his faith, his life, and his teachings, he criticized Western doctrines and practices while envying Western organizational structure and academic rigor. He admired—and emulated in his own life—the typically Protestant qualities of industry, discipline, and order. He was wary of the influence of Western proselytizing on the Coptic people, but maintained many contacts among the missionaries. He took note of their superior educational curricula and models such as the Lancastrian schooling system, adapting them to Coptic Orthodox beliefs and doctrine. Many in the Coptic Church opposed such appropriation of Protestant innovations, and Girgis faced much resistance.

Early in his career, while he was still a student in 1897, churches would not even allow him to preach from their pulpits. They perceived his reforming ways and educational attainments as a threat to their position.

Despite efforts by Girgis and others to counter their efforts, Western denominations were successful to some extent in establishing churches and schools, and gaining converts among the Copts. After a century of work in this direction, by the mid-1950s they claimed a mere 200 living converts from Islam, but some 20,000 from Coptic Orthodoxy (about 2 percent of the Coptic population of around one million). It was evident that, despite the stated goal of converting Muslims, much missionary activity actually targeted the Copts. There were obvious reasons for this: by now the missionaries had realized that any attempt to evangelize among Muslims was dangerous in Egypt, and in any event Muslims were unlikely to leave the religion of state power. So they turned their attention to an easier target: the Copts.

Girgis' other apologetic writing can be found in his 1934 book *The Seven Sacraments of the Church*, an anthology of his articles published in *The Vine*. In this volume, Girgis defended Coptic Orthodox teachings on priesthood, including the tenet that only a canonically ordained priest could administer the sacraments, backing up his arguments with Scripture verses and quotations from many patristic writings. Girgis did not mention the Western missionaries explicitly, but his criticism was implied in the assertion that it was a grave error to allow the laity, including women, to perform such rites, for in so doing one had strayed far from the teachings of the Scriptures.

Girgis' strong faith, as expressed in this type of theological writing, informed all his work, regardless of whether it was on behalf of the seminary, the Sunday School movement, Church reform, or the Coptic community in general. For instance, in his struggle to improve the seminary, he asked, "How can a person be elected to the position of sublime pastoral care while not being qualified for it? Is it appropriate for such exalted positions to be given to people who, we say, have no knowledge and experience? The most humble vocation in the world cannot be practiced unless one learns it, trains for it, and studies its principles."[6] Priests continued to be ordained without any theological training, in many cases inheriting their position from their father, a dangerous tradition that Girgis worked diligently to

[6]Girgis, *Practical Means Toward Coptic Reform*, 31.

change, in order to "put an end to the chaos of priestly ordinations."[7] For him, priesthood was a position of huge significance; a candidate needed extensive education and training because he would be dealing with people's souls, their salvation, and eternity. Such work should not be left to ignorant or uneducated men. In this way, poor clerical education was having a detrimental effect on the Copts, and Girgis identified it as a great obstacle to reform. He argued:

> There is a grave danger in the ordination of someone who has not graduated from the Theological College. It is an impudence against truth, unworthy of praise, a resistance to religious reform, and a blatant violation of divine laws that oblige a priest to be an erudite scholar in religious subjects, as well as other subjects—in order to perform his divine duty in a perfect way, and to perform his duty toward God and the community in the best way.[8]

Girgis at the same time commended those metropolitans who opposed nominations to the priesthood of men from their communities who were not graduates of the seminary. Unfortunately, however, many graduates of the seminary remained unemployed and unable to find suitable work in the Church. Girgis wanted the Copts to realize that the priesthood was neither a position to be inherited like a possession, nor one's birthright. Rather, it was an honor that had to be earned.

Similarly, Girgis reminded his readers that Bishop Yusāb had suggested to the Holy Synod in the 1920s that monasteries should not accept novices before they had completed studies at the seminary. This guideline was intended to ensure that young men would be properly formed and theologically trained before beginning monastic life. Girgis wanted the seminary to be run as a boarding school and administered much like a monastery, so that at the end of his studies a student could decide whether to be ordained a priest or enter monastic life. The seminary would provide the Church with righteous pastors and the monasteries with educated monks, from whose ranks an enlightened Church leadership could be formed and bishops and popes chosen.

[7]Ibid., 83.

[8]Girgis, *The Coptic Orthodox Seminary*, 103.

Girgis' rock-solid Orthodox faith was built upon the ancient rites and traditions of the Egyptian Church: liturgy, music, and iconography. In his efforts to bring the Copts back to their faith through popular education, he employed a three-pronged approach: liturgical catechesis, religious pictures, and hymnology. Liturgical catechesis featured prominently in his curricula, in his books on the sacraments, and in several other books, including *The Prayers of the Congregants During the Liturgy* and *The Spirit of Supplications in Worship and Prayers*. Through this type of catechesis, the faithful could be educated through the senses of seeing, hearing, and touching.

Girgis appreciated Coptic hymnology as an ancient tradition dating to the Fathers of the Church. Believing that the seminary could play a significant role in preserving that tradition, he set up a cantors' school to teach those men to read and interpret musical notation so that they might master the hymns and chant them according to firm musical principles.

Girgis tried throughout his life to inspire Copts to attend church regularly, regardless of whether they were illiterate villagers in Upper Egypt or seminarians in Cairo. He saw how from the beginning of the service the faithful were surrounded by a multitude of experiences that engaged all their senses. It is what a child sees, hears, and experiences in church that brings him or her into a relationship with the Almighty—or, as St John remarked, "That which was from the beginning, which we have heard, which we have seen with our eyes, which we have looked upon, and our hands have handled, concerning the Word of life" (1 Jn 1.1). In using the Liturgy in this way, Girgis' goal was not merely to instruct people about Christianity, but rather to use rites, symbols, and stories to integrate them into the Church. During the readings, even the illiterate parishioner could hear the New Testament and learn about the seasons of the Church and the life of Christ. The sermon also served as pedagogy, with the preacher involving his listeners in the significance of the day by tying the readings together. On the feast day of a major saint, for example, that saint's life story would be read from the *Synaxarion* and connected to the Gospel reading and the Epistles. The sermon also provided an excellent opportunity for the preacher to expound upon key theological teachings, give moral and practical guidance and instruction, and connect it all to the local context of his listeners.

Similarly, the eucharistic prayers and rituals reminded the faithful of the story of salvation, taking the believer on a journey from the birth of Christ to his death and resurrection. Other Christological and theological concepts—for example, that the body and blood of Christ, present in the bread and wine, were shed for their salvation—could be learned by taking part in this central ritual.

Girgis wrote two books on liturgical teaching, one directed at adults and the other at children and youth. In his introduction to the latter book, he explained its purpose.

> I have compiled this small booklet for the benefit of the school students and youngsters who cannot use my larger book, The Spirit of Supplications in Worship and Prayers, as a guide to them in individual and common prayer. I have placed at the end the responses that the congregation recites in the church during the Liturgy in the Coptic language, with the Arabic pronunciation for the benefit of those who do not know their Coptic language, and also translated into Arabic.[9]

Icons and religious images were another educational tool firmly established in the repertoire of the Coptic Church, and used constantly by Girgis. Called "the gospel to the illiterate," icons taught people not only about the lives of the saints, but also doctrinal matters, such as the doctrine of the Theotokos, which is exemplified in the icon of the Mother of God carrying the Christ Child. Icons called believers to reclaim the "likeness" of God, which was lost after the fall. That aspiration—to become once again the likeness of God—is central to iconography and its role in catechesis (through the example and study of icons, as well as reflection and meditation upon them,).

Icons allow the "reader" to learn from them by "encountering" them. Through their innate and artistic storytelling, icons encourage people to listen to their stories, memorize their details, and finally imitate the lives of the transformed humans who are depicted within their frames. For Girgis, an icon told a story and became a living example for a student to live by. Girgis started by importing colored religious pictures from Europe, on the

[9]Habib Girgis, *Murshid al-madāris fī al-ṣalawāt wa-ḥuḍūr al-Kanā'is* [A School Guide for Prayers and Attendance at Churches] (Cairo: Maṭba'at al-Tawfīq, n.d.), 2.

backs of which he would print a short story in Arabic. Later he began to print the pictures locally, distributing them by the millions across Egypt, Sudan, and Ethiopia. They played an important part in the Sunday School movement and were particularly useful for educating the illiterate population, who were concentrated in the villages. Girgis would reinforce the message of the icon by giving a student a related biblical verse to learn, along with a summary of the lesson inspired by the religious figure. Children enjoyed collecting these religious cards in a manner akin to trading cards; rather than bearing a photograph of an athlete with his statistical highlights on the back, these cards bore images of saints on the front, with a summary of their pious lives and scriptural passages on the reverse.

A third type of popular catechesis that Girgis used was music and hymns, which he wrote in order to educate young and old in the tenets of the faith. He wrote five books full of such hymnology, plus a shorter book to describe the appropriate Coptic tunes to be used to chant each hymn.

* * *

When Girgis wrote his *Practical Means Toward Coptic Reform: Hopes and Dreams* in 1942, he was already in his mid-sixties. The Church was at a crossroads: Pope Yu'annis had recently died, and the papal throne was vacant. The Copts numbered one million members.[10] Disagreement between the government and the Patriarchal offices (as well as between the Patriarchate and the Lay Community Council) on matters such as endowments, the constitution for electing a new pope, and marital laws, had reached a crescendo. So Girgis directed his book to the future pope, the Holy Synod, the members of the Lay Community Council, the heads and members of the Coptic societies, and to all those who desired reform.

Girgis begins the book by imagining that, on a summer's night before dawn, his spirit is flying over the whole See of St Mark, hearing everything that is being said without anyone seeing him. He flies in an instant from Alexandria to Sudan, and from there to Ethiopia and Eritrea. During his journey, he passes over every diocese, monastery, church, school, society, and Coptic family, seeing everything that concerns his Coptic community. He then explains with deep sadness: "Immediately I envisioned how great

[10]Girgis, *Practical Means Toward Coptic Reform*, vi.

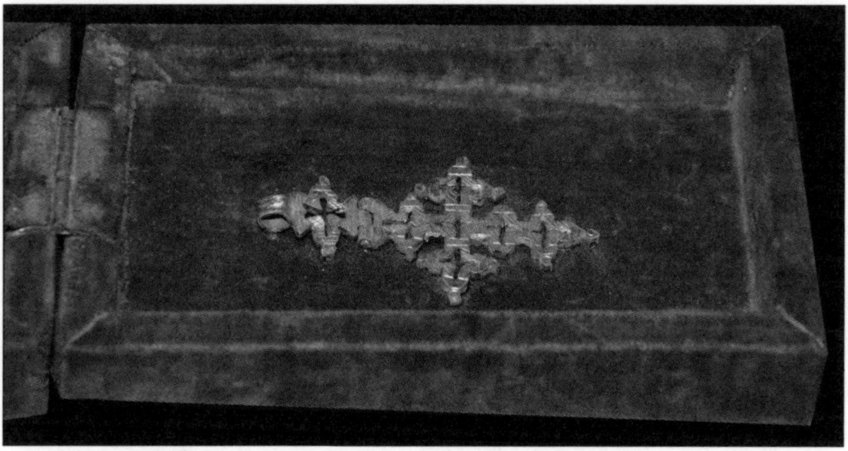

A cross presented to Habib Girgis as a gift during one of his trips abroad. (St Mark Coptic Orthodox Cultural Center, Dayr al-Anbā Ruways; photograph by Hani Gadoun.)

and glorious my Church was in previous eras. How the Coptic people were strong in their faith, determination and knowledge. Then I encountered where we were, and what we have become. So I became sad, in pain, and my hurt increased, since I spent all of my past life in suffering, and struggled as much as I was capable of, to do what was required for the good of my people."[11]

Along his imaginary journey, he listens to what the pastors and congregation are saying, observing with pleasure: "I did not find one, among those to whom I came close, who was accepting of the general state of the Church, but all of them desired and wanted their affairs to be reformed and to move forward with long steps toward advancement and perfection."[12] Girgis is overjoyed to hear everyone calling for reform, for a unified Church led by a unified spirit, sharing one faith: "I was happy to see these feelings, for it is the first sign of success toward reform. The life of the nations is built upon their religious and social desires and feelings, and the desires of men are the measure of their abilities. Who are the reformers, other than creative men with their desires, replacing one desire for another?"

Girgis was correct in his assertion that reform could not take place unless a community desired it and worked toward its achievement. This is what

[11]Ibid., 24.

[12]Ibid., 2.

he attempted to inspire throughout his career, although he was not always successful, and his insights and reforming ideas were met with resistance in some circles. Some of those resisting were seeking to protect their jobs, fearing that they would be replaced by better-educated young men and women. Others wanted to keep the status quo because it was the only thing they knew. Fear of the unknown was a deep threat for many Copts. But just as great leaders tell the truth, so did Girgis, both in his books and through his deeds. He was willing to upset people's expectations in order to push for change, because he knew that if change did not occur, his people were doomed to failure.

One of the main obstacles to reform in the Coptic Church was the rift between the clergy and the laity. There was great friction between the educated lay reformers and the uneducated clergy. How could poorly educated religious leaders lead those who were more advanced in education and knowledge? The lay reformers saw that the clergy did not have the skills for reform, while the clergy believed that the congregation encroached upon their rights and priestly authority, which should be respected and appreciated. This discord was causing the reform movement to freeze.

Girgis offered a way to heal this division. He acknowledged that wherever there were differing minds and varying opinions, conflict was inevitable. However, he argued that such conflicts would not lead to rifts and factions if everyone's guiding principle was reform and the common good. He then asked a vital question: "What harm is there if issues can be simplified and discussed by all with complete freedom and sincerity, and the decision of the majority becomes the accepted decision? If the resolutions do not fulfill the purpose, and were beset with obstacles, what harm is there in reviewing the matter once more?"[13]

Of course, not all parties were acting according to these guiding principles of reform and the common good. Many of the conflicts became personal, reflecting on the honor of individuals. In some cases, an individual's particular interests took priority over the wider interests of the Coptic people. Girgis understood this. "Regrettably, these divisions among us take on unacceptable forms and surpass their limits, general issues become personal and in turn create factions, vilification, and false accusations, and

[13]Ibid., 24.

all involved desire to support their own point of view, being concerned with protecting their own dignity even if it means losing the dignity of the Church and community."[14] The sheer magnitude of that crisis led Girgis to ask: "Don't you see that these divisions have harmed the Church, isolated many from her service, and resulted in division and failure?"[15]

The title of Girgis' book reflects his zeal for the Church and his optimistic outlook for a brighter future, which the rising generation might take up. He decorated the book's cover with quotations from the Scriptures, choosing verses that inspired hope, trust, and determination, such as, "The God of heaven is the one who will give us success, and we his servants are going to start building" (Neh 2.20). The book takes the form of a dream narrative so that "the Church and the Coptic community will be transferred from a painful reality to a better future."[16] He begins by describing the nature of the reform movement and the obstacles that stand in its way, then diagnoses the diseases prevalent in the Church community, and suggests effective remedies.

The first fifty-six pages of the book are presented as five sessions of conversation between three persons of contrasting backgrounds and perspectives. In each session Girgis tackles a particular issue requiring reform. Readers of Girgis' day would soon realize that each of these three imaginary characters represented real attitudes, or perhaps even individuals that they had encountered in their own community. Girgis uses telling names for his protagonists. The first, *Ghayyūr bin Ra'd*, meaning "Zealous, the Son of Thunder" is a twenty-five-year-old man, sincere in his feelings and full of zeal for reform. He places all blame for the Church's backwardness upon the shoulders of the clergy, and pushes for reform through force and violence. The second character is *Ādil bin 'Ārif*, meaning "Just, the Son of Knowledge." Just over forty years of age, he has been knowledgeable about Church matters from a young age, serves peacefully, and continues to search for practical solutions. The third character is *Wuḍāḥ bin Rajā'*, "Luminous, the Son of Hope." This experienced and dignified elder has spent his life serving his community. A thoughtful man, he wishes to see

[14]Ibid.
[15]Ibid., 24–5.
[16]Ibid., xiii.

reform implemented before his departure from the world. These three men discuss matters such as the origins of the reform movement, the repercussions of neglecting religious education, and the reasons behind the misunderstandings between laity and clergy, to name but a few.

After this fascinating interchange between imaginary characters, Girgis moves on to the promising vision of the future, or the beginning of new life. The majority of the book, however, is taken up with Girgis' detailed explication of his reform philosophy, which covers twelve main areas in great need of change. Significantly, Girgis does not see reform as the duty only of the hierarchy and clergy. He calls for the entire community to participate in that work, in various ways. Most importantly, he asks members of the Lay Community Council and the archons (prominent lay leaders) of the Church to participate in twelve committees to be set up by the Holy Synod.

Each committee, led by a metropolitan and comprising two members of the Lay Community Council, members of subcommittees, and several lay leaders, would work in cooperation with the Holy Synod so that everyone would have a share in the task ahead. Girgis envisions the laity and the clergy as partners, not only in the ministry and its implementation, but also in making decisions. Democracy, as seen in the Scriptures, in the apostolic practices of the early Church, and as handed down through generations of Coptic tradition, is essential for reform. Girgis wants every Copt to feel that he or she is an active member of the Church, with an important role to play. He wants men and women to participate in the life and decision-making functions of the Church by joining societies. He also encourages everyone to send suggestions to any or all of the twelve proposed committees.

However, Girgis was naive to think that he would wake up from his dream to find that this idealistic utopia of unified opinion and cooperation had become a reality in the Coptic community. Mistrust, resistance, and antagonism between clergy and laity had continued for decades, and it was wishful thinking to imagine that this could change overnight. Girgis was right to want the person on the street to feel that his or her voice could be heard by the Holy Synod, but was the Holy Synod willing to listen to opinions that might differ from its own? Were its members willing, for the good of the community, to listen to the needs of the people? Or would they see this as a challenge to their authority? For a democracy to work, there must be processes in place to resolve conflict, a constitution that every citizen of the country lives by, and fair and open elections. Perhaps Girgis envisioned some of these prerequisites, but he discussed none of them explicitly in his 1942 book on church reform. That the laity would participate in the work of the Holy Synod was a bold, daring, and yet vital suggestion on Girgis' part. It would move the Church toward reform, but the Church was not yet ready for such a vision.

Girgis' book, and his dream, conclude with a depiction of the Holy Synod—with the participation of the entire Coptic community—realizing his vision within a period of ten years. One of the clergymen suggests holding a new feast, the Feast of Renewal, near the beginning of the Coptic year, and including it in the Synaxarion with the lives of the saints.

Sadly, Habib Girgis' calls for reform went largely unheeded. There is still a need today for the Coptic Church to reclaim, deconstruct, and reconstruct Girgis' innovative reform policy, and to expand upon it for the twenty-first century. Girgis was an inclusive leader who wanted to involve every member of the Coptic community. This was a refreshing new approach, but the resistance with which it was received underscored one of the main obstacles that prevented him from carrying out his reform agenda. Were all strata of the Church prepared to enter into dialogue with those whose roles they perceived to be subordinate or superior to their own? Were the Holy Synod and other clergy willing to sit at the same table as the laity and members of the wider Coptic community, and to listen to each other in a spirit of humility? The answer was, sadly, no.

But even in the face of this and other obstacles, Girgis never accepted defeat. The very title of his book, *The Practical Means Toward Coptic Reform: Hopes and Dreams*, demonstrates his persistence. He describes in detail his thoughts on areas in the Church that are in particular need of reform: the family, religious and theological education, and the print media, among others. He is hopeful until the end that his vision and legacy for the Church will be taken up by the next generation. In the words of Pope Shenouda III,

> Habib Girgis established a strong foundation, and many built upon it. . . . He labored and all of us have entered into the ministry upon his labor.

> . . . He believed in religious education to the fullest extent. . . . He will remain across our modern history, the pioneer of religious education in our land. . . . Habib Girgis was not a mere teacher, but was a school, even a university. . . . He was a symbol for positive work in the Church, a symbol of love for education, a symbol for meekness, zeal, and many virtues.[17]

The strong foundation that Girgis built was the spread of religious knowledge. He achieved this by various means: training clergy in the seminary, publishing school curricula, preaching across Egypt, and nurturing the Coptic Sunday School movement. Girgis' students were inspired by his vision and followed in his footsteps, the clearest example being Pope Shenouda III himself. Girgis was a pioneer in the sense that he saved the Coptic Church from losing its identity. He was the first person in the Coptic Church in the modern era to have a clear vision for religious education, and he did his best to have it implemented. Girgis can be characterized as a school, because his particular educational philosophy would have led to tangible reform in the Coptic Church if only there had been sufficient cooperation between the laity and hierarchy. His legacy is like a university curriculum in the sense that he worked in many fields simultaneously and had an astonishingly broad vision.

* * *

Girgis dedicated a section of *The Practical Means Toward Coptic Reform* to education and teaching. He also discussed the subject in other books, particularly *Educational Studies for Teachers of Coptic Orthodox Sunday Schools, General Visitations to the Village*, and *The History of Preaching and Its Importance in the Christian Church Generally and the Coptic Church Specifically*. In his book on reform, Girgis begins by citing a verse from St Paul the Apostle to remind his readers about the nurturing of children: "Bring them up in the discipline and instruction of the Lord" (Eph 6.4). He maintains that "giving concern to their education is the greatest purpose of their presence, and the school is the blessed place that embraces

[17]His Holiness Pope Shenouda III, "al-Iḥtifāl bi-murūr arbaʿūn ʿāmman ʿalá niyāḥat al-Arshīdyākūn Ḥabīb Jirjis" [The Commemoration of the Fortieth Anniversary of the Death of Archdeacon Habib Girgis], *Majallat al-Kirāzah* 19.29–30 (August 16, 1991): 1.

the child and in which he receives his education in order to be qualified as a man in society."[18] In order to achieve the desired community, Girgis explains, it is important to identify its desired principles and ideologies in the future, and to train and educate children toward achieving them.

Girgis has a clear vision for urban education. "It is imperative that schools are not only for education, that is, the cultivation of the mind, but their objective must also be for the education of the spirit and the body. They should raise the value of the human being and make him a perfect, virtuous man, capable of living."[19] Most schools at that time were concerned only with producing skilled tradespeople, whereas Girgis felt that young people should be taking up leadership opportunities and creating their own pathways to the future, for example, by setting up their own businesses.

Throughout his life, Girgis was disappointed that the majority of Coptic schools were not working to serve the Church, comparing them adversely in this regard to Western missionary schools. He emphasized that, unless Coptic schools served also as a tool for the advancement of the Coptic community and Church, they were useless. He fought hard, and successfully, to ensure that religion was taught, even going so far as to call the lack of religious education in some Coptic schools a "crime," "a plague toward humanity," and "communal suicide." He believed that the presence of such schools in their current state endangered the very future of the Church, for believers had strayed because of lack of religious education. Pope Kyrillos V established a committee responsible for religious education, of which Girgis was a member, to review books and publications and to ensure that the religious lessons in schools were consistent with Coptic Orthodox doctrine. Girgis quoted one Christian scholar as saying, "Give me all the children of the world from a young age, and I will make the whole world Christian,"[20] and also cited the words popularly attributed to Victor Hugo: "Whoever opens a school, closes a prison."[21]

[18]Girgis, *Practical Means Toward Coptic Reform*, 76.

[19]Ibid.

[20]Yūsuf Manqariyūs, *Tārīkh al-ummah al-Qibṭiyah* [History of the Coptic People in the Last Twenty Years from 1893 to 1912], (Old Cairo: s.n., 1913), 208–11.

[21]Habib Girgis, ed. "al-Madāris wa-al-dīn" [Schools and Religion], *al-Karmah* [The Vine] 2.6 (1906): 242.

Girgis' vision for education in urban areas involved, first, the establishment of a general administration to supervise education in all Coptic schools, led by individuals possessing the necessary technical and administrative skills. He wanted to make schooling accessible to all children by opening an elementary school in each locale and a secondary school at the headquarters of each diocese, and increasing the number of schools offering education free of charge. He proposed teaching and organizing religious education in government schools, and endeavored to return religious education to the curriculum of those institutions responsible for preparing teachers: the Education Institute and the Higher Teachers' School. He advocated for the right to teach Christian religion to Christian students attending government schools. Girgis also wanted to increase the number of industrial schools, suggesting there should be at least one each in Cairo, Alexandria, Minyā, and Asyūṭ in Upper Egypt, and encouraging other dioceses capable of establishing such schools to do so. These schools should give greater attention to religious education as well, seeking to edify the students with a spirit of piety and virtue since their graduates would be placed in an environment that required such an education to protect them.

Since the greatest need for any community, after bread, is education, Girgis argued that as many night schools should be opened as possible, located either in Coptic schools or in halls near churches. These should teach basic reading, writing, and Christian piety. Many youths were willing to donate their time to this worthy cause. Similar secular schools existed in Egypt at that time, offering classes after students had attended vespers at church. A committee was set up for the purpose, and the pastors of churches were delegated to facilitate these schools, which would provide one of the most important means of advancing the Church. In Cairo, it was suggested that one should be established in every suburb, especially in the poor areas such as Būlāq and Old Cairo. Specific meetings were also to be held for skilled workers and tradesmen. Finally, Girgis envisaged conducting spiritual meetings every night, beginning with vespers and then short lessons, with one night for Bible study, another for studying Church doctrine, and another for studying Church history. He also proposed holding spiritual meetings specially for women.

At this time women, being half the population, were viewed primarily as mothers by the other half. They had a great influence on communal life and an undeniably important role in the family, so it was essential that they receive spiritual instruction and proper guidance in building a Coptic family on a solid religious foundation. Time was set aside each week in churches for sermons and spiritual teachings directed at the particular needs of women, with women in the Bible often cited as exemplars to which their modern counterparts should aspire. The right influence of women on their husbands and children was believed to improve the family unit. Priests were also encouraged to establish societies for women to help the Church in its work through activities such as charitable projects, assisting the poor, and teaching orphans.

Girgis' view of the role of women reflected the broadly held views of his time. At the turn of the twentieth century, mothers were seen as responsible for ensuring the proper physical, moral, and intellectual development of children, all within the context of an emerging nationalism. Motherhood was redefined in scientific terms according to hygienic and rational principles for developing productive members of society. A mother now had to be equipped to raise a child capable of physical, mental, and moral work, and infused with an ethic of industry, discipline, and order. This new notion of child rearing put a great responsibility on mothers. In colonial Egypt, uneducated mothers were viewed both by colonial administrators and indigenous modernizing reformers as particularly unsuited to raising the next generation.

Girgis' vision for urban education was comprehensive. It was also scripturally based: it included spiritual formation, was squarely founded upon the Orthodox tradition, and tied religious education to liturgical life by encouraging attendance at vespers, for example. Because Girgis cared about the nurturing of each and every Coptic soul, he used every means possible to make religious education available to the whole community. He also envisaged a strong system of adult education, catering to poor and rich alike, paying attention to the educational needs—both spiritual and material—of tradespeople by calling for the establishment of trade and industrial schools.

There is no doubt that Girgis' vision for urban education, if implemented the way he described it—with generous funding, well-qualified teachers, theologically trained priests, Sunday School leaders, youth leaders, and people with good administrative skills—would have had a profound effect on the Coptic community. And indeed, he succeeded in implementing elements of his vision, but only to a limited extent and at a relatively low level of sophistication. His frustrations come across in his writings, especially near the end of his life, when he looked back at his work, reflected, and was saddened by the state of the Coptic community. Yet he still hoped that the community had at least realized that it needed to implement the sweeping reforms he had suggested, and that future generations would turn his dream into reality.

Girgis wanted religious education to reach every soul. Nobody should be disadvantaged, no matter how remote his or her location. In Girgis' time, the village was still central to life in Upper Egypt. Several decades were to pass before Egyptians moved in large numbers from the villages into the cities as modernization accelerated. Girgis felt that villagers needed help, and they needed it urgently. He took a different approach to education in rural areas, catering to the different social and economic circumstances outside Egypt's major cities. He did not write a set curriculum, but rather prepared a detailed guide for teachers to follow, entitling his booklet *Visitations to the Village*.[22] Written in 1947, near the end of Girgis' life, this publication reveals his meticulousness in caring for every soul in a village. It further demonstrates how Girgis' educational reforms could transform a village, enlighten its families, and fortify it to resist external forces.

Girgis envisaged pairs of trained male Sunday School teachers from the city visiting every Coptic household in a village, to deliver the message of the Church. Such an intensive mission needed lengthy and meticulous preparation. First, the teachers were to plan and pray, discuss the situation of the village with colleagues, and form pairs to visit during the summer. They would then seek a letter of blessing from the bishop of the diocese if their parish was close by, or from their parish priest if in a more remote area, before contacting the Higher Committee of Sunday Schools in order to seek advice, gain support, and benefit from its publications and experience. This preparation would be followed by attending meetings in the local ministry

[22]Subsequent editions of this booklet, printed from 1949 onwards, bear the title *Iftiqād al-ʿāmm lil-qaryah* [General Visitations to the Village].

center (usually located in a central church in one of the large cities such as Cairo and Alexandria) each night for a week, in order to pray and seek God's guidance, study methods of visiting households, and prepare a timetable. The teachers were to fast and pray in order to appreciate the seriousness of the work upon which they were about to embark. They learned chapters of the Scriptures, most importantly the Sermon on the Mount, the Ten Commandments, some psalms, parts of the prayers of the saints, sections from St James' Epistle, the First Epistle of John, the four Gospels, and the Acts of the Apostles. The teachers also had to buy a copy of the census book for the relevant governorate or city, in order to know how many families they would be expected to visit, along with a map of the region to use in planning their route and transport. They needed a series of forms to complete for each family, and religious pictures to distribute.

Girgis wanted to be absolutely sure that no household missed out on religious instruction, believing that it was his duty to educate as comprehensively as possible. In his instructions to the teachers he stated: "It is better that the exposition be in the form of a Sunday School lesson and include an introduction, a story, a conclusion, and a practical application, rather than be in the form of a sermon."[23] Teachers were to emphasize the depth of the divine love that drove Christ to be born and to suffer for our sake. Because there was no set curriculum, much would depend on the skill and level of training of the teachers.

The teachers were to be mainly university students and Coptic Orthodox Seminary students who would dedicate their three-month summer vacation to this important ministry. Some regular city Sunday School teachers also took a break from their full-time jobs to take part. While the majority went out into the countryside, a few remained in the ministry center to receive and process the completed forms, prepare the materials and other necessities for the groups of teachers, and try to find solutions to problems that arose during the visits.

The whole region was to be mapped out carefully, with each pair of teachers choosing one transportation line and visiting every village on the way, so that no community would be missed. Upon arriving in a village, the pair was to separate and each teacher would visit, on average, approximately 1000

[23]Girgis, *General Visitations to the Village*, 12.

souls (that is, around 200 homes) in a period of four weeks, working from Sunday to Thursday. Each diocese was divided into regions, and the number of weeks needed to cover every household could be easily calculated. Every evening the teachers would preach in a village and get to know one Coptic family, whose members would introduce him to other families. The teacher would teach the family a hymn about the love of Christ, pray a simple prayer with them, and conclude with the Lord's Prayer. He would then read a chapter from the Gospels and explain it in clear and simple language, giving practical examples drawn from village life. The family was to be asked whether they owned a Bible, and whether they read it. If they did not own the Book, one of the Gospels was to be given to them to read every night. The teacher was to explain to the family members the significance of the lengthy form that they were asked to fill out, recording information about the family, its social status, education, illnesses, needs, church attendance, and the like. He was also to impress upon them the importance of attending church, taking their children to Sunday School, fasting, and partaking of Holy Communion. Each family visit should last no longer than forty minutes, and the teachers should not waste time socializing or drinking coffee or tea. Before leaving the house, the teacher should invite the family to attend the nightly community prayer meeting.

Teachers were also ordered to gather together all the youth of the village for a meeting, since it was from among these young villagers that future Sunday School teachers might be recruited. The teachers were instructed not to differentiate between the poor and the better off—they should be stringent in delivering the message of the Church to every household, no matter how large or small. And this was all to be done free of charge.

Girgis' philosophy was to engage an entire village in discussion; he discouraged the teachers from repeating a lesson, so that when the villagers got together they could exchange various ideas and learn something new from their neighbors. In addition, young villagers were encouraged to read and study, so that they could arrive at the youth meetings feeling ready to integrate fully into the community of believers. Girgis wanted to create a "buzz" that would ignite a sense of awe and wonder. He hoped that villagers would begin to examine the gospel stories and relate them to their own lives and situations. This would give meaning to their own struggles, inspiring them to look within to understand their lives and to think of what lay beyond.

On the face of it, expecting teachers to achieve all this in such a short period of time seems not only impossible but even presumptuous on Girgis' part. A university student on his summer holidays was to enter a stranger's home, having no idea what problems the family might be facing and what level of faith they nurtured, if any. That household might be plagued by family problems and unrest, matters of apostasy, proselytization by Western missionaries, unbaptized members, non-attendance at church, extreme poverty, unemployment, disease, lack of sanitation and health care, illiteracy, or divorce. Girgis was aware that such problems would arise and included in his booklet suggestions on how to deal with them.

Girgis' vision was a lofty and idealistic one, but he lacked the resources, both financial and human, to achieve his goals. Many rural Copts had never even seen a priest, nor gone to church, nor been baptized; such villagers were nominal Christians only, knowing little about their faith or Orthodox worship. Many were fully preoccupied with the struggle for survival. Their main occupation was farming. Poor hygiene and disease would have made many breadwinners unemployable by modern standards. This primitive rural culture fostered a vicious circle that Girgis was attempting to change and transform through education, but he succeeded only to a very limited extent.

From the reports filed by the Sunday School teachers, it became evident that illiteracy was an enormous problem in the villages. As recently as 2009, some 26 percent of Egypt's population was illiterate.[24] What must it have been in the 1940s? Illiteracy not only prevented Copts from participating fully in their native religion and hindered their social and economic progress, but it also placed them at higher risk of conversion to Protestantism, through the influence of Western missionaries, or to Islam.

Girgis was familiar with the success of American Protestant missionary Frank Charles Laubach (1884–1970), who was known as "the Apostle to the Illiterates," in improving literacy rates among Philippine tribespeople.

[24]*Daily News Egypt*, "Egypt's Illiteracy Rate Drops Slightly to 26 pct." The Free Library by Farlex, 2009. <http://www.thefreelibrary.com/Egypt's+illiteracy+rate+drops+slightly+to+26+pct.-a0212009019>, accessed February 1, 2014.

Frank Charles Laubach (1884–1970), who improved literacy rates among the Philippine tribespeople and was known as "the Apostle to the Illiterates." (https://en.wikipedia.org/wiki/Frank_Laubach. Accessed January 31, 2017.)

Laubach's method, called "Each One Teach One," taught people to read and write in their own language and became popular in many countries around the world. Some of his texts had been translated into Arabic. Girgis proposed a similar scheme for the villagers of Egypt. He instructed the teachers to find in each village several youths who were educated, or who could at least read and write. These youngsters were to teach the illiterate Copts in the village to read the Bible and other spiritual books so that they could improve their spiritual lives. The Sunday School teacher assigned to the region was to monitor progress from time to time.

The plan was a good one, but the challenge was to find enough literate youths in each village to teach their illiterate neighbors. Another problem that would be encountered was the cultural divide that existed between the educated, city-based teachers and the village populations. Most villagers were unaccustomed to dealing with outsiders. They probably felt a sense of unease or distrust that would have to be overcome if the teachers were to have any influence.

But the big question was, how could such an ambitious program be paid for? There were costs for transport, religious pictures, Bibles, and other expenses. To save on accommodation costs and travel time, teachers would be billeted with village families during the week. In the end, much of the responsibility for raising the necessary funds was placed on the shoulders of the teachers themselves. They were expected to contribute from their own tithes (calculated as at least 10 percent of their earnings) and, since these Copts came from urban areas and were relatively wealthy compared to the villagers, they were also encouraged to seek donations from members of their urban parishes. The Lay Community Council supported the mission for only the first couple of years, from about 1938 to 1940, after which it withdrew its funding, much to Girgis' disappointment.

So, how effective was Girgis' program for rural religious education? In 1944 he reported that teachers had built churches in many villages and hamlets; established primary offices for teaching village children the principles of their faith; set up Sunday Schools; encouraged village children through the distribution of religious pictures and publications; reclaimed many souls who had renounced their Christian faith, after confronting the reason for their renunciation; and convinced many who had left the Coptic Church for Western denominations to return. Girgis stressed that the work should be continued and expanded, for "the need is immense these days to multiply the efforts to spread religious preaching and teaching to a wider circle, to snatch the sons of the community from the pit of spiritual ignorance, and to preserve the will of God."[25]

[25]Habib Girgis to Lay Community Council, February 4, 1938, Patriarchal Archives 4–6.35/5.

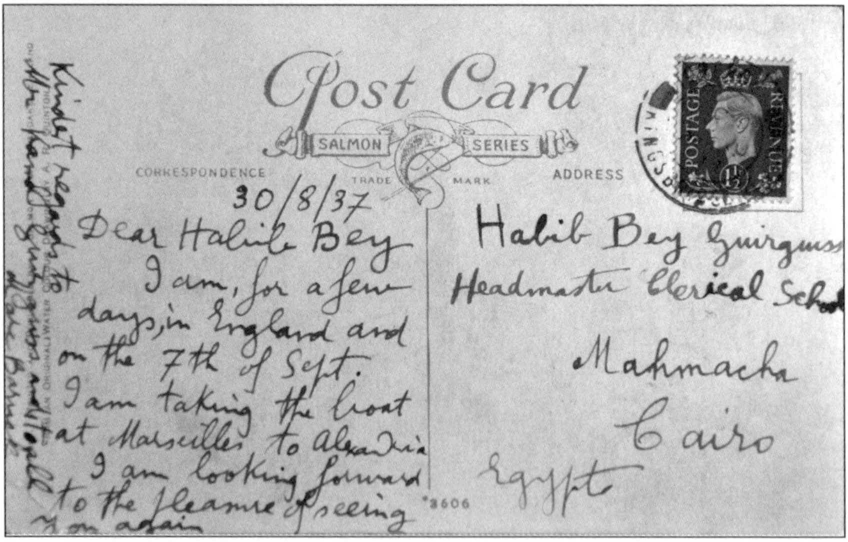

A postcard dated 30 August 1937 from Marc Baruck who was the English teacher at the Clerical School. The card is addressed to Habib Girgis and sent from the United Kingdom in which Baruck explains his forthcoming trip from Marseilles to Alexandria. (St Mark Coptic Orthodox Cultural Center, Dayr al-Anbā Ruways; photograph by Hani Gadoun.)

Epilogue

How can we evaluate the long-term legacy of the dedicated work of Habib Girgis? The seminary that flourished under his guidance is still in operation today. Its most influential leader since the time of Girgis was Pope Shenouda III, of blessed memory. In 1962 Shenouda (then Father Antonius El Souriany) was ordained as Bishop of Theological Education, and one of his main duties was to oversee the seminary. Today, it is headed by Pope Tawadros II. Located at the Patriarchate in Cairo, it is open to both women and men for theological study. But Girgis' dream that the seminary reach the highest academic standards still has not been fulfilled, and although the seminary does train aspiring priests, a theological education is not yet a compulsory prerequisite for ordination.

Sunday Schools continue to prosper, both in Egypt and in other countries to which Copts have emigrated. The schools follow a different administrative structure from that devised by Girgis, for each school is now independently run. Curricula continue to be developed in various regions of Egypt, North America, and Australia, and a new unified curriculum in Arabic is currently being implemented.

The Coptic Youth League is known today as the Bishopric of Youth Affairs. In 1980 Pope Shenouda III ordained the first Bishop of Youth, Bishop Mūsá, who continues to lead a vibrant and successful Coptic youth ministry across the globe. The Bishopric of Youth Affairs continues to take the holistic approach fostered by Habib Girgis, whose philosophy is reflected in its many successful conventions, leadership courses, and publications. Annual international competitions, with participants now totaling almost one million, include events and activities involving spirituality, faith, doctrine, sports, drama, music, theater, and a wide variety of arts. The Bishopric of Youth also serves young women, with some forty consecrated deaconesses fulfilling this role in Egypt.

* * *

Habib Girgis in his latter years c. 1940's. (Private collection, courtesy of Emad Asad—Helwan, Egypt.)

One of Habib Girgis' disciples, Murād Wahbah, sums up Girgis' life as follows: "The great teacher has failed in his reform . . . but he failed where shortcoming and failure are considered an honor. It was the failure of a martyr."[1] The Copts take great historical pride in their martyrs; even their "failures" are a source of strength and courage. Girgis had a clear goal and vision to make the Coptic Orthodox Seminary rise to the highest international standards of the day. One can feel his heartache, pain, and struggles that he had not achieved his goal despite doing everything within his power to succeed. There is a sense of sadness in his expressions of hope that the next generation would continue the effort and bring his work to fruition. However, Girgis sums up his life's work at the seminary with words that are nevertheless inspirational, revealing inner strength and a passion for education and self-sacrifice despite the hardships and failures that he and his community endured.

> Despite efforts that sapped my health and crushed my strength, I did not surrender for one day to anyone who resisted or envied me. This is a great grace that I do not deserve, as one cannot be envious, or resistant, except the one who does not have grace. Stones are thrown only at the trees that are filled with fruits, and birds peck only at ripe fruits. I thank God Almighty that, through his grace, despair never penetrated my soul for even one day, but in fact I constantly smile at the resistances. I have forgiven, and will continue to forgive, from the depth of my heart, everyone who desires to be my enemy in vain, knowing that it is inevitable that obstacles will come along the path of those who desire to serve God and people. It is inevitable that there is no honey without the bee sting, and he who abandons positive work for the sake of the murmurings of people

[1]Quoted in Yanney, "Light in the Darkness," 51.

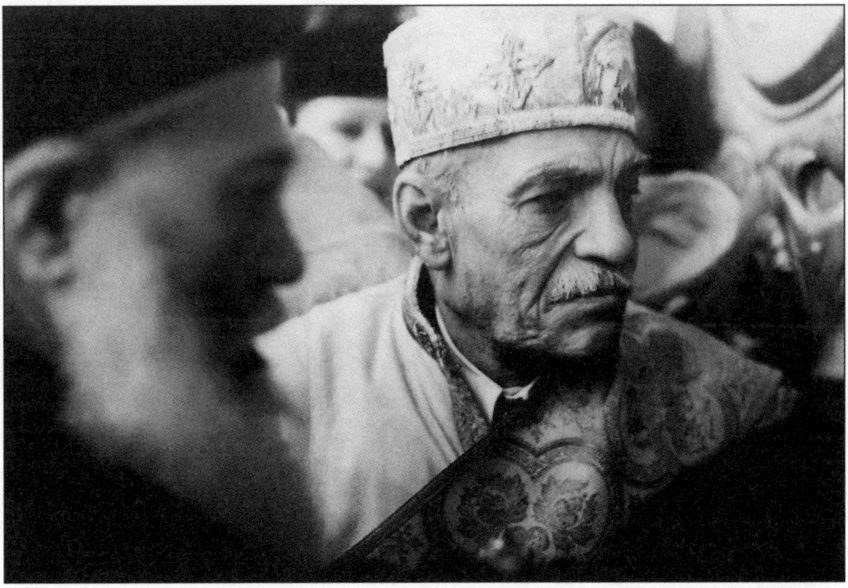

Habib Girgis passing on the keys of the cathedral to Pope Macarius III, on 19 February 1944, as part of the enthronement rite of a new pope. This is the last known photograph of Habib Girgis (Church of the Virgin Mary el-Mu'allaqa, Cairo, courtesy of Nash'at Nisīm Ṣubḥī.)

> resembles the horse that bolts when it sees its own shadow. Gold does not lose its value if it is rejected by animals, and the sun is not blemished if you cannot see it one day. It is imperative that we do not fail in doing good, for we shall reap the harvest in due time, if we do not weary. "Do not be overcome by evil, but overcome evil with good" [Rom 12.21].[2]

In fact, while historians consider Pope Cyril IV to be the Father of Coptic Reform, Habib Girgis should be considered the Father of Education—both religious and theological—in the modern Coptic era. Moreover, he is to be regarded as the educational administrator par excellence of his time. This is evident through the efforts that Girgis exerted at the Coptic Theological College, through the statutes that he designed to run the College in 1912, through his efforts as dean to operate the Theological College on sound administrative principles, as well as through his organizing the Sunday School Movement.

[2]Girgis, *The Coptic Orthodox Seminary*, 157.

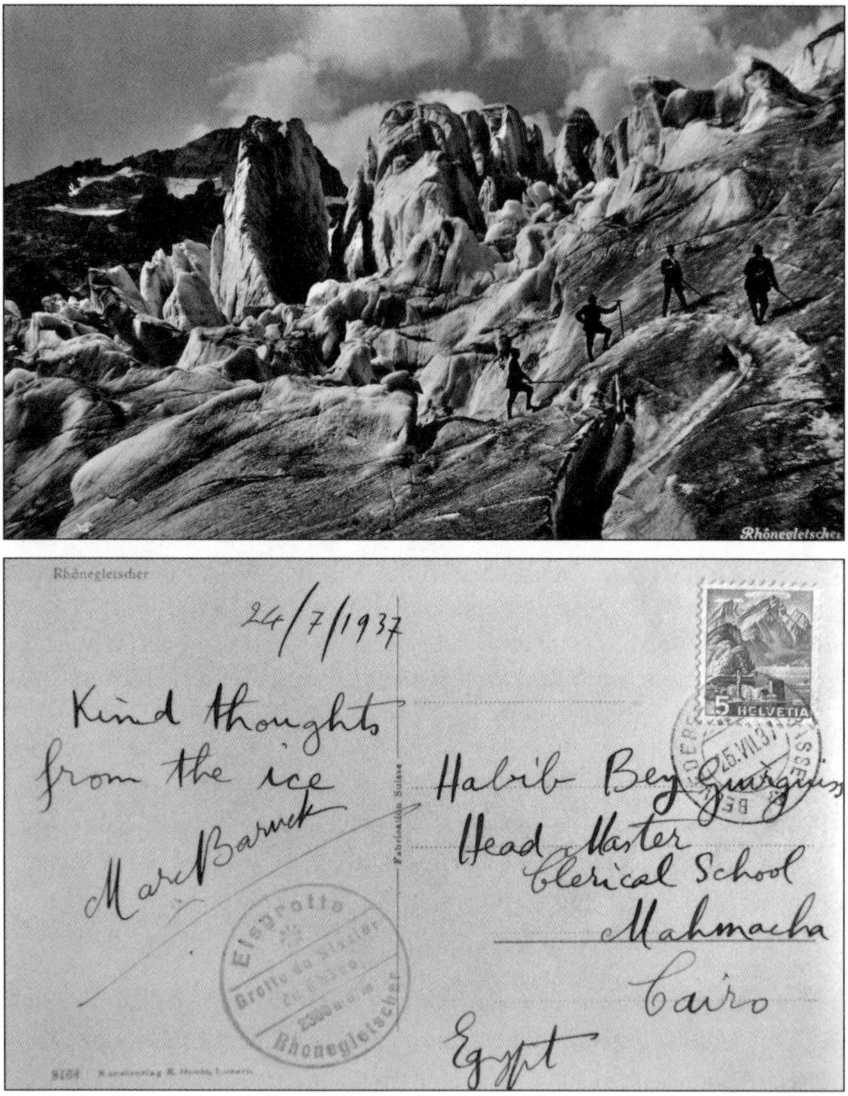

A postcard dated 24 July 1937 from Marc Baruck who was the English teacher at the Clerical School. The card is addressed to Habib Girgis and sent from Luzern, Switzerland. Baruck sends greetings from the ice. (St Mark Coptic Orthodox Cultural Center, Dayr al-Anbā Ruways; photograph by Hani Gadoun.)

APPENDIX ONE

Glossary of Terms Used in the Coptic Orthodox Church

ABBOT A monk considered as a spiritual father; the head of a *monastery*. Today an abbot can also be a *bishop*, which is indeed the case in all Coptic Orthodox monasteries today, although historically this was not the case.

ARCHON A lay member of the Church who, through long years of experience and dedication, has earned honored status as a leading member of the Coptic community.

ARCHPRIEST The middle rank of the three ranks of *priest*; the senior priest in a parish who takes a leadership role in administration and the spiritual guidance of the parishioners. Also known as hegumen.

AWQAF (singular WAQF) Land or other property bequeathed to a church, religious institution, *monastery*, or the *Patriarchate*, held in trust for ecclesiastical and charitable use. Such endowments are inalienable and cannot be used for any other purpose.

BISHOP A clergyman of the highest order, higher in rank than a *priest* or *deacon*, and the main spiritual leader of a *diocese*, although today a bishop may have a general ministry (such as a youth ministry) rather than a specific diocese. Bishops are drawn from the ranks of *monks*. They are celibate and cannot have been married.

CALENDAR The Coptic calendar was introduced on September 11, 284 AD at the beginning of the reign of the Roman Emperor Diocletian, who persecuted and martyred many Christians in Egypt. Christmas is celebrated on January 7.

CANTOR Leader and director of the chanting of the choir and congregation during the *Liturgy* and other ceremonial occasions. A cantor is usually a *deacon*, but may be a layman. He also teaches hymns to other deacons and members of the congregation.

COPTIC CATHOLIC CHURCH A semi-autonomous Eastern Catholic Church in full communion with the Roman Catholic Church. Founded in 1824, it is based in Cairo and has about 200,000 followers. It uses the Coptic language in its liturgy.

DEACON The lowest of the three ranks of orders in the Coptic Church. There are five ranks of deacon: epsaltos (hymnist), ognostis (reader), epideacon (subdeacon), deacon (full deacon), and archdeacon (leader of deacons). A deacon may assist the *priest* and the *bishop* at the sacraments, but may not perform them himself. In recent times the Church has also consecrated deaconesses, though these do not have any liturgical role.

DIOCESE An ecclesiastical district under the jurisdiction of a bishop.

HEGUMEN see *archpriest*.

HOLY SYNOD The highest authority in the Church: a body chaired by the pope and comprising the *metropolitans, bishops, abbots* of *monasteries, khoori episcopi*, and Patriarchal deputies (vicars-general). It deals with spiritual, ecclesiastical, structural, management, and financial matters.

KHOORI EPISCOPOS (chorepiscopus) The highest of the three ranks of *priest*; assistant to a *bishop*.

LAY COMMUNITY COUNCIL (*Majlis millī*) Now called the Coptic Community Council.

METROPOLITAN The leader of a group of bishops, and also bishop of a large city.

MONASTERY A building or complex of buildings comprising the domestic quarters and workplaces of *monks* or nuns (monastics), who live under religious vows, either in communities or alone, as hermits.

MONK A man who lives apart from the world in an all-male community, devoting himself to prayer, contemplation, and the performance of religious duties. He may live as a hermit, dwelling alone and meeting other members of the community only occasionally in church and at mealtime in the monastery refectory. A cenobitic monk, on the other hand, lives in a cloistered community and follows a strictly organized pattern of daily life.

A monk may be ordained a *priest* and can then officiate at the sacramental rites for public worship.

LITURGY A rite or body of rites prescribed for public worship.

PATRIARCHATE The residence and headquarters of the *pope*. During Girgis' time this was located at al-Azbakiyyah.

PATRIARCHATE CHURCH COUNCIL At the time of Habib Girgis this was the administrative body that supervised the day-to-day operation of the Church as a whole.

PATRIARCH see *pope*.

PATRISTIC Of or relating to the church fathers, or to their writings.

POPE The Pope of Alexandria and Patriarch of the See of St Mark, head of the Coptic Orthodox Church. His Holiness Pope Tawadros II was consecrated as the 118th Pope of Alexandria and Patriarch of the See of St Mark in 2012.

PRIEST There are three ranks of priest: priest, *archpriest* (hegumen), and *khoori episcopos*. Priests are usually married, although in modern times in particular there are some celibate priests.

SACRAMENTS The seven sacraments are baptism, confirmation or chrismation, confession or repentance, the Eucharist or Holy Communion, unction of the sick, matrimony, and priesthood.

SAINT A person who, by virtue of sacrifice and quest for God during his or her lifetime, has attained a prominent place in the divine hierarchy. The Coptic Church honors a very large number of saints. During his or her time on earth, a saint might have lived as a patriarch, monk, nun, layperson, or even a child. Many early Coptic saints were martyrs who died for their faith. Canonization is by majority vote of the Holy Synod of the Coptic Orthodox Church at any time after the person's death.

SCRIPTURE Biblical texts.

SEE The seat of a *bishop*.

SEE OF ST MARK The seat of the *pope* (patriarch) of the Coptic Orthodox Church.

SYNAXARION A liturgical book recording the lives of the *saints*.

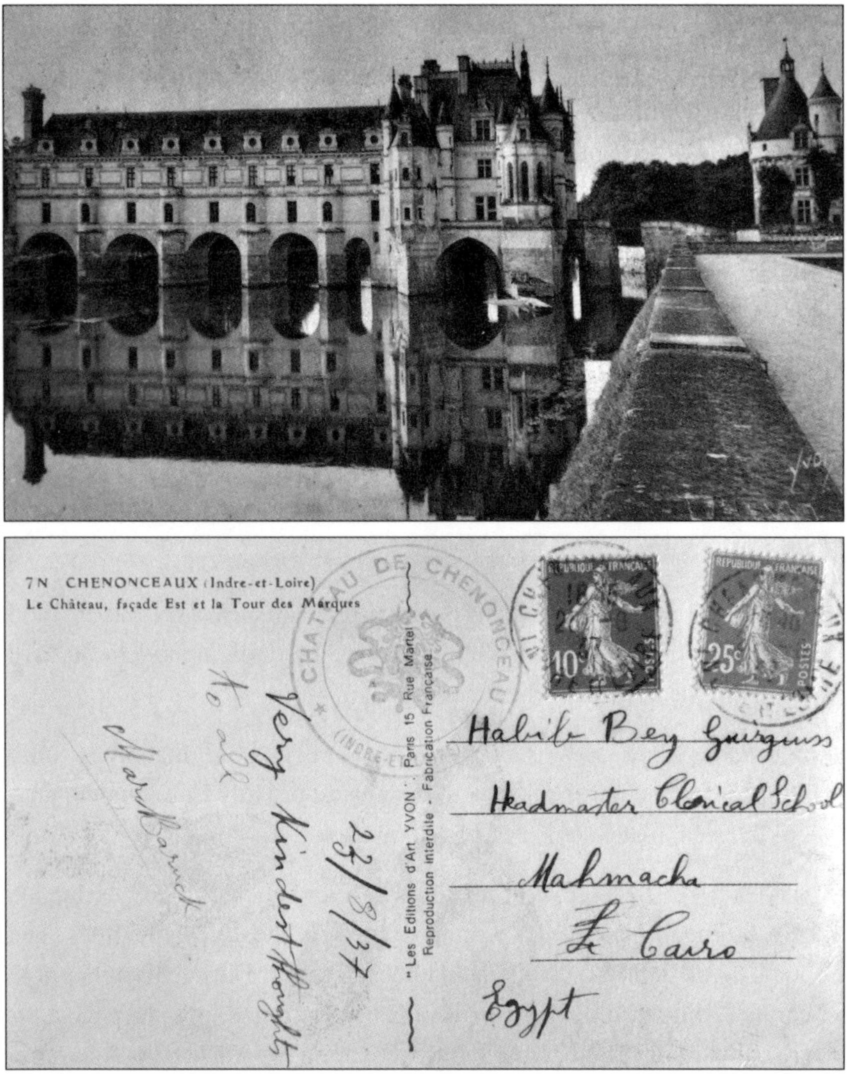

A postcard dated 23 August 1937 from Marc Baruck who was the English teacher at the Clerical School. The card is addressed to Habib Girgis and sent from France in which Baruck sends his best wishes. (St Mark Coptic Orthodox Cultural Center, Dayr al-Anbā Ruways; photograph by Hani Gadoun.)

APPENDIX TWO

Chronology of Events in Egypt: 1798–1951

1798–1801	French occupation of Egypt under Emperor Napoleon Bonaparte.
1799	Church Missionary Society (CMS) is founded in England.
1801–4	Civil war in Egypt.
1805	Reign of Khedive Muḥammad ʻAlī begins.
1808	Joseph Lancaster, Joseph Fox, and William Corston form the British and Foreign School Society (BFSS).
1809–52	Reign of Pope Buṭrus al-Jawlī (Peter) VII.
1819–20	William Jowett arrives as the first Anglican missionary in Egypt.
1824–64	Lutherans from Basel set up educational missions in Egypt.
1825	Protestant missionaries arrive in Egypt, sent by the Church Missionary Society.
	Reverend John Lieder arrives in Egypt and establishes a monitorial school.
1826	(December) First British mission school opens in Alexandria.
1828	William Krusé establishes a school for boys in Cairo, using the Lancaster system; it closes in 1848.
1829	(February) Mrs Krusé establishes a school for girls; it closes in 1860.
1837	Khedive Muḥammad ʻAlī establishes the Ministry of Schools.

1840	Reverend Lieder reports that there are seven Coptic schools, which he supplies with publications from Malta.
1843	Church Missionary Society opens a seminary in Cairo for Coptic clergy.
1848	End of the reign of Khedive Muḥammad ʻAlī.
	Church Missionary Society closes the seminary for Coptic clergy.
1849–1905	Life of Muḥammad ʻAbduh, jurist, religious scholar, liberal reformer and intellectual pioneer of Egyptian modernity. He led Islamic reform in Egypt in parallel with reform movements that had begun in the Coptic Church.
1854	American Presbyterian missionaries arrive in Egypt.
1854–61	Reign of Pope Kyrillos (Cyril) IV.
1855	Kyrillos IV establishes the Great Coptic School in Cairo.
	Kyrillos establishes boys' schools in ʻĀbidīn and al-Manṣurah, and also girls' schools next to the Patriarchate and in ʻĀbidīn.
	Jizyah (the poll tax or capitation tax imposed on all able-bodied, non-Muslim subjects of the Islamic state) is abolished for Copts. The tax was one of many injustices faced by Copts under Islamic rule; its abolition significantly alleviated daily hardship for many Copts.
1856	The *Haṭṭ-i Hamāyūn* decree places onerous conditions on the building and repair of churches, but does not apply to mosques.
	The *dhimmī* title is removed from the Copts. *Dhimmīs* were Christians or Jews living in Muslim territory who, in exchange for submitting to Muslim rule and paying special taxes, were offered some protections including limited freedom of religious worship. Removal of this degrading title gave the Copts

some sense that they were not considered strangers in their own land.

Copts are officially conscripted into the Egyptian army.

1859 Pope Kyrillos IV imports printing press from Austria.

1860 (April) American Presbyterian Mission (APM) is formally established in Cairo.

1861–62 American missionary Reverend Gulian Lansing sells many Bibles and tracts to Coptic clergy and laity.

1862–70 Reign of Pope Demetrius II.

1863 The reign of Khedive Ismāʿīl Pasha begins.

1865 Reverend John Lieder dies in Egypt.

American missionaries establish boys' and girls' schools in Asyūṭ.

1867 Khedive Ismāʿīl Pasha opens government schools to non-Muslims and donates 1,500 acres of land to the Coptic Church.

Pope Demetrius II visits Coptic adherents in Upper Egypt to caution them against the missionaries; he issues a papal bull against Protestantism (see Appendix 4).

Khedive Ismāʿīl declares bankruptcy of the Egyptian state.

American missionaries establish a theological seminary in Asyūṭ, Upper Egypt, for converts sent from Cairo to Alexandria.

1873 Number of students in Egyptian schools (both government and non-government) rises to 90,000.

1874–1927 Reign of Pope Kyrillos (Cyril) V—the longest-reigning Coptic pope.

1874 Lay Community Council (*Majlis millī*) is inaugurated.

Reverend B. F. Pinkerton breaks away from American Presbyterian Mission and begins a charismatic movement, following the Plymouth Brethren movement.

1875 The Lay Community Council opens a Coptic theological seminary; it is shut down by Pope Kyrillos V only months later.

1876 Birth of Habib Girgis.

1877 *Al-Waṭan* Coptic newspaper established.

1878 End of Khedive Ismā'īl Pasha's reign; beginning of Khedive Tawfīq Pasha's reign.

There are now twenty-five Coptic schools and thirty-five Protestant schools in Egypt.

Khedive Tawfīq Pasha officially recognizes the Protestant community of Egypt as a distinct Christian sect.

1881–82 The 'Urābī revolt, which is followed by seventy years of British rule in Egypt.

1888 Missionaries observe that Orthodox Copts are following the Protestant custom of organizing Bible study and prayer groups.

1891 The Tawfīq Coptic Society, whose main concern is schools, is established.

1892 (September 1) Pope Kyrillos V is banished to al-Bārāmūs Monastery.

End of Khedive Tawfīq Pasha's reign.

1893 (February 4) Pope Kyrillos V returns in triumph to his see in Cairo.

(November 29) The Coptic Orthodox Seminary is (re)opened by Pope Kyrillos V in a house in al-Fajjālah owned by the al-Muḥarraq Monastery. Yūsuf Manqariyūs is the first dean. Habib Girgis is one of the first students to enroll.

1894	Catholic converts in Egypt number 5,000.
	The Coptic Orthodox Seminary moves to the Patriarchal Center.
1895	First Coptic Catholic patriarch appointed by the Vatican.
	Establishment of *Miṣr* Coptic newspaper.
1897	Egyptian national census counts 608,000 Copts (around 7 percent of the population).
	American Protestants claim 5,355 Egyptian converts, mainly Copts.
	Habib Girgis begins his career with an impressive lecture entitled "The Christian Religion."
1898	Habib Girgis begins teaching at the Coptic Orthodox Seminary while in his final year of study.
	Habib Girgis completes his studies at the seminary.
	Holy Synod issues a statement on the importance of religious education for Coptic youth and children.
	Girgis publishes a three-volume curriculum: *Kitāb khilāṣat al uṣūl al īmāniyah fī mu'taqadāt al Kanīsah al Qibṭiyah al Urthūdhuksiyah* [The Doctrines of the Coptic Orthodox Faith: A Foundational Synopsis] (question-and-answer catechesim), Grades 1–4.
1899	Protestants form the Presbyterian Synod of the Nile.
1900	Missionaries have now identified Egypt as a "strategic center" for Muslim evangelization worldwide.
	Girgis travels to Upper Egypt to give a series of lectures in defense of Orthodox doctrine.
	Habib Girgis begins to teach Sunday School lessons to children in the suburb of al-Fajjālah in al-Azbakiyyah district of

central Cairo. This date is considered the beginning of the Sunday School Movement.

1902 The Coptic Museum collection is brought together in a temporary gallery in the Bulāq Museum.

1903 The Holy Synod reaffirms the importance of religious education for Coptic youth and children.

1904 (September 11) Habib Girgis launches the religious journal *al-Karmah* (The Vine).

The seminary relocates to Mahmashah site.

1905 Annie Van Sommer and Arthur T. Upson, British missionaries connected to the evangelical, interdenominational North Africa Mission, establish the Nile Mission Press in Egypt.

1907 Egyptian government conducts a census.

Number of Coptic schools grows to forty-six.

Pope Kyrillos V issues a pastoral letter stressing the importance of children's education.

1908 The Coptic Museum moves to its permanent home in the suburb of Old Cairo.

Sa'd Zaghlūl, Egyptian minister of education, agrees to have Christian religion taught in public schools.

1908–10 Buṭrus Ghālī Pasha serves as Egypt's first and only Coptic prime minister.

1910 World Missionary Conference takes place in Edinburgh.

1911 (March 6–8) Coptic Congress takes place in Asyūṭ.

Catholic converts in Egypt number 25,000.

1912 Samuel M. Zwemer establishes the Cairo Study Center to train Protestant missionaries in Arabic and Islamic studies.

	Coptic Orthodox Seminary is temporarily relocated to the Patriarchal Center, then returns to Mahmashah.
1914–18	World War I, which ends with the defeat of the Ottoman Empire.
1914	It is estimated that 50 percent of Egypt's wealth is in Coptic hands. However, such wealth is held by a small, business-savvy elite; the majority of Copts are poor.
1918	Yūsuf Manqariyūs, first dean of the Coptic Orthodox Seminary, dies.
	Habib Girgis becomes dean of the seminary.
	Formal establishment of the Sunday School movement, with the formation of a central Sunday School Committee.
1919	Nationalist revolution, with Copts joining the nationalist *al-Wafd* party and Egypt's political movement for independence from British rule.
1922	Egypt declares independence.
1926	Presbyterian Synod of the Nile becomes the Evangelical Coptic Church.
1927	Habib Girgis is chosen as general secretary of the Sunday School Committee.
	The Young Men's Muslim Association (YMMA), an Islamic operation similar to the Young Men's Christian Association (YMCA), established.
1928–42	Reign of Pope Yu'annis (John) XIX.
1928	Habib Girgis is nominated to the papacy.
	Pope Yu'annis XIX opens a theological school for monks in Hulwān.
	Muslim Brotherhood founded by Ḥasan al-Bannā.

1930s	The Great Depression.
1931	The Coptic Museum is taken out of the hands of the Coptic Church and becomes a national museum under the jurisdiction of the Egyptian Department of Antiquities.
1933	Muslim Brotherhood holds its first conference.
1934	Ten conditions restricting the building and repair of churches in Egypt are added to the *Haṭṭ-i Hamāyūn* edict.
	Egyptian government issues Law 40, regulating foreign private schools.
	Girgis publishes *The Seven Sacraments of the Church.*
1935–42	Sunday School movement grows rapidly; centers in Shubrā, Giza, Jazīrat Badrān, and Damanhūr play important roles in its future direction and growth.
1936	The Anglo–Egyptian treaty is signed, providing for the withdrawal of most British troops from Egypt.
1937	Catholic converts in Egypt number 39,000.
	Girgis publishes an eight-volume curriculum for elementary and secondary schools called *Christian Orthodox Principles.*
1938	Lay Community Council introduces a personal status law that infuriates the Holy Synod.
	Habib Girgis publishes his history of the seminary on the occasion of its forty-fifth anniversary.
1939	Outbreak of World War II.
1940	Qur'ān study becomes compulsory for Muslim students in every elementary school in Egypt, including Christian mission schools.
1941	Habib Girgis participates in the first conference for Sunday School teachers.

1942	Girgis publishes *The Practical Means Toward Coptic Reform: Hopes and Dreams*.
1944	American missionaries in Egypt claim 24,504 converts.
1944–45	Reign of Pope Macarius III.
1945	End of World War II.
1946–56	Reign of Pope Yusāb (Joseph) II.
1946	The Coptic Clerical School officially becomes the Coptic Orthodox Seminary.
1948	(March 18) Pope Yusāb (Joseph) II asks Habib Girgis to create a Higher Committee for Sunday Schools.
	Girgis publishes *The Orthodox Rock.*
1948	Egyptian minister of education officially recognizes graduation from Coptic Orthodox Seminary as equivalent to a bachelor's degree.
1949	Habib Girgis participates in the second conference for Sunday School teachers.
1951	(August 21) Habib Girgis dies at the age of seventy-five.

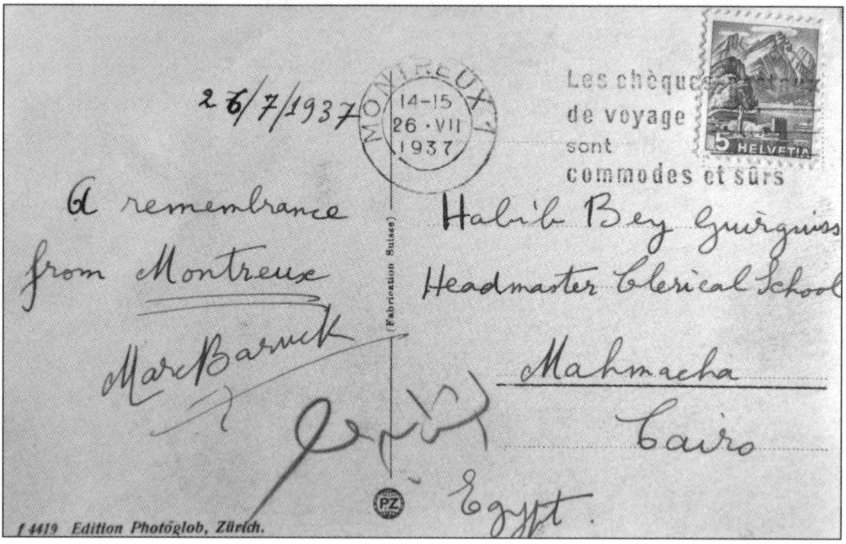

A postcard dated 26 July 1937 from Marc Baruck who was the English teacher at the Clerical School. The card is addressed to Habib Girgis and sent from Montreux, Switzerland in which Baruck shares an image of a beautiful spot that he is visiting along his journey. (St Mark Coptic Orthodox Cultural Center, Dayr al-Anbā Ruways; photograph by Hani Gadoun.)

APPENDIX THREE

Certificate of Authenticity for the Relics of St Habib Girgis, the Archdeacon

Coptic Orthodox Patriarchate, Cairo.
Churches of the Eastern Region of the Railway
Mahmashah – al-Sharabiya – al-Zawya al-Hamra

بطريركية الأقباط الأرثوذكس
بالقاهرة
منطقة كنائس شرق السكة الحديد
مهمشة - الشرابية - الزاوية الحمراء

15 January 2014
7 Tubah 1729 A.M.

Certificate of Authenticity for Relics of St. Habib Girgis, the Archdeacon

His Grace Bishop Martyros, the General Bishop for the Eastern Region of the Railway-- Cairo, testifies that these relics are of the great saint Archdeacon Habib Girgis (1876 – 1951). He is the pioneer of Church renaissance in the twentieth century and was the dean of the Coptic TheologicalCollege and established the Sunday School Movement. He departed on the eve of the Feast of Saint Mary, the Virgin on 21 August 1951 (15 Misra 1667 A.M.).

The sainthood of Archdeacon Habib Girgis was recognised during the Holy Synod Meeting headed by His Holiness Pope Tawadros II, the 118th Pope of Alexandria and Patriarch of the See of St. Mark on Thursday 20 June 2013.

It gives us great joy to receive with honour the blessed father, His Grace Bishop Suriel, Bishop of Melbourne and its Affiliated Regions in the continent of Australia on the morning of Wednesday 15 January 2014 (7 Tubah 1729 A.M.). We received him with love and hospitality at the Church of the Virgin Mary in Mahmashah, al-Sharabiya – Cairo.

His Grace received the relics from us – and the relics are: the complete upper right arm bone (humerus), the handkerchief that was wrapped around the head, an embroidered cross-decorated with silver thread, the glove that was on the right hand and a section of the liturgical vestment, to be a source of blessing and grace for the Diocese of Melbourne.

His Grace will place these relics in a church named after Saint Habib Girgis, the Archdeacon in his Christ loving diocese, and we ask of God to preserve the life of:

His Holiness Pope Tawadros II
Pope of Alexandria and
Patriarch of the See of St. Mark

As we also ask for the intercessions and prayers of the great saint Habib Girgis, the Archdeacon.

Archon:
MagedKamel
BishaySaad

Archon:
AttiaBishay
AttiaBishay Hanna

Archon:
HishamFathy
Abdelmessih

Bishop Martyros
General Bishop

Bishop Suriel
Bishop of Melbourne and
its Affiliated Regions

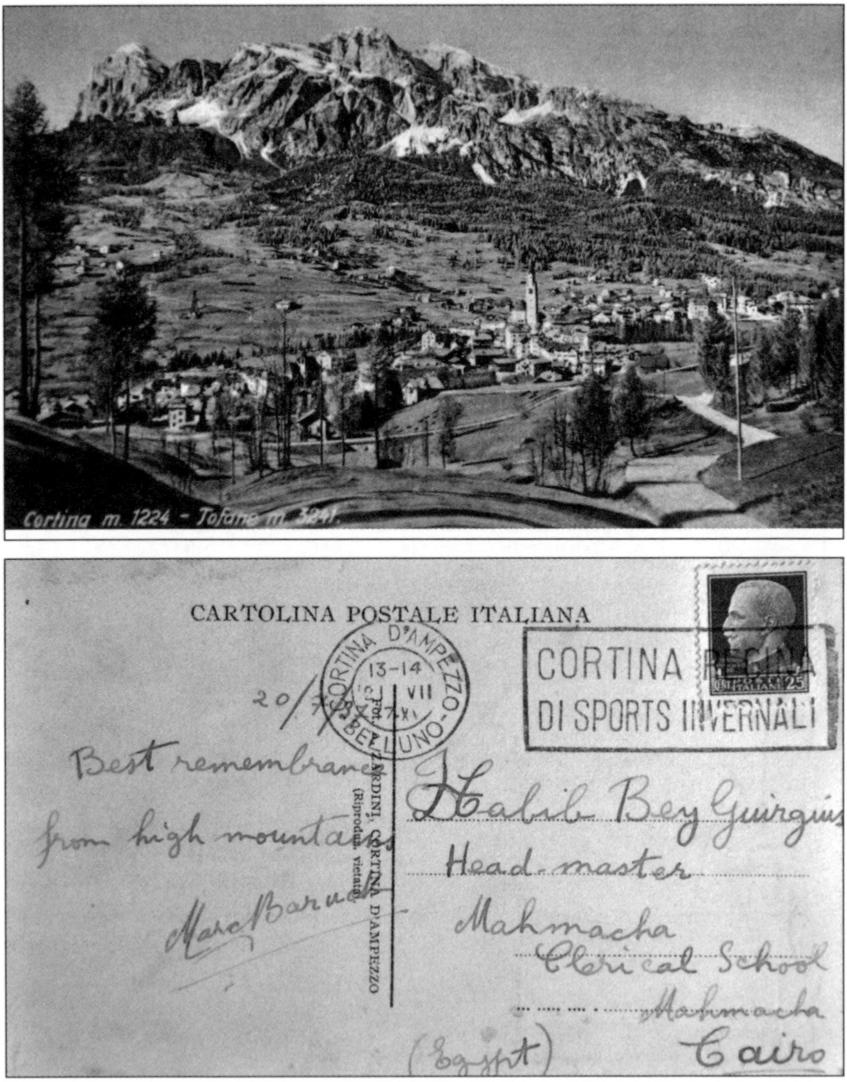

A postcard dated 20 July 1937 from Marc Baruck who was the English teacher at the Clerical School. The card is addressed to Habib Girgis and sent from Cortina, Northern Italy in which Baruck sends greetings from high mountains. (St Mark Coptic Orthodox Cultural Center, Dayr al-Anbā Ruways; photograph by Hani Gadoun.)

APPENDIX FOUR

Patriarchal Bull Against Protestantism Issued by Pope Demetrius II, Patriarch of the Copts, in 1867

From Demetrius, the servant of Jesus Christ, called by the high grace of God, Patriarch on the Chair of Mark in Alexandria and the Egyptian and adjoining Provinces, to our blessed children, the trusted priests and renowned pillars and honoured deacons and respected scribes and merchants and artisans and peasants, and all the orthodox people, great and small, rich and poor, who are in the city of Osiout and its surrounding villages, and towns and hamlets and churches, even all our Christian children,—the peace of God the Father Almighty, and the grace of his only Son, our Lord Jesus Christ, the Eternal Word, and the communion and gifts of the Holy Ghost the Comforter descend upon you and rest on you and abide among you,—you and your children and your relations,—and may supernal blessings be poured out upon you, and abundant heavenly benefits be multiplied unto you, and may you ever continue in all health, safety and peace, enjoying security and respect and honour, steadfast in your pure orthodox faith, being fruitful in every good and precious work, being preserved from all temptations and cares and griefs, profiting by your beneficent works, prospering always in your laudable enterprises, while being accounted children of the kingdom and of the blessed everlasting life in the paternal exuberant glorious joys,—by the intercession of the pure Virgin Lady St. Mary, the mother of God, the Supreme incarnate Word, and by the prayers of the high archangels and the masters, the apostles, the exalted high priests and the happy just crowned martyrs and all the blessed saints. Amen.

O our spiritual children, beloved in the Lord, since it is a matter acknowledged and known by high and low legally, and popularly that the pastor is the watchman of his flock and pastoral visits are part of his duty, I therefore, although I have always been in assurance in respect of my children dwelling in these parts by means of epistles and letters and constant inquiries, yet since in these days we have determined to establish schools in different quarters for the children of our sect, and among them in your place, and also since certain causes have intervened causing contentions and controversies, my religious zeal and paternal affection have stirred me up to arise and endure the fatigues of journey, only to visit our children in the southern provinces: and we have continued by the providence of the Most High passing through the cities and villages and churches from Cairo until we reached this place, and thanks be to God that you are all in the possession of all security, peace, stability, and integrity, and we have reached your town and witnessed your profound respect for us and your joy in meeting us, and your pleasure at our approach, and your exultation before us, and your filial preparation, and the signs of your rejoicing beaming in your faces.—We have therefore thanked the bounties of the Most High. May he be praised, glorifying his grace and benefits and bounties, offering to his Majesty all supplications, that he may increase you and bless you, in your merchandise and servants and trades and possessions and children and houses, and render you blessed in both worlds,—and as ye are all joyful in us, we are far more so in each one of you, and we will never cease to offer these prayers to the exalted Creator.—But O our children, our joy and rejoicing and the boast of our preaching, although the conditions of you all are joyous and pleasing, and ye are abiding in the true orthodox faith and established in the honoured sacraments of your church, and respecting exceedingly its spiritual ordinances, and rites and ceremonies, yet in this spiritual garden which the right hand of the Lord Christ planted by means of his priestly apostles, and their righteous disciples and successors, and in the spiritual cultivation of which they laboured, there are to be found two things which are displeasing, nay exceedingly grievous, and depressing, and heart-rending.—The first of these is the reception by some of you of the doctrines of those opposers who follow the Protestants, sometimes by receiving and reading their books, and sometimes by hearkening to their words, and being made to doubt by them and follow them. The second, that it has not sufficed that the adults have looked upon these poisons, but with your own hands you have cast your little ones into their deadly snares, since one gives over his boy to their school, and another his daughter unto them, that they may cause them to drink from their childhood the milk of error, and while from your city itself there are no boys in the school of that schism there are in it fifteen or more of your daughters, and from the surrounding towns and villages there are in it a number of boys.—These, then, are the two evils which I have witnessed as occurring among you. Therefore, O my children, my heart is not at peace, nor are my joys full since the fulness of joy is, that I hear, as said the Apostle John, that my children walk in the truth, not in doubts and corrupting confusions. In respect of the school, since there has been opened in your city and church a Coptic school, and we have placed in it a fitting teacher,—a man adept in the desired languages and renowned sciences, and we have further strengthened it and filled it by sending to it many of the children of the common schools, and we are purposing to do all that may be necessary for its increased prosperity and efficiency. Why, then, since you have your own school, which necessarily will irrigate the lands of your children's hearts with pure and sweet waters, do ye turn aside and cast them into these snares, the teachers of which water your branches with foul water or rather with deadly poison,—and especially those pure maidens, how can you allow yourselves to cast them with your own hands into those pernicious perils, the evil consequences of which will yet come upon you, and cause you to repent when repentance will not profit you. Since, therefore, it is my duty, in accordance with the rule of my calling, to preach to you and proclaim in your ears what is necessary for the purity of your consciences, and salvation of your souls from the guilt of your children, I therefore proclaim to you by the word of God, that you take your sons out of these snares, and deliver your daughters from this pit of destruction, and train them up in your own houses in politeness and modesty and the fear of God. As for your sons, therefore, behold the school is open before them, and I by His grace am always prepared to assist it with books and teachers and the orders necessary for its respectability and prosperity, of the truth of which ye are my witnesses. But the girls bring up, in fear and modesty and humility, in your own homes, and deliver them not into the hands of those ravenous ones who cause them to drink cups of wickedness instead of morality. Therefore, from this time henceforth, whoever transgresses and dares to take his son or daughter from his own church or school, and introduce him into the school of the Protestants, in order to abide therein and learn its detestable sciences, let him be under the excommunicating word of God. Therefore beware of transgression, and take heed unto yourselves, O company of my children, and abide in obedience, that blessings may descend upon you and let not one of you be like unto the Jews, who, not content with the crime of the blood of the Son of God upon themselves alone, placed it upon their children also. Wherefore beware exceedingly thereof, and inasmuch as ye have respect unto your own souls, and desire their salvation, so also have respect unto your sons and daughters; for while they are minors, you will be judged for them.

Then also in respect of the implication of certain ones of you in this obstinate schism, I know that your consciences and enlightened and unprejudiced minds, are not in ignorance concerning their true character, since every wise, prudent, God-fearing man knows well their abominable heresies and confused divisions,—a company who come to you, as said the Lord, clothed with sheep's clothing, and within they are ravening wolves,—a company who feign humility and wisdom, while they cast into the hearts of believers the poisons of doubt and uncertainty,—a company who claim to be preachers of the gospel, while they fight against the Author of the gospel, the Son of God, the Word incarnate by the Holy Ghost and St. Mary, since they believe concerning his honourable incarnation what is opposed to the truth, for they say that the Word of God did not descend into the womb of the virgin and assume humanity, and deny the word of the gospel with which Gabriel addressed the virgin lady: "The Holy Ghost shall come upon thee, and the power of the Highest shall overshadow thee; therefore also that holy thing which shall be born of thee shall be called the Son of God." And they are people who claim to be evangelical, while they abolish the doctrines of the Lord of the Gospel, who says, "The bread which I give you is my body," and his saying, "Verily, verily, I say unto you, except ye eat the flesh of the Son of man, and drink his blood, ye have no life in you. He that eateth my flesh and drinketh my blood dwelleth in me, and I in him. My flesh is meat indeed and my blood is drink indeed." And thus, also, when he delivered his sacrament to his disciples, he hallowed the bread and wine, and said to them, "This is my body; eat it: this is my blood; drink it." But these persons say sometimes, that this is the sacrament of the body of Christ, and sometimes that it is the memorial of the body of Christ. Then away with such false evangelicals, who have given diligence to pervert the word of God; but they are the perverted ones, who have deceived themselves. But the words of God are a firm and sure foundation which cannot be shaken nor changed, and who is he that opposes the words of God himself, and abolishes his plain teachings, which are brighter than the sun? Is not every one that does this a stranger to the true faith? A company who claim that they are the apostles of our Lord in the last times, while they themselves prevent the believers from honouring the apostles and the saints of the Most High, who himself blessed them and prepared for them the glory which is unutterable. They persuade the simple that they teach the true religion, while in truth the end of all their teaching is the abolishing of the precious sacraments without the participation in which a Christian can by no means be a Christian;—such as baptism, by which we are regenerated, and the holy mysteries by which we live, and our souls are enlightened, and we are united to Christ,—and such as penance, by which our hope is renewed and our purposes strengthened, and the priesthood, by which all the mysteries are perfected and bestowed upon us according to the necessities of each one,—and matrimony, by which we are kept and preserved, and as long as we are united by it in purity, we resemble the union of Christ with his church. And thus, as to the rest of the sacraments, they abolish them, and in order that they may convince a few, they claim that they believe in baptism, and the offering,—but what a faith is it? It is nothing but a pretense and a deception; for they believe that in baptism we have only a mark and sign, and some of them have dared to equalize it to the baptism of John, and they have denied that by it a man is regenerated, thus rejecting the plain saying of Christ concerning it. And they believe that the offering is simple or blessed bread, and deny the sayings of our Lord, (the alone Mighty,) who took that bread, and said, "Take, eat of it all of you, this is my body;" and so also the cup, "Take ye, and drink of it all of you, this is my blood, a new covenant." And the apostle Paul also confessed the same in his first epistle to the Corinthians, Chapter x. 11, "That it is not lawful to draw near to this honourable sacrament unworthily, so that to him that approaches without preparation abound diseases and sudden death."[1] Has, therefore, O, my children! simple or blessed bread alone efficacy to such an extent? Is there in bread the power

[1][Summary paraphrase of 1 Cor 11.27–30.—*Ed.*]

of everlasting life? Is there in simple bread the forgiveness of sins? Is common bread able to harm or heal? Our Lord has taught us concerning common bread, saying, that not by bread alone does a man live, but by every word that proceedeth from the mouth of God. But concerning the holy offering which is replenished with the mysteries of wisdom, which is in truth, as the Creator of all creatures has revealed his own precious body; he hath said, "He that eateth this bread shall live for ever." It is not like the manna which the fathers of the Jews ate and died. Therefore judge ye, O wise brethren, concerning the doctrine of these new prophets. Truly a wise man is confounded by the mixture of their opinions and doctrines; for their books contradict each other. Their histories sometimes establish and sometimes refute their doctrines. Their verbal sayings disagree with the contents of their compositions. Let God, therefore, judge justly this company, who come to you claiming that they will enlighten your darkness, and address you with words which in appearance are good, but within they are whitened sepulchres. Let us mention some of their enlightenments, that their true character may appear. Among them is, that they deceive the priest who has become a soldier for Christ, and has vowed chastity and celibacy, strip him of the honour of his priesthood, take from him the robe of his chastity, and plunge him into the sea of lusts, offering him certain women in the semblance of marriage of those women whom they have caught in their snares, and in which, as we have before said, we fear they may entrap some of your daughters. And no doubt you have heard what their marriage is. Are these, then, the spiritual lights? Where is the saying of the Master, by his own mouth, that no man having put his hand to the plough, and looking back, is fit for the kingdom of God? And how is it fitting that a priest of theirs, claiming to be a disciple, should disgrace himself by marriage after having become a disciple of His? By the judgment of the Savior, he has been stripped of the purity of the disciples of the kingdom. And where is his saying, "There be eunuchs which have made themselves eunuchs for the kingdom of heaven's sake?" And where is "the church of the first-born," [the word for first-born and virgin in Arabic is one,] "which are written in heaven," which Paul mentioned in the last of his epistle to the Hebrews? And where is the honour of the virgins, who have not been defiled with women, and the glory prepared for them, as John, the speaker of divine things, indicated in his Revelation? Judge, O my wise children, whether these are enlighteners, or rather preachers of the darkness of their own lusts. Then we also see these new spiritual ones dissuading the believers from temperance in food and fasting, opening to men the door of gluttony. Nor are they ashamed thereof, that the chief of bodily sins is gluttony, and it is that which drove our first grand father from Paradise, and therefore our Lord came fasting for us a long time, that he might abolish the works of Satan, and lay for us a good foundation, that we might follow his example. These claim that they are preachers, and they are not ashamed of the state of the true preachers who traversed the world in hunger and thirst and much fasting and nakedness, and the like, in comparison with the state of these new ones of luxury and greediness, and letting loose the reins of their lusts in clothing, in drunkenness, in superciliousness, in anger, in schemes, in deception, in backbiting. Are these spiritual preachers, or rather those teachers whom the Master rebuked, saying, "Woe unto you, for ye compass sea and land."

But it is not our purpose to exhibit all their vanities, one by one, in this short epistle; but it will suffice for every believer to have respect to the rule given by the Savior, namely, "By their fruits, shall ye know them," and it is enough for every believer to know that the Savior has given woe and lamentation to every one casting doubt into the heart of any one of the believers in his name; and since the aim and end of this company is to cast doubts and stumbling blocks and quenching into the hearts of the faithful servants of God, let it, therefore, be judged whether these are evangelical, or rather deserving from God of that with which he has threatened those who offend his servants.

Further, the glorious Master has redeemed his honourable church with his precious blood, adorned her with his divine sacraments, established her upon the orthodox faith in him, and promised that the gates of hell shall not prevail against her; and he gave her over to his apostles, and commanded them to disciple others, that they might feed her, and promised them that he would not leave them unto the end of the world. Therefore neither the heresy of Arius, who denied the divinity of the Son, could conquer this church, nor could the heresy of Manes, the liar, disturb her, nor the infidelity of Macedonius in the Holy Spirit deceive her, nor the error of Sabellius, nor others who invented heresies, nor did the wandering of Nestorius quench the new faith; but by the supreme providence these heresies have been annihilated, and the church established upon her true faith, sacraments and ceremonies, and the Lord himself, who in olden times visited Egypt, has preserved his church which is in it, as he foretold by the prophet, that "My altar shall be in the midst of thee, O Egypt!" and especially that the cruel foreign Governments of former times were not able to extinguish the candle of faith in the Egyptian Church. How then, O my children, is it that some of you are deceived by this heresy, which is so patent to every wise person?

Since, by the grace of God, I have been called to the pastorate of the preaching of Mark, and ye have heard the sayings of God to the prophet Ezekiel concerning his obligation to warn the people, we therefore, in executing the high behest, and by the power given by the Most High, in his saying, "Whatsoever ye bind on earth shall be bound in heaven, and whatsoever ye loose on earth shall be loosed in heaven," do exhort you and all, rich and poor, learned and simple, that you entirely abstain from them.

First, therefore, receive not at all their books, which teach their doctrines; and if any one has any of them, let him burn them with fire. Secondly, by no means receive their teaching, whether oral or by letters or signs. Thirdly, have no communications with them in the matter of a livelihood, nor receive them into your houses, on any other pretense, which would result in your own injury, nor assist them in obtaining a foothold, nor in opening houses or schools nor any thing of the kind, the evil consequences of which will come upon you; and, finally beware of them inwardly and outwardly, that ye may be the children of peace and obedience, and the divine blessing may rest upon you.

And let the obstinate and refractory one who despises this our epistle and transgresses the laws of his church, and denies the seven holy sacraments, or is deceived in the truth of the orthodox faith delivered unto us by the honoured apostles, by the mouths of the holy councils of Nice and Ephesus, and established by that of Constantinople, or dares to disrespect the mother of God, who is worthy of the blessing and honour of all ages, or disrespects the saints, who are the temple of the Holy Ghost, and, in fine, everyone who is obstinate, and still holds the false doctrines of the Protestants, and does not return nor recant his errors, nor respect the commands of his honourable church, know that he is under the bond of the excommunicating word of God.—But if he returns and repents, acknowledges his error, and repents towards God, the church will then receive him among her children, and will rest upon him the grace and blessing of God, who never yet sent back the wanderer, and the Most High, in his bounty, will forgive the past, of which he has repented, and he shall be absolved and blessed.

Take heed, therefore, O my children, priests and people, great and small, whether they be men or women, from falling into these nets. And the God of peace strengthen you by his providence, and protect you by his care, and preserve you by his own right hand, and grant you perpetual peace; and grace and honour and glory be to the Father and the Son and the Holy Ghost, now and ever and unto all ages. Amen.[2]

[2]Translated from the Arabic by Gulian Lansing, in *The Evangelical Repository and United Presbyterian Review* 6.6 (1867): 353–8.

May the glad dawn
of Easter morn
Bring holy joy to thee.
Easter Greetings

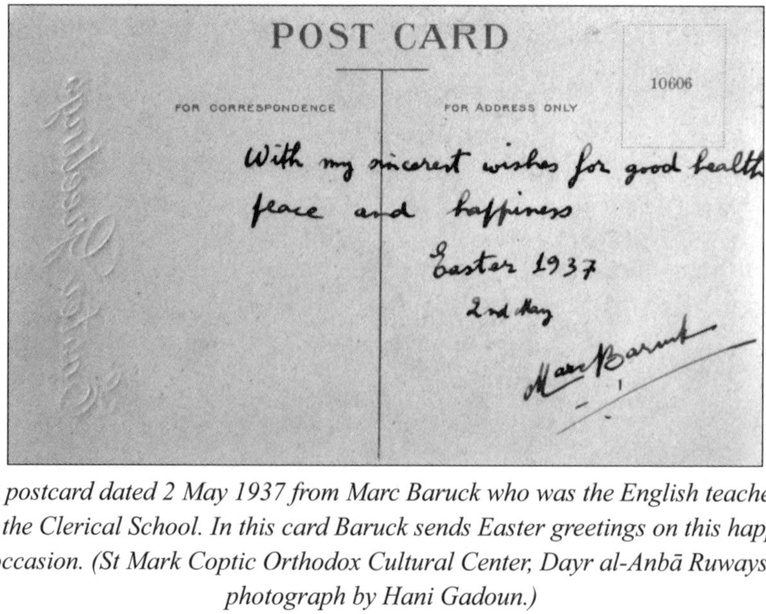
POST CARD
10606
FOR CORRESPONDENCE
FOR ADDRESS ONLY
With my sincerest wishes for good health
peace and happiness
Easter 1937
2nd May
Marc Baruck
Easter Greetings

A postcard dated 2 May 1937 from Marc Baruck who was the English teacher at the Clerical School. In this card Baruck sends Easter greetings on this happy occasion. (St Mark Coptic Orthodox Cultural Center, Dayr al-Anbā Ruways; photograph by Hani Gadoun.)

APPENDIX FIVE

Coptic Orthodox Patriarchal Archival Documents

Introduction

THE DOCUMENTS IN THESE APPENDICES come from a collection of archival documents, dating from between 1909 and 1968, found in the Coptic Orthodox Patriarchate in Cairo. A professional photographer was employed to digitize all of the original documents as ".jpg" files. These, in turn, were appropriately cropped and converted to ".pdf" files by a graphic designer in Melbourne, Australia. The total number of pages of the archival documents consulted in this study numbered 7,130. However, only the most pertinent of these were catalogued, and they number 4,776 pages in total. Each catalog entry, moreover, conforms to the Chicago Manual of Style. The entries in the catalog were ordered chronologically, numbered sequentially and contained five distinct elements. It should be noted that, where a document is undated, its approximate date was estimated from other documents in the same file, context, etc., and was duly noted.

Firstly, the term "**Doc. N°**" refers to the number of every archival document included. These were taken from the cover of each folder, within which the documents were enclosed, as they were discovered in the similarly labelled archival boxes. The number sequence between the period and the forward slash, on the other hand, refers to the pages of documents as they appear in the ".pdf" files. It should be noted, however, that some of these multi-page documents were actually to be found in reverse sequential order in the archival folders. The sequences in the document numbers of such cases, though, have not been reversed. Any text which was included refers to the title on the cover of each folder, where provided. For example, **4-1.5-6/18 General Issues** refers to pages 5 to 6 of the file **4-1/18 General Issues**. Additionally, a comma is used in the number sequence to indicate associated documents that do not immediately follow one another in a particular file. For example, **4-1.5-6, 8-9/18 General Issues** refers to pages 5 to 6 and 8 to 9 of the file **4-1/18 General Issues**. Departure from this convention occurs in one instance only in the case of **4-1./51-52**, which has been referred to as **4-1./51** since all of the documents in that file relate to the title of the former number.

Secondly, the term "**Incepit**" indicates an extract in Arabic from the archival document that appears immediately after any salutation (if present). In the absence of a salutation in the document, the title or other introductory text is written. Thirdly, the term "**Date**" indicates the Gregorian calendar date of the relevant archival document. Where multiple dates are present, the date of the first authorship of the document is used. Fourthly, the term "**Description**" provides a brief and concise classification of the relevant document. For example, this will specify if the document is handwritten, in addition to its genre (letter, memo, list, table, report, booklet, etc.). It will also indicate the author and recipient, where applicable. If either of these is unclear or illegible, then only one has been mentioned.

Furthermore, transliterations from Arabic to English are in accordance with the International Journal of Middle East Studies (IJMES) guide for Arabic transliteration. These guidelines, however, have not been followed in certain circumstances. In particular, when an Arabic place or personal name has already been transliterated in an archival document, then that is preferred. For example, Al-Maaref appears in **4-1.4/7** and is preferred over al-Maʿārif. Also, the transliteration Girgis (جرجس) has been preferred only in the case of the name Habib Girgis. In all other cases, the Arabic letter ج has been transliterated as j—in accordance with IJMES—and not as g as is customary in Egyptian pronunciation.

Similarly, where a particular Arabic phrase or title is translated into English in a letterhead or elsewhere, that particular translation is used consistently throughout the entire catalog. For instance, the name وزارة المعارف العمومية appears translated in **4.1.25/8 Schools General Issues Pt. 1** as the Ministry of Education, rather than the more literal translation Ministry of Public Instruction. Also, the name المدارس القبطية الارثوذكسية بالقاهرة appears translated in **4-1.5/7** as the Coptic schools in Egypt rather than a more literal translation The Coptic Orthodox Schools in Cairo. Moreover, some of the archival documents are in languages other than Arabic, i.e. French and English. Of the English documents, a number are translations of corresponding Arabic documents. Others, however, are not. Such cases are identified as either "translation" or "English" / "French" documents. Fifthly and finally, the term "**Summary**" provides a brief and concise summary in relation to the relevant document.

١٠

٧٥

«هوذا الحقول قد ابيضت للحصاد»
«أطلبوا من رب الحصاد أن يرسل فعلة»

اللجنة العليا المركزية
لمدارس الأحد وجامعة الشباب القبطي
بالكرازة المرقسية

بمركزها بالكلية الاكليريكية مهمشة – مصر

خطاب لفروع مدارس أحد القاهرة بخصوص التطوع للخدمة
فى الرحلات الصيفية

حضرات أبنائنا المباركين مدرسي مدارس الأحد ....

السلام لكم والنعمة من رب السلام . إن قلوبنا تفيض بالشكر العميق لله الذى حسبنا أمناء إذ جعلنا خداماً فى حقل مدارس الأحد ولكن كلما امتد بنا الزمن ازددنا شعوراً بالمسئولية من نحو كل طفل وكل شاب بكافة انحاء الكرازة المرقسية فهوذا الحقول قد ابيضت للحصاد وإننا نريد فعلة .

وقد رتبت اللجنة العليا خلال العطلة الصيفية المقبلة بمشيئة الرب رحلات عامة إلى كافة أنحاء القطر لافتقاد فروع مدارس الأحد القائمة وإنشاء أخرى جديدة وتدعيمها ورسم الخطط القويمة لتربية النشء القبطى .

وسيتم هذا بأن توفد اللجنة العليا من الخدام المتطوعين لهذا العمل الجليل مندوبين إلى البلاد (إثنين فى كل ابروشية) مزودين بكافة اللوازم على نفقتها الخاصة .

وسيكون اجتماع هؤلاء المندوبين بمشيئة الله يوم الجمعة القادم أول يوليو الساعة الخامسة مساء بملجأ مدارس الأحد ٧٠ شارع روض الفرج للتفاهم فى التفصيلات وحصر المتطوعين.

واننا ننتظر من قبلكم من يتقدم الى هذا العمل فالضرورة موضوعة علينا وويل لنا أن كنا لا نبشر . وإننا فى انتظار حضور المتقدمين لهذه الخدمة فى الاجتماع المذكور .

نعمة الرب تشملكم آمين ؟

نائب غبطة الرئيس الأعلى

حبيب جرجس

١٩٤٩/٦/٢٥

Doc. N°: 4-1.385/30 Sunday School Grants Pt. 1
Incipit: خطاب فروع مدارس أحد القاهرة بخصوص التطوع للخدمة في الرحلات الصيفية.
Date: 25 June 1949
Description: A letter by Habib Girgis addressed to the teachers of the Coptic Sunday Schools.
Summary: The letter seeks volunteers for village visitations for the coming summer. The volunteers will visit the existing branches of the schools and establish new ones.

75 250 10 152

"The fields are already ripe for harvest"
"Ask the Lord of the harvest to send out workers"

The Central High Committee for Sunday Schools and the Coptic Youth League in the See of St. Mark
With its Centre at the Clerical College, Mahmashah—Egypt

A message to the Sunday School branches of Cairo about volunteering for service at summer excursions

Our distinguished, blessed children, teachers of the Sunday schools,

Peace to you and blessings from the Lord of peace. Our hearts overflow with deep gratitude to God who deemed us trustees, since he made us servants in the field of Sunday schools. But as time has progressed, we have increasingly felt the responsibility toward every child and every youth all over the See of St Mark. Thus, the fields are already ripe for harvest and we need workers.

The Higher Committee has arranged, with the Lord's will, general excursions to all parts of the country during the coming summer vacation. [This is] because of a lack of the existing Sunday school branches, and to establish and support other new ones, drawing up the right plans for educating Coptic youth.

This will be through the Higher Committee's dispatch of volunteer servants as delegates to the countryside for this honourable work (two in each diocese), supplied with all that is necessary for their personal expenditure.

The meeting for these delegates will be, God-willing, on this coming Friday, the first of July, at five in the afternoon, in the Sunday Schools' home [at] 70 Rawḍ al-Faraj Street. [This will be] to go through minute details and to register the volunteers.

We expect applicants for this work from [among] you because the necessity has been laid upon us and woe unto us if we did not preach. We expect the presence of applicants for this service at the abovementioned meeting.

May the Lord's grace be upon you, Amen.

25 / 6 / 1949 Deputy of His Holiness the Supreme Head
Ḥabīb Jirjis

٧٢
١١٦

٢٤-٧
الجيب
٦ / ١١ / ٩١٨

جناب الاب الفاضل وكيل البطريركية وحضرة صاحب العزة مديرها العام

بعد الاحترام. الخطاب طيه وصلني امس من حضرة الدكتور لوريا بك طبيب المدارس القبطية ارجو الاطلاع عليه

وفي الحقيقة انني استدعيت حضرته في الشهر الماضي عدة مرات وفي كل مرة كان يجد نحو اربعة او خمسة من الطلبة مرضى وفي كل مرة كان يصعب علينا جداً فصل المرضى عن الاصحاء منعاً من سريان عدوى المرض لعدم وجود مكان خاص لذلك وهذه الحالة طالما كنا نشكو منها في الماضي والآن نحن في اشد الحاجة الى اعداد مكان خاص للمرضى وبالمدرسة اوده فسيحة بعيدة عن اماكن النوم اريد ان اخصصها لهذا الغرض وغرفة اخرى خاصة لعيادة الدكتور لفحص الطلبة كل اسبوع مرة على الاقل وايجاد المواد الطبية التي اشار اليها الطبيب المرفقة طيه لاجل الاسعافات الوقتية التي اشار الى ضرورة وجودها وعلى ذكر ذلك اخبر حضرتكم انه من منذ عشرة ايام اغمي على تلميذ في اثناء الدرس ولبعد المسافة عن الاطباء والاجزاخانات تعبنا جداً واوجد الذعر في قلوب الطلبة

ثانياً ان اماكن النوم في غاية القذارة والمراحيض والحمام كلها محتاجة الى اصلاح والتصليح وبما انها لم ترد في المقايسة التي عملت بمعرفة قلم الهندسة فارجو التكرم بالنظر في هذه الامور وتكليف حضرة المهندس بالحضور الى المدرسة وتقديم التقرير اللازم لحضرتكم لعمل ماترونه مناسباً

اما الحالة الغذائية فسأقدم لحضراتكم كشفاً باسماء الفقراء من الطلبة والمرفوضين

واقبلوا وافر الاحترام

ناظر المدرسة الاكليريكية
[signature]

١٦٣٥ ٩١٨
٢٦ بابه ٥ نوفمبر

[handwritten marginal note, partly illegible] ... ١٩١٨/١١/٥

Doc. N°: 4-6.9/2 Theological College Restorations & Repairs Pt. 1
Incipit: الخطاب طيه وصلني أمس من حضرة الدكتور.
Date: 6 November 1918
Description: A handwritten letter from Habib Girgis to the deputy of the Patriarchate.
Summary: The letter is in relation to the poor health of the students at the Theological College. A request was made for the creation of a quarantine room for the sick students. Also, Habib Girgis asked for a maintenance engineer to be sent to report on what work must be done to fix the building.

2403 73 / 116 7
H…
6 / 11 / [1]918

Worthy Reverend Father, Patriarchal Deputy, and his distinguished and respected Excellency, its general director,

After [my] respect—I received the enclosed letter yesterday from the distinguished Doctor Lūryā Bik, Physician of the Coptic Schools. Please examine it.

In truth, I summoned him many times last month and, each time, he would find roughly four or five of the students ill. Every time, it was difficult for me to separate the sick from the healthy, in order to stop the spread of the infection of the disease, since there is nowhere set-apart for that. For as long as we have been complaining about this situation, whether in the past or now, we are in the direst of need for the preparation of a special place for the sick and a spacious room in the school, far from the dormitory, which I want to dedicate for this purpose, as well as another special room for the doctor's clinic, in which to examine the students at least once a week, and the procuration of medical items which the doctor pointed out in the enclosed attachment, for the sake of first aid—which he pointed out must be present. On that note, I must tell you that 10 days ago a student fainted during the lesson and, because of the distance from the doctors and pharmacies we were greatly fatigued and I found the students panic-stricken.

Secondly, the bedrooms are most filthy, and the toilets and bathroom are all in need of painting and repair, since they are not included in the estimate made with the knowledge of the engineering department. Please pay attention to these matters, and commission the distinguished engineer to attend the School and present you the necessary report to do what you see fit.

As for the dietary situation, I am presenting you with a list of the names of the poor among the students and cantors.

Accept [my] utmost respect,

1635 [1]918 Headmaster of the Clerical School
26 Bābah and 5 November [Signature]

(Note from the Patriarchate from 5 November 1908 [sic])

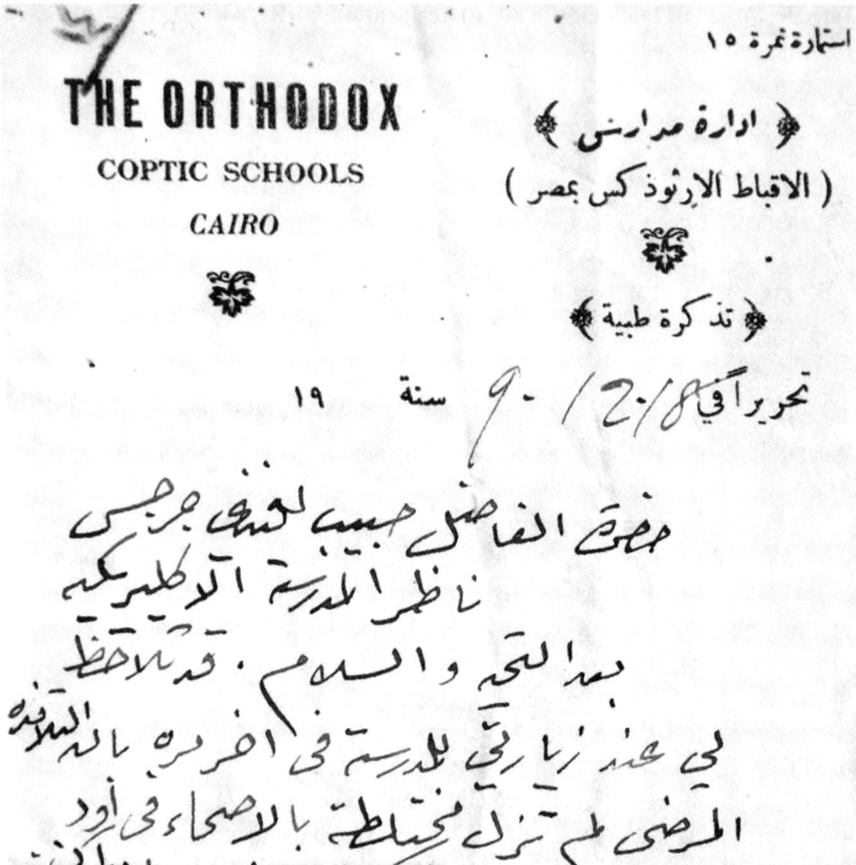

استمارة نمرة ١٥

THE ORTHODOX

COPTIC SCHOOLS

CAIRO

﴿ ادارة مدارس ﴾

(الاقباط الارثوذكس بمصر)

﴿ تذكرة طبية ﴾

تحريراً في 8/12/90 سنة ١٩

حضرة الفاضل حبيب افندي جرجس
ناظر المدرسة الاكليريكية
بعد التحية والسلام . قد لاحظت
لي عند زيارتي للمدرسة في آخر مرة بأن التلامذة
المرضى لم تزل مختلطة بالاصحاء في أود
النوم مع انه حضرتكم تكلمتم لي بأنه لما كنا
وعدت بعمل التصليحات اللازمة لعزل
المرضى في اوده مخصوصة معده لذلك
فالرجا الاسراع في ادخال الاصلاحات
التي لفت نظر حضرتكم اليها لئلا تشتد
وطأة الامراض بالمدرسة ونضطر في آخر
الامر بالالتجاء الى مصلحة الصحة واقفال
المدرسة وفي الختام اقبلوا فائق احترامي الدكتور

Doc. N°: 4-6.13/2 Theological College Restorations & Repairs Pt. 1
Incipit: .قد تلاحظ لي عند زيارتي للمدرسة
Date: 8 February 1919
Description: A handwritten letter from the physician of the Theological College to Habib Girgis.
Summary: The letter is in relation to a designated area for ill students at the college. The physician warns that if this issue is not addressed, he may have to inform the health department.

Form Number 15 14

Schools Administration
Orthodox Copts in Cairo
(Medical Prescription)

The Orthodox
Coptic Schools
Cairo

Written on 8 / 2 / 19[1]9

Distinguished Sir, Ḥabīb Afandī Jirjis, Headmaster of the Clerical School,

After [my] salutations and greetings—It was brought to my attention during my last visit to the School that the sick students are still mixed in with the healthy ones in the bedrooms, even though you told me that the Patriarchate promised to execute the necessary repairs in order to isolate the sick in a special room intended for that purpose. Please hurry in the commencement of repairs, which I draw your attention to, lest the weight of disease at the School intensifies and we are eventually forced to resort to the Health Bureau and close it down. In conclusion, accept my utmost respect, Doctor Lūryā.

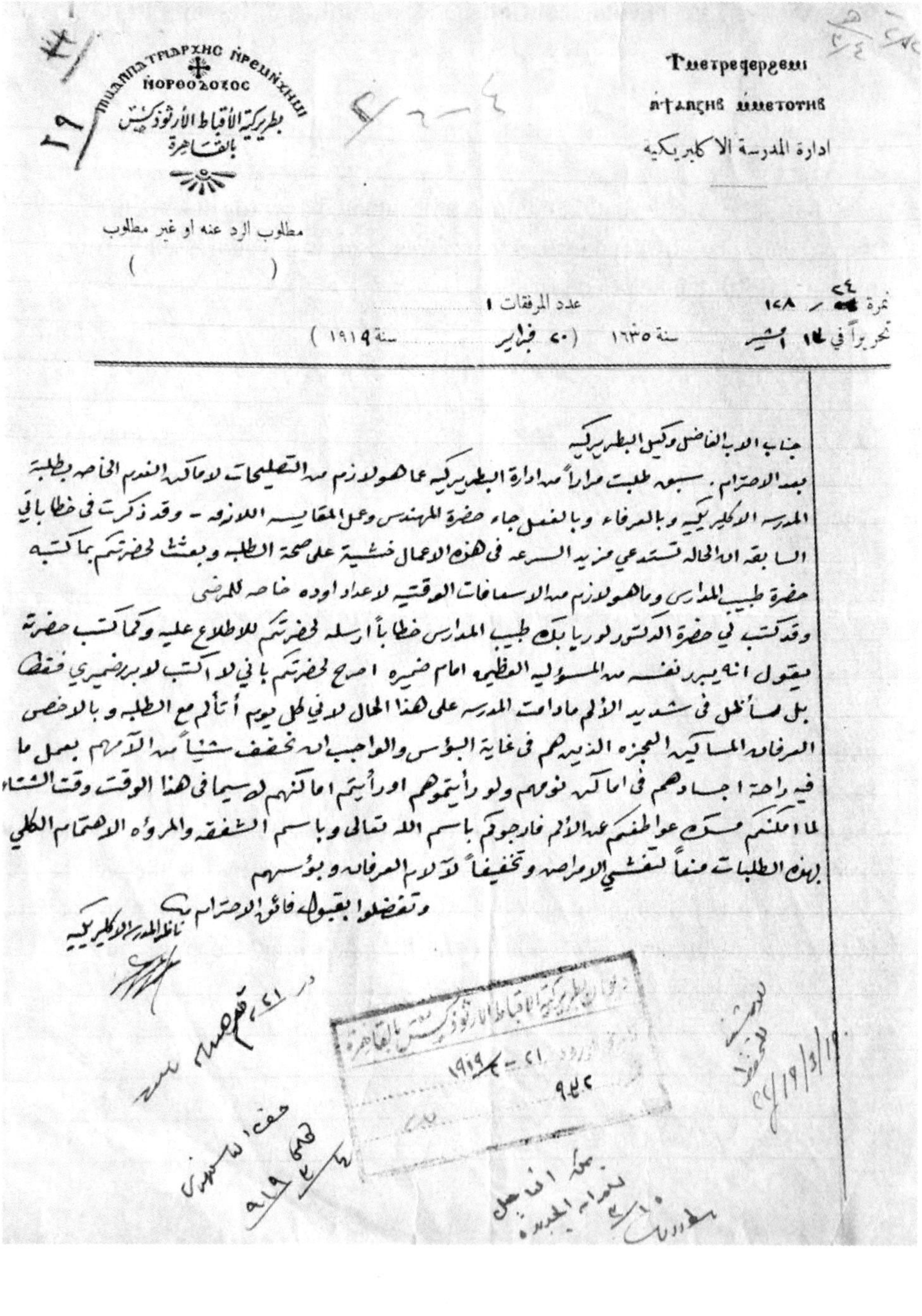

بطريركية الأقباط الأرثوذكس بالقاهرة

ادارة المدرسة الاكليريكية

مطلوب الرد عنه او غير مطلوب
(   )

نمرة ٢٤ / ١٢٨ عدد المرفقات ١

تحريراً في ١٤ أمشير سنة ١٦٣٥ (٢٠ فبراير سنة ١٩١٩)

جناب الاب الفاضل وكيل البطريركيه

بعد الاحترام . سبق ان طلبت مراراً من ادارة البطريركيه عمل ما هو لازم من التصليحات لاماكن النوم الخاصه بطلبة المدرسه الاكليريكيه وبالعرفاء وبالفعل جاء حضرة المهندس وعمل المقايسه اللازمه - وقد ذكرت في خطاباتي السابقه ان الحاله تستدعي مزيد السرعه في هذه الاعمال خشية على صحة الطلبه وبعثت لحضرتكم بما كتبه حضرة طبيب المدارس وما هو لازم من الاسعافات الوقتيه لاعداد اوده خاصه للمرضى

وقد كتب لي حضرة الدكتور لوريا بك طبيب المدارس خطاباً ارسله لحضرتكم للاطلاع عليه وكما كتب حضرته يقول انه يبرر نفسه من المسئوليه العظيمه امام ضميره اصرح لحضرتكم باني لا اكتب لابرر ضميري فقط بل اني اظل في شديد الألم مادامت المدرسه على هذا الحال لاني كل يوم أتألم مع الطلبه وبالاخص العرفاء المساكين العجزه الذين هم في غاية البؤس والواجب ان نخفف شيئاً من آلامهم بعمل ما فيه راحة اجسادهم في اماكن نومهم ولو رأيتموهم او رأيتم اماكنهم لاسيما في هذا الوقت وقت الشتاء لما امكنكم مسك عواطفكم عن الألم فارجوكم باسم الله تعالى وباسم الشفقه والمروءه الاهتمام الكلي بهذه الطلبات منعاً لتفشي الامراض وتخفيفاً لآلام العرفاء وبؤسهم

وتفضلوا بقبول فائق الاحترامات

ناظر المدرسة الاكليريكية

Doc. N°: 4-6.25/2 Theological College Restorations & Repairs Pt. 1
Incipit: سبق طلبت مرارا من ادارة البطريركية.
Date: 20 February 1919
Description: A handwritten letter from Habib Girgis to the deputy of the Patriarchate.
Summary: The letter is in relation to the sub-standard living conditions at the Theological College. **4-6.23-24/2 Theological College Restorations & Repairs Pt. 1** was attached to this letter.

21 / 2, H. 4 / 3 — 29
Administration of the Clerical School — Coptic Orthodox Patriarchate in Cairo
4 – 6 / 2 — Requiring a response or not
( )

Number: 24 / 128 — Number of Attachments: ____
Written on 13 Amshīr 1635 (20 February 1919)

Worthy Reverend Father, Patriarchal Deputy,

After [my] respect—I have repeatedly sent requests to the Patriarchate's administration previously regarding what repairs are necessary for the private bedrooms of the students of the Clerical School and the cantors. Indeed, the distinguished engineer came and took the necessary measurements. But, in my previous messages, I have reminded [you] that the condition calls out for more haste in these works, fearing for the health of the students. I also sent you what the distinguished Physician of the Schools wrote, and what is necessary in terms of first aid, in order to arrange a special room for the sick.

The distinguished Doctor Lūryā Bik, Physician of the Schools, has written me a message, which I am sending you for your own information. Thus, as he has written, he says that he excuses himself of the great responsibility before his conscience. I declare to you that I am not only writing to excuse my conscience, but I will remain in intense pain as long as the School is in this condition, because every day I am suffering with the students, and especially the poor and weak cantors, who are in the utmost misery. It is an obligation for us to alleviate some of their suffering by doing something for their bodily comfort in their bedrooms. If you saw them or their bedrooms, especially in this winter time, how could you hold back your emotions from the suffering? In the name of the Most High God, and in the name of compassion and generosity, I beg you to pay complete attention to these requests, to prevent the fear of illness and to ease the suffering of the cantors and their misery.

Please accept [my] utmost respect,

Headmaster of the Clerical School
[Signature]

[Notes from the Patriarchate from 21 February, and 4, 15 and 19 March 1919]

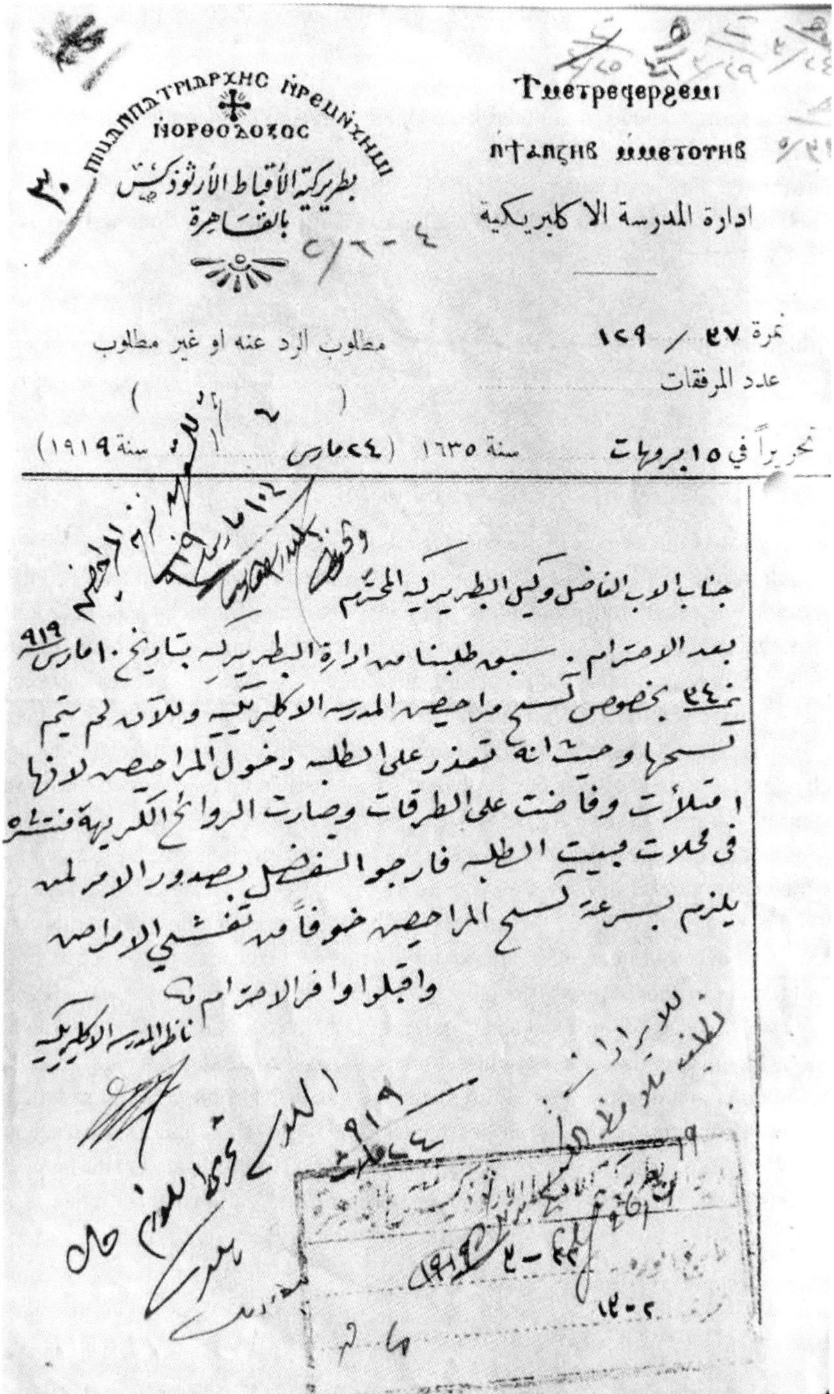

ⲠⲒⲘⲀⲚⲠⲀⲦⲢⲒⲀⲢⲬⲎⲤ ⲚⲢⲈⲘⲚⲬⲎⲘⲒ
ⲚⲞⲢⲐⲞⲆⲞⲜⲞⲤ
بطريركية الأقباط الأرثوذكس
بالقاهرة

Ϯⲙⲉⲧⲣⲉϥⲉⲣϩⲉⲙⲓ
ⲛ̀ϯⲁⲛⲍⲏⲃ ⲙ̀ⲙⲉⲧⲟⲧⲏⲃ
ادارة المدرسة الاكليريكية

نمرة ٢٧ / ١٢٩
عدد المرفقات

مطلوب الرد عنه او غير مطلوب
(   )

تحريراً في ١٥ برمهات سنة ١٦٣٥ (٢٤ مارس سنة ١٩١٩)

جناب الاب الفاضل وكيل البطريركية المحترم

بعد الاحترام. سبق طلبنا من ادارة البطريركية بتاريخ ١٠ مارس ٩١٩ نمرة ٢٤ بخصوص كسح مراحيض المدرسة الاكليريكية وللآن لم يتم كسحها وحيث انه تتعذر على الطلبة دخول المراحيض لانها امتلأت وفاضت على الطرقات وصارت الروائح الكريهة منتشرة في محلات مبيت الطلبة فارجوا التفضل بصدور الامر لمن يلزم بسرعة كسح المراحيض خوفاً من تفشي الامراض

واقبلوا وافر الاحترام

ناظر المدرسة الاكليريكية

Doc. N°: 4-6.26/2 Theological College Restorations & Repairs Pt. 1
Incipit: سبق طلبنا من ادارة البطريركية.
Date: 24 March 1919
Description: A handwritten letter from Habib Girgis to the deputy of the Patriarchate.
Summary: The letter is a reminder to empty overflowing septic tanks at the Theological College.

H. 24 / 3, T. 29 / 3, H. 21 / 4, T. 25 / 4, H. 31 / 5 30

Administration of the Clerical School

Coptic Orthodox Patriarchate in Cairo

4-6/2

Requiring a response or not
(   )

Number: 37/129
Number of Attachments: ____
Written on 15 Baramhāt 1635 (24 March 1919)

Worthy Reverend Father, respected Patriarchal Deputy,

After [our] respect—We have previously made a request to the Patriarchal administration on 10 March 1919, [letter] number 34, regarding unblocking the toilets of the Clerical School and, until now, their unblocking has not been completed. Meanwhile, it has been prohibited for the students to enter the toilets because they have filled up and overflowed onto the walkways, and unpleasant odours have permeated the students' dormitories. Therefore, I kindly ask that you issue an order to whoever is necessary for the quick unblocking of the toilets, in fear of the outbreak of disease.

Accept [our] utmost respect,
Headmaster of the Clerical School
[Signature]

[Notes from the Patriarchate from 22, 24 and 26 March 1919]

٣٩

ⲠⲒⲀⲢⲬⲎⲠⲀⲦⲢⲒⲀⲢⲬⲎⲤ ⲚⲢⲈⲘⲚⲬⲎⲘⲒ
ⲚⲞⲢⲐⲞⲆⲞⲜⲞⲤ
بطريركية الأقباط الأرثوذكس
بالقاهرة

Ϯⲙⲉⲧⲣⲉϥⲉⲣϩⲉⲙⲓ
ⲛ̀ⲧⲁⲓⲥⲭⲏⲃ ⲙ̀ⲙⲉⲧⲟⲩⲏⲃ
ادارة المدرسة الاكليريكيه

مطلوب الرد عنه او غير مطلوب
(   )

نمرة ١٤٧ – ١٥١
عدد المرفقات
تحريراً في ٦ كيهك سنة ١٦٣٦ (١٦ ديسمبر سنة ١٩١٩)

٤ – ٦ / ٢

جناب الاب الفاضل المحترم وكيل البطريركيه

بعد الاحترام. سبقت وكتبت لقدسكم مراراً بشأن الفقراء المساكين واكتب الآن مرة اخرى طالباً شفقتكم على هؤلاء البؤساء

فاولاً حالتهم الغذائيه غاية في البؤس فالرغيف الذي ليس كافياً فيه لغذائهم والرجا النظر في تعيين طباخ وصرف اللازم له لطبخ ما يلزمهم من الطعام وزيادة الخبز

ثانياً اماكن نومهم حتى الآن لم تصلح وكثيراً ما نبهت على المقاول او النجار جوني لملاحظة تصليح شبابيك النوم المكسره لان اودهم بارده جداً وكل يوم اجدهم مرتعشين من شدة البرد والبعض منهم يبولون على انفسهم من شدة ما يصيبهم من البرد وعدم وجود الغطاء اللازم فارجو التكرم بصدور امركم للنجار لسرعة تصليح هذه الشبابيك والابواب

وتفضلوا بقبول وافر الاحترام منى

ناظر المدرسه الاكليريكيه

[signature]

ديوان بطريركية الاقباط [illegible]
تاريخ الورود ١٨/١٢/١٩
نمرة ٤٨٧٥

[illegible]

٤٠١
٨٦

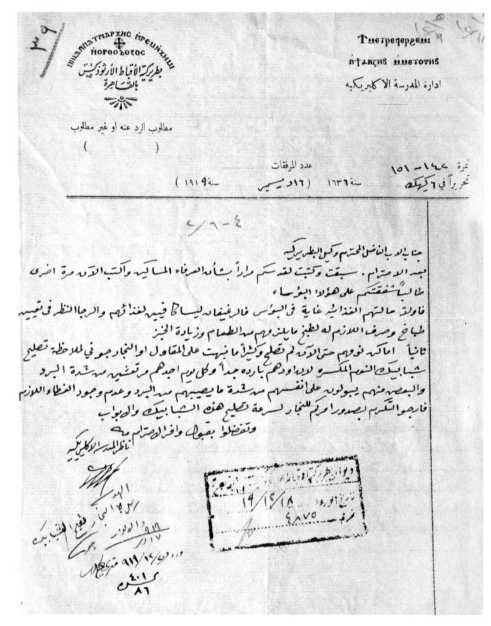

Doc. N°: 4-6.34/2 Theological College Restorations & Repairs Pt. 1
Incipit: سبق وكتبت لقدسكم مرارا بشأن العرفاء المساكين وأكتب الآن مرة أخرى.
Date: 16 December 1919
Description: A handwritten letter from Habib Girgis to the deputy of the Patriarchate.
Summary: The letter is in relation to terrible condition of the cantors' school. Habib Girgis requests immediate intervention from the deputy.

18 / 12 / 19, H. 19 / 12 | 39
Administration of the Clerical School | Coptic Orthodox Patriarchate in Cairo
Requiring a response or not
( )

Number: 142 – 151 | Number of Attachments: ____
Written on 6 Kiyahk 1636 (16 December 1919)
4 – 6 / 2

Worthy and respected Reverend Father, Patriarchal Deputy,

After [my] respect—I have repeatedly written to you previously regarding the poor cantors, and I am writing now, again, requesting you to have compassion on these wretched [souls].

Firstly, their dietary condition is miserable because the two loaves [of bread] are inadequate for their nourishment. Please look into hiring a chef and spending what is necessary for him to cook whatever food is needed, as well as increasing the [amount of] bread.

Secondly, their bedrooms have not been repaired until now and I often reminded the contractor or the carpenter to pay serious attention to repairing the broken bedroom windows because their rooms are very cold and I find them shivering every day from the intense cold. Some of them are urinating on themselves from the intensity of the cold they are suffering from, and the lack of the necessary covering.

Therefore, I kindly ask that you issue an order to the carpenter to quickly repair these windows and doors.

Kindly accept [my] utmost respect,

Headmaster of the Clerical School
[Signature]

[Notes from the Patriarchate from 17, 18 and 20 December 1919]

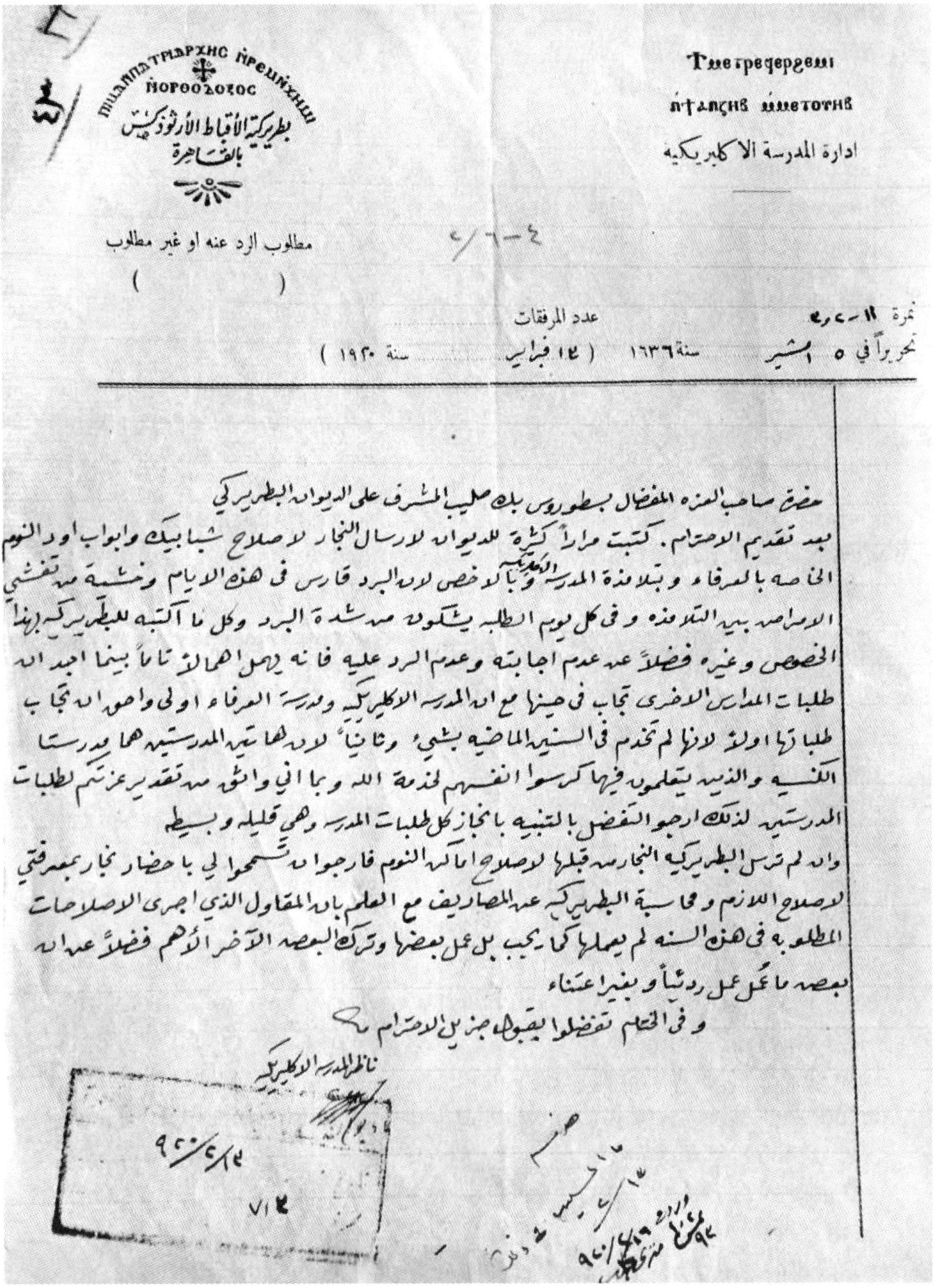

ⲡⲓⲁⲣⲭⲏⲉⲣⲉⲩⲥ ⲡⲁⲧⲣⲓⲁⲣⲭⲏⲥ ⲛⲟⲣⲑⲟⲇⲟⲝⲟⲥ

بطريركية الأقباط الأرثوذكسي بالقاهرة

ⲧⲙⲉⲧⲣⲉϥⲉⲣϩⲉⲙⲓ ⲛ̀ⲧⲉ ⲧⲥⲭⲟⲗⲏ ⲛ̀ⲕⲗⲏⲣⲓⲕⲟⲥ

ادارة المدرسة الاكليريكيه

مطلوب الرد عنه او غير مطلوب ( )

نمرة ١١٠٢

عدد المرفقات

تحريراً في ٥ امشير سنة ١٦٣٦ (١٢ فبراير سنة ١٩٢٠)

حضرة صاحب العزه المفضال بطوروس بك صليب المشرف على الديوان البطريركي

بعد تقديم الاحترام. كتبت مراراً كثيرة للديوان لارسال النجار لاصلاح شبابيك وابواب اودا النوم الخاصه بالعرفاء وبتلامذة المدرسه الاكليريكيه وبالاخص لان البرد قارس في هذه الايام وخشية من تفشي الامراض بين التلامذه وفي كل يوم الطلبه يشكون من شدة البرد وكل ما اكتبه للبطريركيه بهذا الخصوص وغيره فضلاً عن عدم اجابته وعدم الرد عليه فانه يهمل اهمالاً تاماً بينما اجد ان طلبات المدارس الاخرى تجاب في حينها مع ان المدرسه الاكليريكيه ومدرسة العرفاء اولى واحق ان تجاب طلباتها اولاً لانها لم تخدم في السنين الماضيه بشيء وثانياً لان هاتين المدرستين هما مدرستا الكنيسه والذين يتعلمون فيها كرسوا انفسهم لخدمة الله وبما اني واثق من تقدير عزتكم لطلبات المدرستين لذلك ارجو التفضل بالتنبيه بانجاز كل طلبات المدرسه وهي قليله وبسيطه

وان لم ترسل البطريركيه النجار من قبلها لاصلاح اماكن النوم فارجوا ان تسمحوا لي باحضار نجار بمعرفتي للاصلاح اللازم ومحاسبة البطريركيه عن المصاريف مع العلم بان المقاول الذي اجرى الاصلاحات المطلوبه في هذه السنه لم يعملها كما يجب بل عمل بعضها وترك البعض الآخر الأهم فضلاً عن ان بعض ما عمل عمل رديئاً وبغير اعتناء

وفي الختام تفضلوا بقبول جزيل الاحترام

ناظر المدرسه الاكليريكيه

[signature]

١٢/٢/٩٢٠

٧١٢

Doc. N°: 4-6.38/2 Theological College Restorations & Repairs Pt. 1
Incipit: .كتبت مرارا كثيرا للديوان لارسال النجار لاصلاح شبابيك وابواب
Date: 13 February 1920
Description: A handwritten letter from Habib Girgis to the director of the Patriarchate Administration.
Summary: The letter is in relation to a carpenter undertaking maintenance work at the Theological College.

Administration of the Clerical School — Coptic Orthodox Patriarchate in Cairo
4 – 6 / 2 — Requiring a response or not
( )

Number: 11 – 2 and 3 — Number of Attachments: ____
Written on 5 Amshīr 1636 (13 February 1920)

His distinguished Excellency, the favoured Basṭawrūs Bik Ṣalīb, Supervisor over the Patriarchate,

After presenting [my] respect—I have repeatedly written on many occasions to the Patriarchate to send a carpenter to repair the windows and doors of the bedrooms belonging to the cantors and students of the Clerical School, especially because the cold is severe these days and there is fear of the outbreak of illnesses among the students. Moreover, every day, the students complain about the intense cold. Everything that I write to the Patriarchate regarding this and other matters is in addition to its lack of an answer or reply; thus, it is being completely neglectful. At the same time, I am mystified that the requests of other schools are answered immediately, whereas the Clerical School and Cantors' School are prime and more deserving of a response to their requests—firstly, because they have not been served with anything in the past years and, secondly, because these two schools are the Church's schools, and those who are studying in them have dedicated themselves to serving God. Thus I am sure that you will appreciate the requests of the two schools. Therefore, I kindly ask you to pay attention to the fulfilment of all the School's requests, which are few and simple.

Also, the Patriarchate did not send out its carpenter to repair the bedrooms, so please allow me to bring a carpenter that I know, to repair what is necessary. What is the Patriarchate's share of the costs, knowing that the contractor who executed the requested repairs this year, did not do them as required, but only did some of them and left the other more important ones undone. Additionally, some of what was done was done poorly and carelessly.

In conclusion, kindly accept [my] utmost respect,

Headmaster of the Clerical School
[Signature]
13 / 2 / 1920
713

[Notes from the Patriarchate from 13 and 16 February 1920]

[illegible]

ⲠⲒⲀⲘⲠⲀⲦⲢⲒⲀⲢⲬⲎⲤ ⲚⲢⲈⲘⲚⲬⲎⲘⲒ
ⲚⲞⲢⲐⲞⲆⲞⲜⲞⲤ
بطريركية الاقباط الارثوذكس
بالقاهرة

Ϯⲙⲉⲧⲣⲉϥⲉⲣϩⲉⲙⲓ
ⲛ̀ϯⲁⲗⲥⲏⲃ ⲛ̀ⲙⲉⲧⲟⲩⲏⲃ
ادارة المدرسة الاكليريكية

نمرة ———

تحريراً في ——— سنة ١٦٣ (——— سنة ١٩)

المدرسة مفتوحة العمارة والحي جداً بحيث يمكن لأي انسان
من الخارج الدخول اليها . وقد حصل سطو على المدرسة بالأمس
من بعض اللصوص وسرقوا بعض ملابس الطلبة ونقود منهم
وقد حدث مثل ذلك مراراً وبالأخص في العام الماضي في مدة
الأجازة حين تخلو المدرسة من الطلبة وهذا أمر اخشى منه
الآن كثيراً لمناسبة العمارة .

وبناء عليه ارجو رجاءً شديداً بالاهتمام بأمر اتمام العمارة
بكل سرعة .

وتفضلوا بقبول فائق الاحترام

ناظر المدرسة الاكليريكية

[illegible]

[illegible]

Doc. N°: 4-6.123-124/2 Theological College Restorations & Repairs Pt. 1
Incipit: لا يخفي على حضرتكم أن العمارة لاصلاح المدرسة.
Date: 29 May 1923
Description: A handwritten letter from Habib Girgis to the deputy of the Patriarchate.
Summary: The letter is in relation to maintenance at the Theological College. In particular, Habib Girgis laments the slow pace of the work.

Administration of the Clerical School | Coptic Orthodox Patriarchate in Cairo

Number: ___
Written on ____ 163_ (____ 19__)

The school [fence] is very low architecturally, to the extent that any person from outside can enter it. The school was robbed yesterday by thieves, and they stole some of the students' clothes and their money. Things like this have happened repeatedly, especially last year in the final term while the school was empty of students. This is a matter which I am very much afraid of now, in regards to the architecture.

Therefore, I strongly plead that you pay attention to the matter of completing the building as soon as possible.

Please accept [my] utmost respect,

Headmaster of the Clerical School
[Signature]

Patriarchate's Engineer

We point you to another complaint which has come in from his Excellency Jirjis Bik Anṭūn, and he does not know what you have done about it. Your letter did not respond to the note of the Patriarchate. So, we inform you that the Patriarchate cannot help but penalize you, for it is impossible to keep silence after all this.

Iskandar… 29/5

١٤٦/

٢ / ٦ - ٤

١٩٢٢/٥/٢٩

ΟΡΘΟΔΟΞΟΣ
بطريركية الاقباط الارثوذكس
بالقاهرة

Ϯⲙⲉⲧⲣⲉϥⲉⲣϩⲉⲙⲓ
ⲡⲓⲧⲁⲝⲓⲥ ⲙ̀ⲙⲉⲧⲟⲩⲏⲃ
ادارة المدرسة الاكليريكية

نمرة ٧٢ — ٥٩
تحريراً في ٢١ بشنس سنة ١٦٣٩ (٢٩ مايو سنة ١٩٢٢)

جناب الاب الفاضل وكيل البطريركية وحضرة صاحب العزة المتقدم مديرها
بعد الاحترام. لا يخفى على حضرتكم أن العمارة لاصلاح المدرسة
الاكليريكية بدأت في شهر سبتمبر الماضي وقد مضت مدة طويلة ولم
تتم الأعمال المطلوبة وحيث أن العمل جاري بغاية البطء فضلاً
عن عدم وجود من يلاحظ العمل ويراقبه من قبل البطريركية. وحيث
أن اجازة المدرسة السنوية ستبدأ في هذا الاسبوع. فارجو التكرم
بصدور الأمر لحضرة المقاول بأن يسرع في اتمام الأعمال المطلوبة
منه وملاحظة تنفيذ الاتفاق الذي عقد معه لهذا الغرض لأني لا
أستطيع الصبر أكثر مما صبرت ويكفي اننا صرفنا السنة من اولها
الى آخرها في شدة التعب ولا اقدر أن أصف لكم مقدار ما عانيناه
نحن والمدرسون والطلبة من جراء ذلك واخشى أن هذا البطء يؤخر
العمل الى السنة القادمة ولا تكون المدرسة مستعدة في شهر
سبتمبر للدراسة.

وفضلاً عن ذلك فان هناك فتحات كثيرة بالمدرسة وسور

يتبع

H. 29 / 5 / 1923 4 – 6 / 2 148

Administration of the Clerical School

Coptic Orthodox Patriarchate
in Cairo

Number: 270 – 59
Written on 21 Bashans 1639 (29 May 1923)

Worthy Reverend Father, Patriarchal Deputy, and his distinguished and respected Excellency, its administrator,

After [our] respect—It is no secret to you that the building campaign to repair the Clerical School began last September and a long time has passed but the requested works have not been completed. Rather, the work is progressing very slowly, in addition to the absence of someone from the Patriarchate to oversee and monitor it, and whereas the School's yearly vacation will begin this week. Therefore, I kindly ask that you issue an order to the distinguished contractor that he may hasten in the completion of the works requested of him, with attention to fulfilling the agreement which was contracted with him, because I cannot wait any more than I already have. It's enough that we spent the year, from its beginning to its end, in intense fatigue, and I cannot describe to you in words what we have suffered, we and the teachers and students, as a result of that. I am afraid that this delay will postpone the work until the coming year, and the School will not be ready for [commencement of] study in September.

In addition to that, there are so many openings in the school and the [external] wall!

٤-٦-٥

حضرات أصحاب السعادة والعزة وكيل وأعضاء المجلس الملي العام
بعد الاحترام — تعلمون حضراتكم أن القرية القبطية منذ وقت
بعيد كانت في فقر روحي مدقع فلا رعاية للنفوس ولا عناية بالنشء
ولقد كانت مكاتبنا القبطية في القديم الغابر تعالج ذلك الفقر الروحي
بما تبثه في أبنائها من الروح الدينية والتعاليم العقائدية القويمة.
ومنذ أن خفتت أصوات تلك المكاتب المباركة، خفتت معها أصوات
التسابيح والمزامير في القرية، وبالتالي فترت الروح الدينية وأصبحت
القرية مع الأسف تورد لنا عشرات الرجال والسيدات يرتدون عن
دينهم، بعد أن كانت تنجب للكنيسة مئات الأراخنة الأتقياء.
كل هذا يا حضرات الزملاء راجع الى أن القرية القبطية كانت قفراً
من الرعاية الروحية الحقة.

لاحظت الاكليريكية ذلك بعين الأسى والحزن، فأخذت على
عاتقها التقدم بخدمة القرية خدمة مرضية، فمنذ سنة ١٩٢٠ أرسلت
طلبتها الى القرى والدساكر فكان من أثر ذلك أن انتشرت
الجمعيات في كثير منها، وفي سنة ١٩٢٨ قام الطلبة بوضع الأحجار
الأساسية في بناء كنائس عين شمس والقناطر الخيرية و[illegible]
وفي سنة ١٩٢٢ قامت حركة مباركة أيضاً كان من نتيجتها بناء كنيسة
أخرى في بلدة الأقواز مركز الصف.

وما أن جاء عام ١٩٢٧ حتى وحدت الاكليريكية جهودها ونظمت
صفوفها فأرسلت جنودها فرقاً فرقاً الى خمسة وثمانين فرعاً
في شتى نواحي الابروشيات المجاورة

والى حضراتكم يا أصحاب السعادة والعزة بياناً بهذه الفروع:

١- ابروشية الجيزة: امبابه - الوراق - بشتيل - ميت عقبة
الهرم - الأخصاص - عمازه - أسكر - الأقواز - الصف -

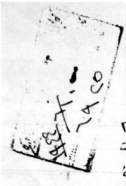

Doc. N°: 4-6.41-43/5

Incipit: علمون حضراتكم أن القرية القبطية منذ وقت بعيد.

Date: 15 May 1944

Description: A handwritten letter from Habib Girgis to the Lay Community Council.

Summary: The author laments the state of religious education in rural areas. Important information regarding the welfare service of the Theological College is also contained therein.

4 – 6 / 5

Your distinguished excellencies, deputy and members of the Lay Community Council,

After [our] respect—You know that the Coptic village, for a long time, was in extreme spiritual poverty without care for souls and no attention to the young generation. In the olden days, our Coptic schools would treat that spiritual poverty with the religious spirit and strong doctrinal learning that their children would study. Since the voices of those blessed schools have faded, however, the sounds of hymns and psalms in the village have faded with them. Subsequently, the religious spirit languished and the village, unfortunately, began to supply us with tens of men and women that would abandon their religion, after it had given birth to hundreds of pious lay leaders for the Church. All this, O distinguished colleagues, goes back to the fact that the Coptic village was a wilderness for true spiritual care.

The Clerical [College] observed this with an eye of sorrow and grief, so it took it upon itself to render a satisfactory service unto the villages. So, since 1920, it sent its students to the villages and hamlets. One of the effects of that, therefore, was the spread of associations in many of them. Then in 1932, another blessed movement began, the result of which was the construction of another church in the town of al-Aqwāz, dependent on al-Ṣaff.

By the year 1937, the Clerical [College] began to unite its efforts and organized its ranks, sending its soldiers, section by section, to eighty five branches in various townships of the surrounding dioceses.

Here is a list of these branches for your distinguished excellencies:

الوادي - أبو خار - طناح - الجزيرة الشقراء

(ب) القاهرة وضواحيها: الدرب الإبراهيمي - درب البرابرة - حوصه
الزهور - جمعية الوفاء ببرهتم - أرض ونيس - المساكن الخيرية
النهضة الروحية بشبرا - روضة الفرج - حارة زويلة - أبناء النهضة بمصر الجديدة
عين شمس - الحلمية - المرج - الخصوص - المنية.

(جـ) إيبارشية القليوبية: القناطر الخيرية - المنير - السموت - الرملة
سندنهور - القشيش - سندوه - طحا - كفر مستول - الحصافة -
نوى - شبلنجة.

(د) إيبارشية المنوفية: المنيل - الفرعونية - سنتريس - برهيم
بن العرب - سبك الأحد - كفر الحما - محلة سبك - جريس - طاليا
منشأة سنوان - كفر المضارة - عزبة القسيس - سرس الليان - فيشا
تتوانة - هيتة - سبك الضحاك - كفر الباجور - عزبة حنين.

(هـ) إيبارشية الدقهلية: كفر شكر - المنشأة الكبرى - المنشأة الصغرى
صهوه - صهرجت - كفر الشهيد - ميت يعيش - حصفا - ميت أبو خالد
البيوم - كفر عطا الله - الحلمية - مسكا - تفهنا.

(و) إيبارشية الشرقية: هريا - كفر هريا - السماقية - الشانية
كفر الحبش - عزبة حنا - عزبة بدوي - القلزم.

يا حضرات السادة:

لا يمكنني في مذكرة وجيزة كهذه أن أقدم لحضراتكم صورة واضحة
لتلك الجهود الجبارة التي بذلها الإكليريكيون في مضمار الوعظ بالقرى
ولقد كان من آثار تلك الجهود المباركة ما يمكنني تلخيصه فيما يلي:

١- بناء الكنائس في كثير من القرى والكفور
٢- إنشاء بعض المكاتب الأولية لتعليم أبناء القرى مبادئ عقيدتهم
٣- نشر مدارس الأحد وتشجيع أطفال القرى بتوزيع الصور والنشرات
٤- رد كثيرين ممن ارتدوا عن طريق المسيحية بعد علاج أسباب الارتداد

A. The Diocese of al-Jīzah: Imbābah, al-Warrāq, Bashtīl, Mīt ʻAtbah, al-Haram, al-Ikhṣāṣ, Ghammāzah, Askar, al-Aqwāz, al-Ṣaff, al-Widī, Abū Fār, Ṭanān, al-Jazīrah al-Shaqrā.

B. Cairo and its Outskirts: al-Darb al-Ibrāhīmī, Darb al-Bazbūz, Ḥawḍ al-Zuhūr, the Understanding Association in Mahmashah, Arḍ Wanīs, Charitable Efforts of the Spiritual Renaissance in Shubrā, Rawḍ al-Faraj, Ḥārat Zuwaylah, News of Grace in Miṣr al-Qadīmah, ʻAyn Shams, al-Ḥilmiyah, al-Marj, al-Khuṣūṣ, al-Manbah.

C. The Diocese of al-Qalyūbiyah: al-Qanāṭir al-Khayriyah, al-Munīrah, al-Shimūt, al-Ramlah, Sandanhūr, al-Qashīsh, Sundūrah, Ṭaḥā, Kafr Mashtūl, al-Ḥaṣāfah, Nawá, Shiblanjah.

D. The Diocese of al-Munūfiyah: al-Manyal, al-Firʻawniyah, Sintrīs, Bahnāy, Bayy al-ʻArab, Subk al-Aḥḥad, Kafr al-Ḥimā, Maḥallat Subk, Jurays, Ṭāliyā, Munsha'at Shinwān, Kafr al-Naṣārá, ʻIzbat al-Qissīs, Sirs al-Layyān, Fīshā, Tilwānah, Hīt, Subk al-Ḍaḥḥāk, Kafr al-Bājūr, ʻIzbat Ḥunayn.

E. The Diocese of al-Daqahliyah: Kafr Shukr, al-Munsha'ah al-Kubrá, al-Munsha'ah al-Ṣughrá, Halāh, Ṣahrajt, Kafr al-Shahīd, Mīt Yaʻīsh, Jaṣfā, Mīt Abī Khālid, al-Bayyūm, Kafr ʻAṭāllah, al-Ḥākimiyah, Miskā, Tiṣfā.

F. The Diocese of al-Sharqiyah: Hihyā, Kafr Hihyā, al-Saḥāyiqah, al-Shanāyinbah, Kafr al-Ḥibsh, ʻIzbat Ḥannā, ʻIzbat Badawī, al-ʻAkzam.

Distinguished gentlemen:

I cannot present to you a clear picture of those great efforts which the Clerical [College] exerted in the course of preaching in the villages in a brief memorandum such as this, but I can summarize the effects of such blessed efforts as follows:

1. The construction of churches in many of the villages and hamlets.
2. The spread of some primary schools to teach the children of the village the principles of their doctrine.
3. The diffusion of Sunday schools, and the encouragement of village children through the distribution of pictures and bulletins.

٥- اقناع المتذبذبين ممن تركوا كنيستهم القبطية الى مذاهب اجنبية وتثبيتهم فى عقيدتهم المستقيمة.

٦- ايجاد الصلح والسلام وقطع اسباب الخصام بين العائلات

٧- ابطال بعض العادات المستهجنة المنتشرة بوفرة بين القرويين

يا أصحاب السعادة:

لقد وقفتم حضراتكم فيما مضى على هذه الجهود المباركة وتفضلتم فى يناير سنة ١٩٢٨ فقررتم اعانة لهذا المشروع عشرة جنيهات شهرياً وبعد نحو عشرين شهراً فقط من تقرير الاعانة فوجئنا بقطعها فانقطع حبل الجهاد واقفرت خمسة وثمانون قرية من بشارة الانجيل المقدس لها وحرمت نحو عشرة آلاف نفس على أقل تقدير من ماء الحياه فتضاءل المشروع وتقلصت الفروع حتى الى اثنى عشر فرعاً يصرف عليها الطلبة من أجرة أكلهم الشهرية الضئيلة، وليس هذا من العدالة فى شئ أن نكلف الطالب بمجهود عقلى وروحى وجسمانى وعوضاً أن نبذل له المكافأة المادية، نثقل عليه بدفع اشتراك شهرى.

يا أصحاب السعادة:

تضاعفت أجور السفر والانتقال، وتراكمت علينا طلبات الفروع التى هجرناها مضطرين وأصوات ضمائر أولادنا تنبع من الداخل مستغيثة مع الرجل المكدونى قائلة «اعبر الينا وأعنا»

لهذا أضم صوتى الى أصوات أبنائى التى ضمنوها التماسهم المرفوع بمذكرتى هذه آملاً أن ينال تقديركم ويلاقى استعداداً قوياً فى نفوسكم، سعياً لخلاص النفوس ومجداً لاسمه القدوس

وتفضلوا يا حضرات الزملاء الأجلاء بقبول فائق الاحترام والتقدير

١٥ مايو ١٩٤٤

حبيب جرجس

مدير الاكليريكية

4. The return of many of those who apostasized from the gravity of Christianity, after addressing the reasons for [their] apostasy.
5. Convincing many of those who left their Coptic Church for foreign sects and confirming them in their correct doctrine.
6. The finding of reconciliation and peace, and the severing of reasons for quarrelling between families.
7. The revocation of some deplorable outrages, abundantly widespread among villagers.

Your excellencies:

You have previously stood by these blessed efforts and, in January 1938, you decided to subsidize this project with ten pounds a month. Then, only twenty months after the decision to subsidize, we found that this had been suspended. Thus, the cord of the effort was cut and eighty five villages became void of the preaching of the Holy Gospel, nay, roughly ten thousand souls, at the very least, were deprived of the water of life.

The project waned and the branches dwindled. The students are funding up to twelve branches with their meagre monthly subscriptions, and this is not fair at all, since we entrust each student with intellectual, spiritual and physical efforts. Instead of providing him with a material reward, we are adding to his burden through the payment of a monthly subscription.

Your excellencies:

The costs of travel and transportation have doubled and the requests of the branches, which we have been forced to abandon, have accumulated against us. The voices of the consciences of our children dismay us internally, pleading, with the Macedonian man, saying, "Come across and help us."

So, I add my voice to the voices of my children who have included their plea enclosed with this memorandum of mine, hoping that it receives your attention and finds strong willingness in your hearts in striving to save souls and in glorifying His holy name.

Please, O distinguished colleagues, accept [our] utmost respect and appreciation,

15 May 1944 [Signature]

Director of the Clerical [College]

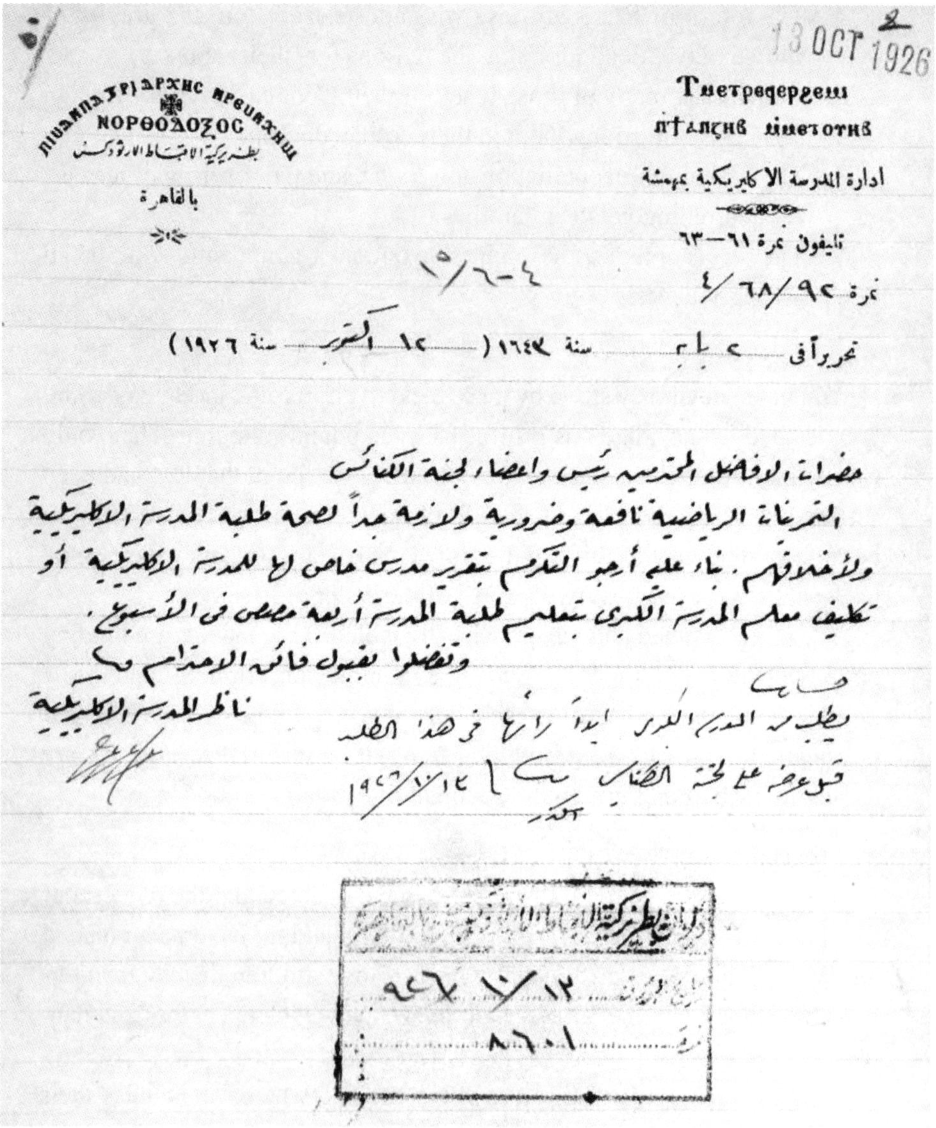

13 OCT 1926

بطريركية الأقباط الأرثوذكس

بالقاهرة

ادارة المدرسة الاكليريكية بمهمشة

تليفون نمرة ٦١–٦٣

نمرة ٩٢/٦٨/٤

تحريراً في ٥ بابه سنة ١٦٤٣ (١٢ اكتوبر سنة ١٩٢٦)

حضرات الأفاضل المحترمين رئيس وأعضاء لجنة الكنائس

التمرينات الرياضية نافعة وضرورية ولازمة جداً لصحة طلبة المدرسة الاكليريكية ولأخلاقهم. بناء عليه أرجو التكرم بتقرير مدرس خاص لها للمدرسة الاكليريكية أو تكليف معلم المدرسة الكبرى بتعليم طلبة المدرسة أربعة حصص في الأسبوع.

وتفضلوا بقبول فائق الاحترام

ناظر المدرسة الاكليريكية

يطلب من المدرسة الكبرى [illegible] رأيه في هذا الطلب قبل عرضه على لجنة الكنائس [illegible] ١٢/١٠/١٩٢٦

بطريركية الأقباط الأرثوذكس

تاريخ الورود ١٢/١٠/٩٢٦

نمرة ٨٦٠١

Doc. N°: 4-6.71-86/15 Theological College Pt. 1

Incipit: تمرينات الرياضية نافعة وضرورية ولازمة جداً لصحة طلبة المدرسة الاكليريكية.

Date: 12 October 1926

Description: A handwritten letter from Habib Girgis to the director and members of the Patriarchate Church Council.

Summary: The letter is in relation to the importance of teaching physical education as a part of the curriculum at the Theological College.

Administration of the Clerical School
in Mahmashah
Telephone Number 61—63

Coptic Orthodox Patriarchate
in Cairo

Number: 92 / 68 / 4 4 – 6 / 15

Written on 2 Bābah 1643 (12 October 1926)

To the distinguished and honourable president and members of the Churches Committee,

Exercise is lacking but essential and very necessary for the health of the students of the Clerical School and for their manners. Therefore, kindly determine a specialized [sport] teacher for the Clerical School or commission an instructor from the Great School to teach the students for four periods per week.

Please accept [our] utmost respect,

Headmaster of the Clerical School
[Signature]

It is requested of the Great School to support this request before it is presented to the Churches Committee [Signature] 13 / 10 / 1926

بيـــــان لا بد منه

(١) تمهيـــد ·

لم يدر بخلدى يوما من الأيام انى اضطر فى وقت ما الى الاشارة الى أى مأثرة أسديتها لكنيستى أو خدمة قمت بها لطائفتى على حد قول ربنا ومخلصنا له المجد "مهما عملتم فقولوا اننا عبيد بطالون انما عملنا ما يجب علينا · على هذا القياس خدمت كنيستى مدة الخمس والثلاثين سنة فى صمت وهدو · ولكن جد فى الأمر ما أجبرنى أن أخرج عن صمتى مقتديا بالرسول بولس الذى لما أمطره بعض الكورنثيين وابلا من انتقاداتهم المرة اضطر أن يرد سهامهم بلطف وتؤدة فقال من بين ما قال "اننا لا نجترئ أن نعد أنفسنا بين قوم من الذين يمدحون أنفسهم ولا أن نقابل أنفسنا بهم بل هم اذ يقيسون أنفسهم على أنفسهم ويقابلون أنفسهم بأنفسهم لا يفهمون · وقال من افتخر فليفتخر بالرب لأنه ليس من مدح نفسه هو المزكى بل من يمدحه الرب وقال ما أفعله سأفعله لأقطع فرصة الذين يريدون فرصة كى يوجدوا كما نحن أيضا فى ما يفتخرون وقال لا يظن أحد انى غبى والا فاقبلونى كغبى لأفتخر أيضا قليلا ··· ان أردت أن افتخر لا أكون غبيا لأنى أقول الحق ··· وبعد أن عدد الرسول أعماله وبين جهوده فى خدمة الرب قال أخيرا قد صرت غبيا وأنا أفتخر · أنتم ألزمتمونى لأنه كان ينبغى أن امدح منكم · ٢ كو ١٠ و ١١

ودحضا لافتراءات المفترين أكتب هذا البيان لألقى قبسا على بعض الأعمال التى قمت بها نحو المدرسة الاكليريكية التى كرست ذاتى لخدمتها منذ صباى · حتى أكون فى الحاضر وفى المستقبل كما كنت فى الماضى الخادم الأمين لكنيستى والمضحى بصحته وماله فى سبيل خدمة آمته ·

ولقد أضطررت أن آتى هنا بالمامة عن بعض مجهوداتى الماضية متوخيا الايجاز بذكر ما أديته للمدرسة فى الماضى البعيد وبعض الاطناب فيما كان خاصا بالماضى القريب · فأقول ·

(٢) تاريخ انشاء المدرسة الاكليريكية ·

أنشئت المدرسة الاكليريكية فى سنة ١٨٩٣ وخصص لها منزل بالفجالة ملك دير المحرق (سكنت به مدرسة البنات القبطية فيما بعد وأخيرا بيع لحضرة الدكتور فريد عبد الله) ظلت المدرسة فى ذلك المنزل سنة من الزمان ثم نقلت الى الدار البطريركية واحتلت ثلاث غرف أرضية رطبة بجوار الكنيسة الصغرى وبعد ذلك نقلت الى سوق القبيلة ثم أعيدت الى الدار البطريركية ثم نقلت الى بيت الهيجمن بحالته القديمة وبعد ذلك نقلت الى ثلاث غرف فوق مطابخ البطريركية وليس هذا محل ذكر الادوار التى مرت بها المدرسة لأن ذلك متروك للتاريخ ·

وكانت حالة المدرسة العلمية تستدعى العناية ورفع المستوى والنهوض بها من كافة الوجوه الى الدرجة اللائقة بالطائفة غير أن هذا التحسين وهذا الاصلاح كانا يتطلبان مالا كثيرا وخزانة البطريركية المكلفة بالصرف والانفاق على المدرسة ما كانت تسمح بالانفاق على هذا المشروع الجليل ولقد كانت المدرسة مرمى آمالى وموضوع أحلامى وكان حبها يملأ شغاف قلبى أتمنى أن أضحى حياتى لأجل تقدمها لأن بتقدمها تقدم كنيستى المحبوبة ·

(٣) تعيينى مدرسا بالمدرسة ·

تعينت مدرسا بالمدرسة الاكليريكية سنة ١٨٩٨ فى وقت كانت فيه الكنيسة عطشى لسماع كلمة الله وكنت أقضى أوقات الدراسة فى تهذيب الطلبة وتعليمهم الروحى وأقضى أوقات الراحة فى الوعظ بالكنائس وتأسيس الجمعيات الدينية بالقاهرة وخارجها لتوسيع دائرة المعرفة الروحية

Doc. N°: 4-6.60-67/37
Incipit: بيان لا بد منه.
Date: 1 August 1933
Description: A report by Habib Girgis and the treasurer of the Theological College to the Churches Committee.
Summary: The report is in relation to the history, property, donations, dean, cantors' school, and facilities of the Theological College.

Obligatory Statement

(1) *Introduction:*

It did not come to my mind that I would one day, at any time, be compelled to refer to a favour that I offered my Church, or a service that I did for my community, because of the saying of our Lord and Saviour, glory be to Him, "When you have done all those things which you are commanded, say, 'We are unprofitable servants; We have done what was our duty to do'" [Luke 17:10]. Following this standard, I silently and calmly served my Church for thirty-five years. But a new matter forced me out of my silence, following the example of the Apostle Paul who, when some of the Corinthians showered him with a barrage of their bitter criticisms, was compelled to return their darts gently and slowly. So he said, among other things, "For we dare not class ourselves or compare ourselves with those who commend themselves. But they, measuring themselves by themselves, and comparing themselves among themselves, are not wise", and he said, "But 'he who glories, let him glory in the Lord.' For not he who commends himself is approved, but whom the Lord commends." He also said, "But what I do, I will also continue to do, that I may cut off the opportunity from those who desire an opportunity to be regarded just as we are in the things of which they boast," and he said, "Let no one think me a fool. If otherwise, at least receive me as a fool that I also may boast a little… For though I might desire to boast, I will not be a fool; for I will speak the truth…" Then after the Apostle had numbered his works and showed his efforts in serving the Lord, he finally said, "I have become a fool in boasting; you have compelled me. For I ought to have been commended by you" (2 Cor. 10 and 11). So, in refutation of the slanderers' defamations, I write this statement to throw light on some of the works that I have done for the Clerical School, which I devoted myself to serving since my youth, in order to be—in the present and future—as I have been in the past; the faithful servant of my Church, who sacrifices his health and money for the sake of serving his nation.

I have thus been compelled to bring here details regarding some of my past efforts, taking into consideration to briefly mention what I offered the School in the distant past, and some elaboration of what was specific to the near past. So I say:

(2) *History of the Clerical School's Foundation:*

The Clerical School was established in 1893, when a house in al-Fajjālah owned by al-Muḥarraq Monastery was assigned for it (later on, the Coptic Girls' School

(٣)

نستفيد من كلمة الله أكبر عدد من أبناء كنيستى المحبوبة وذلك من غير أجركما يعلم ذلك كل من عرفنى ولقد سافرت على نفقتى الخاصة الى أغلب مدن القطر مرارا واعظا ومرشدا حاضا على الانتباه الروحى ومستنهضا الهمم لخدمة الكنيسة والأمة ٠

(٤) وقفية ستة أفدنة للمدرسة ٠

وفى سنة ١٩٠١ كانت تسكن بجوار مسكنى سيدة متقدمة فى السن هى الطيبة الذكر المرحومة خرسته جرجس جوهره ورثت عن والدها أطيانا بجهة الحمم فسعيت لاقناعها بأن توقف للمدرسة الاكليريكية وللجمعية الخيرية القبطية شيئا من أطيانها ضمن وقفيتها فأوقفت من أطيانها ستة أفدنة للمدرسة الاكليريكية وثلاثة أفدنة للجمعية الخيرية ٠

(٥) جمع تبرعات للمدرسة الاكليريكية والصناعية ٠

درست حالة طائفتى ورأيت من ميول أفرادها الصالحة نحو المدرسة الاكليريكية ما أكد لى بأنهم مستعدون لكل خدمة تؤدى الى تقدمها ورقيها وهذا ما دعانى فى سنة ١٩٠١ أن أسعى مع الطيب الذكر المرحوم ارمانيوس بك حنا لجمع تبرعات من الطائفة لوضع أساس لمدرسة لاهوتية تليق بطائفة ذات تاريخ مجيد وكنيسة كان لها شأن يذكر فى عالم المسيحية ٠ ولقد زرنا كثيرا من بلاد القطر لهذا الغرض وقضيت ثلاث سنوات وأنا أصرف يومى السبت والأحد فى البلاد للوعظ وجمع التبرعات وبلغ وقتئذ مجموع التبرعات حوالى احدى عشر ألفا من الجنيهات كانت تودع فى حينها بخزينة البطريركية ٠ ومن هذه المبالغ اشتريت سراى مهمشا فى سنة ١٩٠٢ ومساحتها وقتئذ ٣٠٨٨ مترا بمبلغ ١٥١٨ جنيها و٥٦١ مليما لتكون دارا للمدرسة الاكليريكية بدل انشاء مدرسة من جديد ٠ كما بنيت من تلك المبالغ مدرسة الصنائع ببولاق واشتريت ٣٦٥ فدانا لذمة المدرستين الاكليريكية والصناعية بمبلغ ٢٢٨٠٠ جنيها دفع من ثمنها جزء والباقى دفع على أقساط من ريعها ٠

وفى سنة ١٩٠٤ بذلت أقصى جهودى لما رافقت الطيب الذكر المتنيح الأنبا كيرلس البطريرك السابق فى رحلته الى الخرطوم لوضع أساس كنيسة قبطية بها وجمعنا فى هذه الرحلة لذمة كنيسة الخرطوم نحو خمسة آلاف جنيه ٠

(٦) تعيينى ناظرا للمدرسة ٠

كنت فى مدة تدريسى بالمدرسة أشعر بالمسئولية الملقاة على عاتقى وألتهب غيرة على تقدمها وزادنى قوة على قوة تقدير حضرات رجال الدين وحضرات أبناء كنيستى لمجهوداتى فكانت ثقتهم الغالية أكبر مشجع لى فى المضى فى عملى المثمر حتى اذا ما لاقى ربه المرحوم يوسف بك منقريوس ناظر المدرسة السابق سنة ١٩١٨ اختارنى المتنيح الطيب الذكر الأنبا كيرلس الخامس البطريرك الراحل ناظرا للمدرسة فقمت بأعباء هذه الوظيفة ونار الأمل الصالح يلهب صدرى فلا أنفك عن خدمة الكنيسة والمدرسة لحظة واحدة ٠

لم تكن المدرسة فى سنة ١٩١٨ بالمدرسة التى تليق لطائفة درجت مدارج التقدم العلمى والأدبى فبلغت غاية تغبطها عليها طوائف شرقية كثيرة ولذلك رأيت أن المدرسة وان كانت أسدت خدمة جليلة للكنيسة قبل سنة ١٩١٨ الا أنها يجب أن تتمشى مع سنة الرقى المنشود حتى تصل الى درجة مرضية وصل اليها نابغوا الأقباط فى دوائر العلم والمال ٠ كانت هذه الأمنية

occupied it, and it was finally sold to the distinguished Doctor Farīd 'Abd-Allāh). The School remained at that house for one year and was then moved to the Patriarchal Residence, where it occupied three damp rooms on the ground floor, next to the small church. After that, it was moved to Sūq al-Qabīlah, then it was returned to the Patriarchal Residence, then it was moved to al-Hajīn House, in its old condition. After that, it was moved to three rooms above the Patriarchate's kitchens. It is not the place here to mention the stages through which the School passed, since that is left to history.

The academic state of the School was in need of care and the raising of its standards, as well as its overall promotion to a level befitting the community. This improvement and reform, however, required a lot of money but the Patriarchate's treasury, which was assigned to the School's finances and expenditure, was not in a position to fund this great project. The School, therefore, was the aim of what I hoped for and subject of my dreams. Its love, which filled the depths of my heart, made me wish to sacrifice my life for its progress because, through its progress, my beloved Church would progress.

(3) *My Appointment as a Teacher at the School:*

I was appointed as a teacher at the Clerical School in 1898, a time in which the Church was thirsty to hear the word of God. I used to spend class time disciplining the students and educating them spiritually, and I would spend rest times preaching in the churches and establishing religious societies in and around Cairo, in order to expand the circle of spiritual knowledge, so that a greater number of children of my beloved Church could benefit from the word of God. [I did] that for free, as everyone who became acquainted with me knows. I have travelled several times at my own expense to most cities in the country preaching, guiding and urging for spiritual awareness, and awakening the will to serve the Church and nation.

(4) *Endowment of Six Acres to the School:*

Then in 1901, there was an elderly lady living next door to me. She was the late Khristah Jirjis Jawharah, of blessed memory. She had inherited agricultural lands from her father near Akhmīm. I thus sought to persuade her to endow some of her agricultural lands to the Clerical School and the Coptic Charitable Society as part of her will, and she did endow six acres of her agricultural lands to the Clerical School and three acres to the Charitable Society.

(5) *Collecting Donations for the Clerical and Trades School:*

I studied my community's situation, and observed the righteous inclinations of its individuals toward the Clerical School. It affirmed to me that they were prepared for any service that would lead to its progress and promotion. This then is what encouraged me, in 1901, with the late Armāniyūs Bik Ḥannā, of blessed memory, to strive for the collection of donations from the community to lay the foundation for a Theological School worthy of a community with a glorious history, and a Church that had a memorable role in the Christian world. We thus visited many of the country's districts for this purpose, and I spent three years devoting Saturdays

(٣)

نصب عيني فقمت أجدد المدرسة تجديدا لأبلغ بها درجة تتفق وميول الشعب الاصلاحية ولذلك وجهت مجهوداتي الى انشائها من جديد . فتناولت يد الاصلاح جميع شئونها المادية والعلمية كما ترى مما يأتي . —

(٧) تحسين حال العرفاء .

تسلمت ادارة المدرسة الاكليريكية وبها وقتئذ نحو خمسين طالبا وستين عريفا . وكانت حالة العرفاء تستدعي علاجا سريعا شافيا اذ كانوا لا يأكلون الا القليل من الطعام مما يجمعونه بأنفسهم من بيوت المحسنين ولقد رأيت بعيني رأسي بعضهم يجلسون في فناء المدرسة في الشمس يتدفأون بحرارتها مما يصيبهم من البرد ويقطعون حشائش قذرة من الحديقة يأكلونها عند ما يعضهم الجوع بنابه وفوق ذلك يزجون عند النوم في حجرات رطبة كانت في الأصل مرابط للحيوان متهدمة ليس لها من التحوطات الصحية شيئ ما وكانت هذه الحجرات أقرب الى مذاود البهائم منها الى ملاجئ الانسان فكمف بالضرير الأعمى الذي لا ناصر له فانه علاوة على غضب الطبيعة عليه وحرمانها له أعز ما يتمتع به الكائن الحي لا يجد من يعطف عليه ليخفف عنه شيئا من بؤسه ويساعده في حياته . كانت مناظر البؤس التي أراها بعيني كل يوم تمزق نياط قلبي وتعذب نفسي وتزعج ضميري . وكنت أكتب لديوان البطريركية طالبا تحسين حال هؤلاء العرفاء رأفة بالانسانية ولكن الحالة المالية وقفت عن تلبية طلبي فيممت شطر أبناء الأمة الأسخياء وكنت أوصي أهل البر من معارفي بأن يرسلوا الى أولئك العرفاء كل ما يفيض عندهم من طعام ولباس ومن وقت لآخر كنت أجمع ما تيسر لذمة كسائهم ورأيت من الضروري تخفيف آلام الانسانية في هؤلاء البائسين بتحسين حالتهم في أكلهم ونومهم وتعليمهم صنعة يدوية كأشغال الكراسي الخيزران وكراسي الصفصاف والفرش علاوة على ما يتعلمونه في المدرسة من الحان كنسية وقراءة وكتابة بالأحرف البارزة فشرعت في هذا المشروع وكان أصدقائي واخواني الأخصاء يعاونونني في هذه الخدمة أخص بالذكر منهم حضرة صديقي الأستاذ توفيق ابراهيم الذي كان وقتئذ نائبا بقلم قضايا المالية (والآن قاضي بمحكمة أسيوط) وبقوة الله تعالى وجدت معاضدة وعطفا من أبناء الطائفة وبدأت في جمع المال اللازم لهذا الغرض وكنت أودع ما أجمعه بخزينة البطريركية وفعلا تفاوضت لشراء العدد والأدوات اللازمة ولكن قام المعترضون في وجهي ووضعوا من الصعاب ما وضعوا مما لا محل لذكره هنا فاضطرني الحال الى أن اوقف الى حين مشروع الصناعة اليدوية وصرفت مما تبرع به أهل الجود ما دعاه الحال لتحسين لباسهم ونومهم وأودع الباقي في خزينة البطريركية أمانة لذمة هذا المشروع وقدره ١٥٢ جنيها و٨٤٥ مليما وصدر قرار المجلس الملي بضمه لحساب عمارة المدرسة

ولقد نفذت فيما بعد والحمد لله مشروع تعليم العرفاء الصناعة اليدوية بوساطة تبرع سيدة كريمة هي الطيبة الذكر المرحومة السيدة روجه ميخائيل اثناسيوس كما يعرف ذلك حضرات أعضاء المجلس الملي ولا يزال هذا العمل قائما وقد أفاد كثيرين من العرفاء الذين تعلموا هذه الصناعة

(٨) أبنية المدرسة الاكليريكية .

لم تكن أبنية المدرسة في سنة ١٩٢٢ خصوصا ما كان منها خاصا بالتعليم أو بمبيت الطلبة بالقسم الداخلي صالحة لأن يتربى فيها طلبة يصبحون بعد تخريجهم قسوسا وواعظين ومعلمين

and Sundays in the countryside to preach and collect donations. The total amount of donations at the time was about eleven thousand pounds, which were immediately deposited in the Patriarchate's treasury. [Using] some of this amount, I purchased the Mahmashā palace in 1902, the area of which, at the time, was 3,088 metres [square], for a total of 1,518 pounds and 561 millīms, to be a home for the Clerical School, instead of building a new school. Also [using] some of that amount, I built the Trades School in Bulāq, and purchased 365 acres for the sake of the two schools, the Clerical and Trades [Schools], for a total of 22,800 pounds. Part of its price was paid [outright], and the remainder was paid in instalments, using its revenue.

Then in 1904, I exerted the maximum of my efforts when I accompanied the previous patriarch, the reposed Anbā Kīrillus [V] of blessed memory, on his trip to Khartoum to lay the foundation of a Coptic church there. On that trip, we collected roughly five thousand pounds for the sake of the Khartoum church.

(6) *My Appointment as the School's Headmaster:*

During the time in which I was teaching at the School, I realized the responsibility that had been laid upon me. Thus, a certain zeal for its improvement was ignited, and the recognition of my efforts by the esteemed Clergy and sons of my Church increased my strength more and more. Their precious trust, therefore, was my greatest encouragement to continue with my fruitful work. Then, when the late Yūsuf Bik Manqariyūs, the previous headmaster of the School, met his Lord [i.e. departed] in 1918, the late patriarch, the reposed Anbā Kīrillus V, of blessed memory, selected me to be the School's [new] headmaster. I thus carried the burden of this position with the fire of righteous hope burning in my chest. I would, therefore, not be disengaged from serving the Church and the School [for] a single moment.

The School in 1918 was not fitting for a community that had continued to advance in science and letters, and had reached a goal desired by many Eastern communities. I thus supposed that, although it had offered a great service to the Church before 1918, the School should follow a required pattern of progress until it reached a satisfactory level that many brilliant Copts have already achieved in the areas of education and wealth. I had set my eye on this wish, so I began to modernize the School to bring it to a level consistent with the people's reform achievements. I therefore directed my efforts at re-founding it, so all of its financial and educational affairs were reformed, as you will observe in the following:

(7) *Improvement of the Condition of the Cantors:*

I took over the management of the Clerical School, in which there were about fifty students and sixty cantors at the time. The cantors were in a condition that required swift treatment as they were only eating the little food that they collected themselves from the houses of benefactors. With my own eyes, I observed some of them sitting in the schoolyard to keep warm with the sun's heat, all from the effect of the cold, and they were cutting and eating filthy weeds from the garden as they felt the pinch of hunger. Moreover, at bed time, they were cast into damp rooms, originally used for keeping animals, [which were] run-down and lacked sanitary precautions. These rooms resembled mangers for animals rather than shelters for

(٤)

بل كثيرا ما زار المدرسة كبار رجال الدين فى الغرب فكان الجميع يبدى خجلا من وجود هيكل رث لأبنية قديمة العهد مما دعانى الى السعى لدى ديوان البطريركية لترميم ما يمكن ترميمه واقامة مبانى جديدة لتنفيذ الخطة التعليمية الجديدة التى وضعتها نصب عينى وقد نجحت بقوة الله وتأييده، وأصلحت أماكن التدريس وبناء أماكن للنوم ووجدت من المجلس الملى مساعدة فى أعمالى كما انى وجدت مساعدة من الغيورين من أبناء الطائفة وجمعت وقتئذ اعانة لهذه العمارة قدرها ٧٥٠ جنيها سلمت كلها لخزينة البطريركية .

(٩) توسيع نطاق المدرسة .

ولما كانت مساحة المدرسة تضيق عن أن تسع طلبتها ولا يمكن بحالتها القديمة أن تقوم برغبات الطائفة الاصلاحية سعيت فى توسيع مساحتها ووجدت المساعدة الكبرى من الطيب الذكر المتنيح الأنبا كيرلس ومن حضرات أعضاء المجلس الملى وحدث فعلا أن اشتريت بيوتا وأراضى مجاورة للمدرسة وكان الشراء على أربع صفقات كما يأتى —

الصفقة الأولى ٩ س ٦٥٦ مترا أرض فضاء بمبلغ ٧٦٠ مليم ٢٦٢ جنيه من السيدة لوسيه والدة د صرفرعون

الصفقة الثانية ٦٠ ٧١٢ = عليها منزل = ٦٠٠ ٧١٢ من ورثة رزقالله وموسى فرعون

الصفقة الثالثة ٤٠ ٣٣٠ = عليها منزل = ٥٥٠ من ورثة بترو فرعون

الصفقة الرابعة ٦٠ ٦١٣ = عليها منزل على الشارع ١٢٠٠ من احمد جامع

وبهذه الأراضى التى اشتريت أصبحت مساحة المدرسة ٥٣٩٩ مترا أما مساحة الأرض المشغولة بالبناء فصارت ٩٩٢ مترا قدر حضرة صاحب العزة فرج بك امين باشمهندس السرايات الملكية المتر بعشرة جنيهات وقتئذ ووضع تقريرا عن الأبنية فى ٢٢/٦/١٩٢٥

وقد دفع ثمن الصفقة الأولى من خزينة البطريركية .

وأما الصفقتان الثانية والثالثة فدفع ثمنهما من تبرع لغبطة المتنيح الأنبا كيرلس .

وأما الصفقة الرابعة فتاريخها كما يأتى —

فى سنة ١٩٢٦ كان فى واجهة المدرسة من جهة شارع مهمشا قطعة أرض يبلغ مساحتها ٦٢٣ متر ٢٠ س وعليها منزل ملك احمد جامع أراد أن يبنى عليها اربعة منازل فى واجهة المدرسة ورأيت أن فى ذلك ضررا عظيما بالمدرسة اذ يحجب المدرسة من الداخل فتفاوضت معه على شراء المنزل فلم يقبل الا أن يبيعه بمبلغ ١٢٠٠ جنيها وكان غبطة البطريرك الراحل رحمه الله يريد أن تملك هذه الأرض ولكن لا نقود تحت يده، وقتئذ عرضت على المجلس الملى شراء الأرض وتعهدت أن اجمع تبرعات بقيمة النصف فقرر المجلس أن الصفقة ضرورية ولازمة للمدرسة ووافق على الشراء بشرط أن اودع بخزينة البطريركية مبلغ ٦٠٠ جنيها قيمة نصف ثمن تلك الأرض قبل الشراء ولما لم يكن بينى وبين البائع سوى مهلة اسبوعين وكنت عازما على شراء هذه الأرض لذمة بناء كنيسة للمدرسة عليها وكان حضرة صديقى العزيز الاستاذ توفيق ابراهيم الذى عاوننى فى أمور كثيرة لخير المدرسة تعهد لى بأن يتبرع بمبلغ مائتى جنيه لذمة بناء هذه الكنيسة فتسلمت منه حالا هذه القيمة ودفعت الباقى وقدره ٤٠٠ جنيه من مالى الخاص وحررت العقد الابتدائى مع صاحب الملك ودفعت له العربون الابتدائى مبلغ ١٠٠ جنيه وسلمت مبلغ ٥٠٠ جنيه لخزينة البطريركية وفى ذات الاسبوع تم شراء الأرض ومن ثم بدأت فى جمع التبرعات لذمة بناء كنيسة ولتسديد باقى ثمن أرضها .

humans. How is it then that a blind person, who has no patron and who, furthermore, because of the wrath of nature upon him that has deprived him of the dearest thing that a living being can enjoy, cannot find someone to sympathize with him enough to relieve from him some of his misery, and to help him in his life? The scene of misery that I would witness every day was tearing my heart, tormenting my soul and disturbing my conscience. I used to write to the Patriarchate requesting the improvement of the situation of those cantors, having mercy upon [their] humanity. The financial situation, however, halted the realisation of my request. Therefore, I turned toward the generous sons of the nation, and I would exhort the philanthropists I was acquainted with to send whatever extra food and clothing they had to those cantors; also, from time to time, I would collect whatever was available to clothe them. I thus deemed it necessary to relieve the humanitarian suffering among those miserable [people] through improving their eating and sleeping conditions, and teaching them handcrafts such as making bamboo chairs, willow chairs and beds in addition to the Church hymns, and reading and writing with raised letters [i.e. Braille] that they were learning at the School. I thus commenced this project, and my closest friends and brethren were assisting in this service. It is important to mention among them my friend Professor Tawfīq Ibrāhīm, who was an attorney at the Department of Finance at the time (now a judge at the court of Asyūṭ). Through the might of the Most High God, therefore, I found support and kindness from the community's sons, so I began to collect the money necessary for this purpose, and I would deposit whatever I collected in the Patriarchate's treasury. I did indeed negotiate to buy the necessary equipment and tools, but some [people] opposed me and put certain obstacles [in my way], though this is not the place to mention them. The situation thus compelled me to cease the handcrafts project for some time. I then spent some of what had been donated by the generous people [on] what was needed to improve their clothing and sleeping conditions; the rest, 152 pounds and 845 millīms, was deposited in the Patriarchate's treasury [in] trust, for the sake of the project. The Lay Community Council then issued a decree to add it to the School's building fund.

Later on, thank God, I executed the project of teaching handcrafts to the cantors through a generous lady's donation, namely the late Mrs Rūmah Mīkhā'īl Athanāsiyūs, of blessed memory, as the distinguished members of the Lay Community Council know. The work still exists and it has benefitted many of the cantors who have learnt this trade.

(8) *The Buildings of the Clerical School:*

In 1922, the buildings of the School, especially those which pertained to teaching or housing the students in the dormitory, were inadequate for fostering within them, students that would become priests, preachers, and teachers after their graduation. Although many Western religious leaders visited the School, I would hang my head in shame because the structure of the outdated buildings was shabby. This prompted me to pursue the Patriarchate for the renovation of whatever possible, and the construction of new buildings in order to execute the new educational plan which I had set my eye upon. I then succeeded, through God's might and support, in

(٥)

(١٠) الانتفاع بالأرض المشتراة ·

الأرض السابق ذكرها المشتراة من احمد جامع على شارع مهمشا فى واجهة المدرسة من الخارج ويمكن الانتفاع بها فاتفقت مع حضرة عطيه افندى مشرقى المقاول على اصلاح المنزل وازالة بعض الأبنية القديمة التى لا فائدة منها ومد السور وبناء ورشة للعرفاء ودكاكين على الشارع وكان ذلك كله تحت اشراف قلم هندسة البطريركية وكانت جملة التكاليف (جـ ملیم) ٣١٦ ٥١٨ وقد قدر مهندس البطريركية قيمة ايجار المنزل والدكاكين بعد اصلاحها بمبلغ (جـ) ١٣ شهريا وتعاقدت مع المقاول على أن يأخذ قيمة التكاليف التى يستلزمها العمل مما يصرف من ثمن زوائد التنظيم عن الأرض التى تركت فى الشارع وذلك حتى لا نكلف ديوان البطريركية شيئا وقد تم ذلك كله فعلا ·

(١١) بنــاء الكنيسة بالمدرسة ·

بناء كنيسة بالمدرسة الاكليريكية كان أمرا ضروريا جدا لأن المدرسة بدونها لا تزيد عن مدرسة عالمية وكان لابد من وضع أساسها خصوصا وانى ما جمعت المبالغ التى دفعتها لشراء أرض احمد جامع الا لذمة شراء أرض وبناء كنيسة عليها (كما هو مكتوب فى قوائم التبرعات) لم يكن فى يدى نقدية فى ذلك الوقت غير مبلغ مائة جنيه فاتكلت على الله تعالى ودفعت المبلغ لحضرة عطيه افندى مشرقى المقاول الذى بدأ فى وضع الأساس ثم دفعت له مبلغ خمسين جنيها دفعة ثانية ومن حسن حظنا أن شرف غبطة البابا المعظم الأنبا يؤانس المدرسة الاكليريكية وأبدى سروره من بناء كنيسة بالمدرسة وتفضل فتبرع بمبلغ مائة جنيه وأصدر أمره الكريم الى الديوان بتخصيص مبلغ ٥٠٠ جنيه مساعدة لاتمام بناء الكنيسة ولكن المجلس خفض هذه القيمة الى (جـ) ٢٥٠ نظرا للصعوبة المالية وحينئذ اضطررنا أن نكلف بعض طلبة المدرسة فى مدة الاجازة المدرسية بأن يجتهدوا فى جمع تبرعات من بلادهم بقدر استطاعتهم وقد جمع بوساطتهم مبلغ (جـ ملیم) ٧٧ ٥٧٥ وهذا المبلغ مع ما جمعناه نحن بمعرفتنا سلم لحضرة المقاول الى أن تم والحمد لله بناء الكنيسة ودشنها غبطة البابا المعظم مع لفيف من حضرات الآباء المطارنة وأقام قداسته فيها أول قداس والحساب الخاص ببناء الكنيسة مثبوت فى سجلات ديوان البطريركية وكل ما أجرى فى عمارة المدرسة والكنيسة كانا بمعرفة هندسة ديوان البطريركية ·

تمت الكنيسة وهى فى حاجة شديدة الى أثاث ومقاعد وفرش ودهان وايقونات وغير ذلك وما زلنا حتى الآن مهتمين باعداد كل ما يلزمها ·

renovating the classrooms and in building dormitories. The Lay Community Council empowered me in my works, and I also received assistance from the zealous among the community's sons. Thus, at the time, I collected aid for this construction amounting to 750 pounds, all of which was submitted to the Patriarchate's treasury.

(9) *Expansion of the School's Area:*

Since the School's area was insufficient to accommodate its increasing students and it could not achieve the reform desires of the community in its old condition, I sought to expand its area and received the greatest assistance from the reposed Anbā Kīrillus, of blessed memory, and from the distinguished members of the Lay Community Council. It indeed happened that I purchased houses and lands adjoining the School, and the purchase was done over four deals as follows:

	Metres	**Cm.**	
1st Deal	656	9	Empty land for the amount of
2nd Deal	712	60	[Land] with a house on it, [for the amount of]
3rd Deal	330	40	[Land] with a house on it, [for the amount of]
4th Deal	613	60	[Land] with a house on it, on the [main] street
	Pounds	**Millīms**	
1st Deal	262	760	From Mrs. Lūsiyah, mother of Naṣr Fir'awn
2nd Deal	712	600	From the inheritance of Rizq-Allāh and Mūsá Fir'awn
3rd Deal	550		From the inheritance of Bitrū Fir'awn
4th Deal	1,,200		From Aḥmad Jāmi'

Because of the purchase of these lands the School's area became 5,399 metres [square], while the area of the land occupied by the building had become 992 metres [square]. His Excellency Faraḥ Bik Amīn, chief engineer of the royal palaces, estimated the metre value to 10 pounds at that time; he also issued a report concerning the buildings on 22 / 6 / 1925.

The cost of the first deal was paid for from the Patriarchal treasury.

The cost of the second and third deals, on the other hand, was paid for through a donation made by the reposed Anbā Kīrillus [V].

As for the fourth deal, its story is as follows:

In 1926, there was a plot of land with a house on it in front of the School on the side of Mahmashah Street, covering an area of 613 metres and 60 cm [square], owned by Aḥmad Jāmi', who wanted to build four houses on it facing the School. I thought that this would greatly disadvantage the School, since it would enclose it from the inside. I thus negotiated with him to buy the house, but he refused to sell for less than 1,200 pounds. His Holiness the departed patriarch (may God have mercy upon him) also wanted us to own this land but he did not have the money at that time. I therefore propositioned the Lay Community Council to buy the land and I undertook to collect donations for half of the value. The Council then decided that the deal was indispensable and necessary for the School, and agreed to the purchase on the condition that I deposit a total of 600 pounds, half the price of that land, in the Patriarchate's treasury beforehand. But there was a time limit of only

(٦)

هو مبلغ ٥٠٠ ج فرددت الباقى الى الصراف حالا ـ الله شاهد على ذلك . لا أقول ذلك فخرا بل لأؤكد انى ما كنت ماديا يوما من الأيام .

(ب) وانى لأذكر المأثرة الآتية من مآثر الطيب الذكر المتنيح الأنبا كيرلس. وهو اداه قدس الله روحه . كان يقدر مجهوداتى وكان وقتئذ مقيما بالمدرسة بجناح خاص أعدته لغبطته . وكان يجاور المدرسة منزل لورثة المرحوم بترو فرعون وكان معروضا للبيع بمبلغ ٥٥٠ ج وكنت ميالا لضمه الى المدرسة . فأعطانى غبطة البطريرك يومئذ ١٠٠ ج قائلا لى خذ هذه بركة مصروفا لك فتقبلت العطية وقلت لغبطته حالا سأدفع هذا المبلغ عربونا لشراء المنزل فباركنى غبطته ببركات لن أنساها مدى حياتى ودعا لى بالنجاح وأبدى لى النصائح الغالية وأخيرا قال لى اكتب عقد المنزل باسمك وها هى القيمة الباقية من الثمن وأمرنى أن اضيف اليه دورا ثانيا واصلحه كما أشاء على حسابه من ماله الخاص ليكون مسكنا ملكا خاصا لى ولعائلتى من بعدى . تلقاء هذا العطف الأبوى العالى أطعت وقلبى فائض بشكر الله لكسب ثقة وبركة غبطته وكانت ثقته الغالية وبركته أثمن ذخيرة املكها تنسينى متاعبى ولما رأى غبطته تمنعى من قبول ذلك أكد علىّ مرارا بأن يكون العقد باسمى فأظهرت الخضوع ولكنى اشتريت المنزل وحررت العقد باسم غبطته شاكرا له فضله وعطفه . ولما عرف غبطته هذا الصنيع بعد تسجيله دعانى مرارا وأظهر لى رضاه علىّ وتقديره لمجهوداتى وخدماتى للكنيسة وللمدرسة وقال لى يا بنىّ ان هذا البيت بيتك وقد وهبته أنا شخصيا لك وفى كل مرة كنت اظهر الطاعة والامتثال لغبطته نيح الله روحه الطاهرة فى فردوس النعيم . ولكنى كنت مصمما ألا أحيد قيد شعرة فى خدمتى عن الاخلاص لكنيستى وأن اخدمها خدمة لا تشوبها أطماع مادية . وخرجت من لدن غبطته بعد كل مرة وأنا متمسك بمبدأى بينما كان غبطته واثقا باننى قبلت الهبة . وأخيرا تسلمت المنزل وكان مؤجرا فأخليته وأسكنت به الفقراء . يعرف هذه الحقيقة كثيرون من حضرات آباء الكنيسة وأبنائها .

(ج) دعانى حضرة الوجيه داود بك صليب سلامه من أعيان ميت غمر لأن احضر حفلة زفاف ابنه وأن القى خطاب تهنئة عقب الاكليل فرفضت وألح علىّ فاشترطت أن آخذ منه مائة جنيها عقب القاء الخطاب فى الاكليل فقبل فأجبت الدعوة وحضرت الاكليل والقيت كلمة تناسبت المقام وفى الحال بر بوعده وأنقدنى مبلغ المائة جنيه وتبرع لكنيسة المدرسة بمبلغ عشرين جنيها فحررت أنا فى الحال ايصالا بمبلغ ١٢٠ ج تبرعا من حضرته لكنيسة المدرسة الاكليريكية وانتهزت تلك الفرصة وجمعت نحو مائة جنيها أخرى تبرعات من أصدقائى أعيان ميت غمر وأعيان زفتى (واضحة فى كشف التبرعات) .

(د) دعانى المرحوم بطرس افندى جرجس من أعيان بنى سويف لأن أحضر جناز كريمته بكنيسة سويف لالقاء كلمة رثاء وعزاء فاعتذرت ولما رأيت الحاحا شديدا منه ومن كل أفراد العائلة أجبت الدعوة واغتنمت هذه الفرصة فحضرت الجناز وألقيت في الكنيسة الرثاء المناسب وألقيت كلمة عزاء على حضرات السيدات في المنزل وجمعت من تلك العائلة نحو خمسين جنيها تبرعا لكنيسة المدرسة كما اغتنمت الفرصة أيضا وجمعت من أعيان المدينة مبلغا يذكر كما هو واضح فى كشف التبرعات .

two weeks [agreed upon] between the seller and me; and I was determined to buy this land in order to build a church on it for the School. Thus, my distinguished, dear friend Professor Tawfīq Ibrāhīm, who had assisted me in many matters regarding the School's benefit, had promised me that he would donate a total of two-hundred pounds toward building this church, and I immediately received this amount from him. I then paid the rest, totalling 400 pounds, from my own personal funds, and subsequently wrote up the preliminary contract with the owner of the property, paying him a total of 100 pounds as an initial security deposit. I also handed over a total of 500 pounds to the Patriarchate's treasury and the purchase of the land was completed in the same week. I then began collecting donations for the sake of building a church and to settle the rest of its land value.

(10) *Utilisation of the Purchased Land:*

The previously mentioned land, which was purchased from Aḥmad Jāmi', [was] on Mahmashah Street, facing the School from the exterior, and could [now] be utilized. I therefore agreed with the distinguished 'Aṭiyah Afandī Mishriqī, the contractor, to renovate the house, remove some useless old buildings, extend the [external] wall, and build a workshop for the cantors, as well as shops on the street. All this was under the supervision of the Patriarchate's Engineering Department. The total cost was 316 pounds and 518 millīms, and the Patriarchate's engineer had estimated the rental value of the house and shops at a total of 13 pounds per month after their renovation. I thus made an agreement with the contractor that he would take the value of the costs required for the work from what would be spent from the cost of removing extra material from the land that was left on the street, in order not to incur any costs on the Patriarchate, and all this was actually done.

(11) *Building the Church at the School:*

The construction of a church at the School was quite a necessary matter since, without it, it would be nothing more than a secular school. Its foundation had to be laid, therefore, especially because I had specifically collected the funds that I paid to purchase the land of Aḥmad Jāmi', for the sake of buying the land and building a church on it (as it is written in the donations registers). I had no cash at the time except for a total of a hundred pounds, so I trusted in the Most High God and payed that amount to the distinguished 'Aṭiyah Afandī Mishriqī, the contractor, who proceeded to lay the foundation. I then paid him a second amount of fifty pounds. We were fortunate that His Holiness the Pope, Anbā Yu'ānis, honoured the Clerical School [with a visit] and expressed his delight at the construction of a church at the School, kindly donating a total of a hundred pounds. He also issued his gracious order to the Patriarchate to allocate an amount of 500 pounds to assist in completing the church's construction, but the [Lay Community] Council reduced this amount to 250 pounds because of financial difficulty. We were then compelled to assign some of the School's students to work hard to collect as many donations as they could from their own districts during the school holidays. Accordingly, an amount of 77 pounds and 575 millīms was collected by them. This amount, along with what we had collected ourselves, was thus handed over to the distinguished

(٧)

ومن أمثال ذلك كثير لا يحتمله المقام ولقد جمعت ما جمعت من التبرعات من أصدقائى وبوساطة أصدقائى كما استخدمت علاقاتى الودية عند من يقدرونني فى نجاح ما كنت اشرع فيه من المشروعات لخير الكنيسة والمدرسة ·

(هـ) لا أريد أن اذكر هنا جهودى فى المؤلفات التى وضعتها ولا ما كابدت من الأتعاب فى مجلتى الكرمة · يكفى أن أقول هنا انى أنشأتها فى سنة ١٩٠٤ وأعددت لها مطبعة خاصة فكانت النتيجة فى سنة ١٩١٤ أن رأيت المجلة مدينة بمبلغ ١٥٠ جنيها ثمن ورق ولها من الديون على مشتركيها مبلغ ١٥٠٠ جنيها فما لنا من الدين لم نستطع أن نحصل منه قرشا واحدا وأما ما علينا فلا بد من دفعه لأنه بكمبيالات فاضطررت أن أبيع المطبعة لتسديد ما علىّ من الدين قائلا ما قاله اشعياء النبى · أجرى عند الهى · ــ وفى سنة ١٩١٩ ظننت أن الحالة قد تحسنت وان الشعب يقدر جهود من يخدمهم فأعدت صدور الكرمة ثانية الى الظهور وكانت النتيجة بعد تعب عشرة سنوات أن خرجت بالنتيجة الآتية وهى · انى مدين للمطبعة ولتاجر الورق بمبلغ سبعين جنيها لا أزال اسددها حتى الآن من ماهيتى ولنا على المشتركين مبلغ ٩٥٠ جنيها · مضت سنتان ولم نحصل منها شيئا ولا قرشا واحدا لأن الأزمة المالية حالت دون ذلك ولى يقين فى الله تعالى بانى سأعود مرة ثالثة الى الجهاد فى اعادة الكرمة عند تحسن الحالة المالية ·

خاتمة

جهود أضنت صحتى وهدت قواى ومع ذلك لم تخل حياتى يوما من الأيام من مقاوم أو حاسد على أن هذه نعمة كبرى لا استحقها اذ لا يحسد ولا يقاوم الا كل ذى نعمة ولا ترمى الأحجار الا على الأشجار المحملة بالثمار ولا تنقر الطيور الا الأثمار الناضجة وانى لأحمد الله تعالى انى بنعمته لم يتطرق اليأس الى نفسى يوما من الأيام بل ابتسم دائما للمقاومات ولقد سامحت وأسامح من عمق قلبى كل من يريد أن يعادينى باطلا عالما انه لا بد أن تأتى العثرات فى طريق كل من يريد أن يخدم الله والناس· ولا بد دون الشهد من ابر النحل ومن يترك عمل الخير لأجل كلام الناس يشبه الخيل التى تجفل من ظلها · فلا تنقص قيمة الذهب اذا نبذه الحيوان · وليس بنقيصة على الشمس اذا لم ترها البوم · فيجب أن لا نفشل فى عمل الخير لأننا سنحصد فى حينه ان كنا لا نكل ولا يغلبك الشر بل اغلب الشر بالخير ·

ناظر المدرسة الاكليريكية

contractor until the construction of the church was completed, thank God. It was then consecrated by His Holiness the exalted Pope, accompanied by a number of distinguished Fathers, the Metropolitans, and His Holiness then conducted the first liturgy in it. The church's building fund is documented in the Patriarchate's records, and everything that took place during the construction of the School and the church was with the knowledge of the Patriarchate's Engineering [Department].

When the church was completed, it was in dire need of furniture, seating, furnishings, paint, icons and other things, and we are still concerned with arranging everything it needs.

[A section between pages 5 and 6 of the statement has been omitted]

… It is a total of 500 pounds, so I returned the rest [of the money] to the cashier immediately—God is a witness to that. I do not say this to boast but to assert that I have never been materialistic at any time.

(b) I must also mention the following poignant gesture from the reposed Anbā Kīrillus [V], of blessed memory, may God sanctify his spirit, who appreciated my efforts and, at that time, was residing at the School in a private wing prepared for His Holiness. Adjoining the School, there was a house belonging to the estate of the late Bitrū Fir'awn. It was put up for sale for a total of 550 pounds, and I was interested in adding it to the School. So, the patriarch gave me 100 pounds that day, and said to me, "Take this blessing as pocket-money for you." I thus accepted the gift and I said to His Holiness, "I will immediately pay this amount as a deposit to buy the house." His Holiness, therefore, rendered unto me blessings that I will never forget all my life; he prayed for my success and offered me precious advice, and finally said to me, "Write the contract for the house in your name, and here is the remaining amount of the price." He then ordered me to add a second floor to it, and to renovate it as I see fit at his expense, from his own funds, to be a private property for me to reside in and for my family after me. In response to this supreme fatherly kindness, I obeyed, as my heart overflowed with thanks to God that I had gained His Holiness' trust and blessing. His precious trust and his blessing were the most valuable treasures I have possessed, causing me to forget my troubles. But when His Holiness saw that I did not accept this, he repeatedly asserted to me that the contract should be in my name. I therefore showed submission but wrote the contract in His Holiness' name [when] I purchased the house, thanking him for his favour and kindness. So upon its registration, when His Holiness realized what I had done, he repeatedly called me to express his contentment with me, as well as his appreciation for my efforts and services to the Church and the School. He thus said to me, "My son, this house is yours and I have personally gifted it to you."

I would always show obedience and compliance to His Holiness, may God repose his pure spirit in blissful paradise, but I was determined not to turn away one bit from loyally serving my Church, and from offering it a service unmarred by material greed. Thus I would depart from His Holiness' presence after each time, adhering to my principles, while His Holiness was confident that I accepted the gift. I eventually received the house, which was being rented, but I vacated it and settled the cantors in it. Many of the distinguished fathers of the Church, and its children, know this fact.

(٨)

حســـــاب اجمـــــالى الايرادات

مليم	جنيه	
٨٤٥	١٤٩	باقى المتحصل لذمة تحسين حال الفقراء وأودعت أمانة بخزينة البطريركية وصدر قرار المجلس الملى بضمه لحساب العمارة بتاريخ ١٢/٢/١٩٢٣
	٣	قيمة ما تبرع به حضرة نجيب بك تادرس جوهرة لذمة المدرسة وصدر قرار المجلس بضمها لحساب العمارة بتاريخ ١٢/٢/١٩٢٣
٤٩٠	١٩١٥	التبرعات التى جمعت لمساعدة عمارة المدرسة الاكليريكية ولشراء الأرض والمنزل من احمد جامع وبناء الكنيسة
٦٠٠	١٢٦٢	تبرعات المتنيح البابا الأنبا كيرلس الخامس لشراء المنزل والأرض لضمها للمدرسة
	٧٣	تبرع حضرة عطيه افندى مشرقى المقاول باقى حساب الكنيسة
٧١٠	١٢	تبرع جمعية الوفاق القبطية بمهمشا لادخال وتركيب الكهرباء بالكنيسة
٦٤٥	٣٤١٦	جملة الايراد

ناظر المدرسة الاكليريكية　　　　أمين الصندوق

أول اغسطس سنة ١٩٣٣

(c) The distinguished notable Dā'ūd Bik Ṣalīb Salāmah, one of the dignitaries of Mīt Ghamr, invited me to attend his son's wedding party and to give a congratulatory speech after the ceremony. I refused, however, but he insisted on me, so I made the condition that I would take a hundred pounds from him after giving the speech at the ceremony. He agreed, so I accepted the invitation, attended the wedding ceremony and gave a suitable speech. Immediately after, he fulfilled his promise and gave me the total one hundred pounds, and he also donated a total of twenty pounds to the School's church. I then instantly issued him a receipt for a total of 120 pounds donated by him to the church of the Clerical School. I also seized the opportunity to collect about a hundred more pounds as donations from my friends, the dignitaries of Mīt Ghamr and Ziftá (shown in the list of donations).

(d) The late Buṭrus Afandī Jirjis, one of the dignitaries of Banī Suwayf, invited me to attend his daughter's funeral at the Suwayf church to give a speech of condolence and consolation but I excused myself. However, when I noticed his and his family members' extreme urgency, I accepted the invitation and took advantage of the opportunity, so I attended the funeral and gave a suitable eulogy in the church. I also gave a word of consolation to the distinguished ladies at the house, and collected from the family about fifty pounds as a donation to the School's church. I additionally seized the opportunity to collect an amount from the city's dignitaries, which is mentioned clearly in the donations register.

There are many examples of this, but it is not the place here to discuss them. I had collected whatever donations I did, however, from my friends and through their agency. I also utilized my friendly relations with those who appreciate me because of the success of the projects that I have undertaken for the benefit of Church and School.

(e) I do not want to mention here my efforts concerning the books that I authored, nor the suffering I went through with my magazine al-Karmah. It is sufficient for me to say here that I established it in 1904, and I prepared a special press for it. As a result, in 1914, I found that the magazine was in debt by a total of 150 pounds [which was] the cost of the paper, and it was owed a total of 1,500 pounds by its subscribers, not even a single piaster of which could be collected. As for us, we had to pay it since it was in bills, so I was forced to sell the press to settle my debt, saying what the Prophet Isaiah said: "I run to my God." Then in 1919, I thought that conditions had improved and that people would appreciate the efforts of those who serve them, so I released al-Karmah once again. But the consequence after ten years of labour was that I emerged with the following result: I was in debt to the press and the paper merchant by a total of seventy pounds which, until now, I am still settling out of my own pocket. Additionally, the subscribers owe us 950 pounds. Two years have passed and we have not acquired any of it yet, not a single piaster, because the financial crisis has prevented that. I trust, however, in the Most High God that I will return a third time to work hard in bringing back al-Karmah when the financial condition improves.

Conclusion

[These] efforts affected my health and exhausted my strength; moreover, my life was never devoid of adversaries or the envious at any time. This, however, is a great blessing that I am not worthy of, since no one is opposed or envied except for all those who are blessed; thus stones are thrown only at the trees which bear fruits, and birds peck only at the ripe fruits. I must thank the Most High God that I, through his grace, have never been touched by depression at any time, but always smile at adversities. I have forgiven and I do forgive, from the bottom of my heart, everyone who wants to falsely antagonize me, knowing that offences must come in the way of everyone who wants to serve God and the people. Thus, there is no honey without bee stings; and he who abandons charity for the sake of what people say resembles a horse that winces from its own shadow. Gold will not lose its value if it is rejected by animals, and it is not the sun's fault if the owls cannot see it. We should, therefore, not fail in doing-good because we will reap in due time, if we do not give up. "Let evil not overcome you, but overcome evil with good."

Headmaster of the Clerical School
Ḥabīb Jirjis

Account of Total Revenue

Pounds	Millīms	
149	845	The remainder of what was obtained for the sake of improving the state of the cantors. It was deposited for safekeeping in the Patriarchate's treasury and the Lay Community Council issued a decree adding it to the building fund on 12 / 2 / 1923
3		The amount donated by the distinguished Najīb Bik Tādrus Jawharah for the sake of the School, and the Council issued a decree adding it to the building fund on 12 / 2 / 1923
1,915	490	The donations collected to aid in the construction of the Clerical School, as well as to buy the land and house from Aḥmad Jāmi', and [for] building the church
1,262	600	Donations by the late Pope Anbā Kīrillus V for the purchase of two houses and land to be added to the School
73		Donation by the distinguished contractor 'Aṭiyah Afandī Mishriqī for the remainder of the church fund
12	710	Donation by the Coptic Understanding Association in Mahmashah for the introduction and installation of electricity in the church
3,416	**645**	**Total Revenue**

	Headmaster of the Clerical School	Treasurer
First of August 1933	[Signature]	[Signature]

باسم الآب والابن والروح القدس الاله الواحد آمين

الكلية الاكليريكية للأقباط الارثوذكس

حضرات اصحاب السعادة والعزة رئيس واعضاء لجنة الكنائس

بعد التحية والاحترام - قد وقع اختيارنا على ابننا الاستاذ نظير جيد روفائيل لينضم الى هيئة التدريس بالكلية الاكليريكية مدرسا لمادتى تاريخ الشرق القديم وتفسير العهد القديم .

والاستاذ نظير جيد روفائيل يحمل ليسانس الآداب فى التاريخ من كلية الآداب بدرجة جيد . ويحمل كذلك دبلوم الكلية الاكليريكية بتقدير ممتاز . وهو من خيرة شباب الكنيسة روحا وعقلا . يتصف بالنشاط والغيرة وله ميل واضح واستعداد محمود للبحث العلمى المتزن . ولذلك اجمع جميع اساتذته على ترشيحه بحماس بالغ ليكون ضمن هيئة التدريس بالكلية .

ويلاحظ ان الاستاذ نظير يشغل حاليا مركز مدرس للمواد الاجتماعية بمدرسة القناطر الخيرية الاميرية وعلى ذلك نأمل الموافقة على تعيينه بالكلية الاكليريكية براتب لا يقل عن عشرين جنيها شهريا (كخريج للآداب منذ ثلاث سنوات وخريج للاكليريكية ايضا) مع استحقاقه للعلاوات الدورية والدرجات المقررة فى كادر وزارة المعارف العمومية .

وللجنة الموقرة ان توافق اما على انتدابه رسميا للكلية مع احتفاظه بمركزه تابعا لوزارة المعارف او بتعيينه اساسا مع منحه كامل حقوقه المادية على الاعتبارات السالفة .

وتفضلوا بقبول فائق التحية والاحترام!!!

مدير الكلية الاكليريكية

تحريرا فى اول اكتوبر سنة ١٩٥٠ .

Doc. N°: 10-10.2, 5-6/30

Incipit: قد وقع اختيارنا على ابننا الاستاذ نظير جيد روفائيل.

Date: 1 October 1950

Description: A letter from Habib Girgis to the director and members of the Churches Committee.

Summary: The letter is in relation to the nomination of Naẓīr Jayyid as a teacher of history at the Theological College.

In the name of the Father, and of the Son, and of the Holy Spirit, the one God, Amen.

The Coptic Orthodox Clerical College

Your distinguished excellencies, the president and members of the Churches Committee,

After [our] greetings and respect, we have chosen our son, Professor Naẓīr Jayyid Rūfā'īl [Pope Shenouda III of blessed memory] to join the teaching staff at the Clerical College as a teacher for two subjects—the history of the ancient orient and Old Testament exegesis.

Professor Naẓīr Jayyid Rūfā'īl bears a Bachelor of Arts in history from the College of Arts with a good grade. He also bears a diploma from the Clerical College with an excellent evaluation. Additionally, he is spiritually and intellectually one of the finest youth of the Church. He is characterized by vigor and zeal, and he has a clear inclination and enviable preparedness for serious scientific research. So, for this reason, all of his professors supported his nomination with outstanding enthusiasm, that he may be included among the teaching staff of the Clerical College.

It should also be noted that Professor Naẓīr currently works as a social studies teacher at the school of al-Qanāṭir al-Khayriyah al-Amīriyah. For this reason, we hope that you will approve his employment at the Clerical College with a salary of no less than twenty pounds a month (as a graduate of the Arts [College] since three years, and a graduate of the Clerical [College] as well), along with his entitlement to periodic bonuses and grades prescribed by the staff of the General Education Ministry.

It is up to your venerable Committee to approve or to formally second the matter, along with his retention at a centre belonging to the Education Ministry or, basically, his employment with the granting of his full economic rights, according to the above considerations.

Please accept [our] utmost salutations and respect,

Director of the Clerical College
[Signature]

Written on 1 October 1950.

Bibliography

Archival Sources

The principal archival source for this book—and for the PhD dissertation on which it is based—is the Coptic Orthodox Patriarchal Archives, housed under St Mark's Cathedral in Cairo. In 2005 I made my first attempt at searching the archives for documents relating to Habib Girgis and the Coptic Orthodox Seminary, but with little success. The person responsible for administering the archives knew the various sections where such material was kept, but the presence of material on Girgis was largely unrecognized. However, in July 2011, through direct permission from His Holiness Pope Shenouda III, of blessed memory, I succeeded in gaining full access to the archives, where I spent two weeks.

Because the material was not cataloged, the only way to search the contents was to open up hundreds of boxes, each containing several files enclosing hundreds of documents. After copying some documents from the minutes of the Lay Community Council, I inquired further of the archivist: "Are these documents divided into sections? What types of documents are here?" He replied, "Here we have marriage contracts, here are real estate contracts and land titles, and here we have a section on schools." I responded, "What did you just say? Did you say schools?" My eyes lit up, and I felt that the puzzle was about to fall into place. In fact, in a humble way, I felt a bit like Howard Carter when he discovered the tomb of Tutankhamun. Working with a good friend who is a professional translator, fluent in Arabic and English, I began opening up the boxes and discovering treasures. There were thousands of documents on the Lay Community Council, many with Habib Girgis' signature; documents, letters and reports on Coptic schools, the Sunday School movement, and the seminary, also signed by Girgis; correspondence between the Church and government officials; and much more. I believe that I was the first person to locate and use this material, and that, to date none of it has been digitized or officially cataloged.

With the help of several individuals, I cataloged the bulk of the material relevant to my research. At the end of this laborious task, I presented the resulting preliminary catalog as a lengthy appendix to my doctoral dissertation. This archival material proved invaluable, but much remains for further inquiry and research. Citations are ordered as follows: author's name, title of document, date, box and file number, page numbers being cited. For example, **4–1.5–6/18 General Issues** refers to pages 5 to 6 of the file **4–1/18 General Issues**. A comma in the number sequence indicates associated documents that do not immediately follow one another in a particular file. For example, **4–1.5–6, 8–9/18 General Issues** refers to pages 5 to 6 and 8 to 9 of the file **4–1/18 General Issues**.

Other Primary Sources

I found many of my other primary sources in a museum dedicated to Habib Girgis and situated at the Coptic Orthodox Patriarchate in Cairo, which was officially opened by His Holiness Pope Shenouda III on August 22, 1990. These sources include a great number of Girgis' published writings, such as *The Orthodox Rock, The Mystery of Godliness*, and *The Invaluable Treasure: A Summary of the Bible and Biblical History*, plus several unpublished papers and lectures on a variety of subjects, such as *A Study on the Mystery of the Presence of God, A Study On the Nature of God, A Study On the Nature of Man*, and *A Study On the Mystery of the Trinity*, as well as postcards sent to Girgis by Marc Baruck, the English teacher at the Coptic Orthodox Seminary, during Baruck's many trips to Europe. I also collected sources from libraries at the Patriarchate and from monasteries and bookstores.

Secondary Sources

There is a wide variety of useful secondary sources dealing directly with Girgis and his work. Other publications deal with the educational, historical, and socio-political trends during Girgis' time, and offer a wealth of useful information for better understanding Girgis' era.

Coptic Newspapers

In 1877, during a time of reform in the Coptic Church which was led largely by laypeople (and resisted by the pope and clergy), the historian and reformer Ya'qūb Nakhlah Rūfaylah co-founded the pro-clerical Coptic newspaper *al-Waṭan*. In 1895, other reformers launched the *Miṣr* newspaper to counter *al-Waṭan*. In this way several Coptic newspapers began to circulate during Girgis' time, and he would have been well aware of them. Evidence suggests that Girgis even wrote articles about his work for some of these publications. Much information can be gleaned from them about religious education and what was happening in the Coptic Church. Unfortunately, however, a lack of access to these newspapers and their content was a major limitation to my research. Because of political upheavals in Egypt, I could not spend time in the Egyptian National Library and Archives. Any future inquiry ought to include a detailed review of these periodicals for further insights regarding Girgis and his work.

Personal Communications

I was able to interview the late head of the Coptic Orthodox Church, His Holiness Pope Shenouda III, a former student of Girgis'. Another surviving witness who could have been interviewed was Metropolitan Mīkhā'īl of Asyūṭ, who served on the board of directors of the seminary from 1946 onwards. Because of his ill health and advanced old age, however, an interview was not possible, and he passed away in 2015. At the time of publication, I had met with Nādiyah Fulayfil, who was born in the same apartment block as Habib Girgis. Fulayfil's family had a very close relationship with Girgis, and in a future edition of the book further information about Girgis' life will be added.

Arabic Texts

The primary written sources used in this study are in Arabic, the main language in which Girgis wrote. I have provided English translations where necessary. The titles of sources are translated and, where transliterations were essential, I have followed the translation and transliteration guidelines of the *International Journal of Middle East Studies*.

Archival Sources

Coptic Orthodox Patriarchal Archives, Cairo.

Works Written or Edited by Habib Girgis (listed by date of publication)

Many of these works are now rare, and it was not always possible to locate first editions; I have cited only those editions I was able to find.

Jirjis, Ḥabīb [Habib Girgis]. *Khuṭbah dīniyah fī al-diyānah al-masīḥiyah* [A Religious Lecture on the Christian Religion]. Cairo: Maṭba'at Miṣr, 1897.

______. *Kitāb khilāṣat al-uṣūl al-īmāniyah fī mu'taqadāt al-Kanīsah al-Qibṭiyah al-Urthūdhuksiyah* [The Doctrines of the Coptic Orthodox Faith: A Foundational Synopsis] (question-and-answer catechesim). Grades 1–4. 3 vols. Cairo: Maṭba'at al-Tawfīq, 1898.

______. *al-Mar'á al-khaṣīb: al-Nabdhah al-ūlá* [The Fertile Pasture: Booklet 1]. Cairo: Jam'iyat al-Nash'ah al-Qibṭiyah al-Urthūdhuksiyah, 1898.

______, ed. *al-Karmah* [The Vine] 1–17 (1904–31). Girgis contributed numerous articles to the journal, as well as editing it. Individual articles cited in the present volume are listed among the "Other Primary Sources" below.

______, and Wahbī Bik, eds. *Sīrat Barlām wa-Yuwāṣaf* [The Story of Balaam and Jehoshaphat]. Cairo: Maṭba'at al-Karmah, 1909.

______, ed. *Kitāb al-durr al-muntakhib fī maqālāt al-Qiddīs Yūḥannā Famm al-Dhahab* [Selected Pearls from the Writings of St John Chrysostom]. Cairo: Maṭba'at al-Karmah, 1912.

______, ed. *al-Jawharah al-nafīsah fī khiṭab al-Kanīsah* [Precious Jewels of Church Sermons]. Cairo: Maṭba'at al-Karmah, 1914.

______. *Tārīkh al-wa'ẓ wa-ahammiyatih fī al-Kanīsah al-Masīḥiyah 'umūman wa-al-Qibṭiyah khuṣūṣan* [The History of Preaching and Its Importance in the Christian Church Generally, and the Coptic Church Specifically]. Cairo: Jam'iyat al-Īmān al-Qibṭiyah al-Urthūdhuksiyah, 1916.

______. *Rūḥ al-taḍarra'āt fī al- 'ibādah wa-al-ṣalawāt* [The Spirit of Supplications in Worship and Prayers]. 3rd ed. Cairo: Maṭba'at al-Shams, 1920.

______. *Kitāb sirr al-taqwah* [The Mystery of Godliness]. Cairo: Maṭba'at al-Shams, 1922.

______. *al-Kanz al-anfas fī mulakhkhaṣ al-Kitāb wa-al-tārīkh al-Muqaddas* [The Invaluable Treasure: A Summary of the Bible and Biblical History]. 3rd ed. 4 vols. Cairo, 1923.

______. *Ṣalawāt al-sha'b ithnā' al-Quddās* [The Prayers of the Congregants during the Liturgy]. Cairo: Maṭba'at 'Ayn-Shams, 1926.

______. *al-Tarnīmāt al-rūḥiyah lil-Kanīsah al-Qibṭiyah* [The Spiritual Hymns of the Coptic Church]. 5th ed. Cairo: Maṭba'at 'Ayn-Shams, 1926.

______. *Asrār al-Kanīsah al-sab'ah* [The Seven Sacraments of the Church]. Cairo: Jam'iyat al-Maḥabbah al-Qibṭiyah al-Urthūdhuksiyah, 1934.

______, *'Azīz Tādrus, Shinūdah 'Abd al-Sayyid, and Rāghib 'Aṭiyah, eds. al-Kitāb al-Muqaddas: al-'Ahd al-Jadīd; al-juz' al-awwal, al-Bashā'ir al-Arba'* [The Holy Bible: New Testament; Part One, the Four Gospels]. Cairo: Maṭba'at at-Tawfīq al-Qibṭiyah, 1935.

______, and Kāmil Jirjis. *al-Qiddīs Murqus al-Anjīlī: Mu'assis al-Kanīsah al-Miṣriyah* [St Mark the Evangelist: The Founder of the Egyptian Church]. Cairo: Lajnat Murāqabat al-Kutub al-Dīniyah, 1937.

______. *'Azā' al-mu'minīn* [The Comfort of the Believers]. 3rd ed. Cairo: Maktabat Jam'iyat al-Maḥabbah al-Qibṭiyah al-Urthūdhuksiyah, 1937.

______. *al-Mabādi' al-Masīḥiyah al-Urthūdhuksiyah lil-madāris al-ibtidā'iyah* [Christian Orthodox Principles for Elementary Schools] (Grades 1–4). 4 vols. Cairo: al-Lajnah al-'Āmmah li-Madāris al-Aḥḥad al-Qibṭiyah al-Urthūdhuksiyah, 1937.

______. *Tamḥīṣ mā fī "kitāb Jam'iyat Aṣdiqā' al-Kitāb."* [Scrutinizing What Is in the Book of the "Society of Friends of the Bible"]. Cairo: Maṭba'at al-Iqtiṣād, 1937.

______. *al-Madrasah al-Iklīrīkiyah al-Qibṭiyah al-Urthūdhuksiyah bayn al-māḍī wa-al-ḥāḍir, 1893–1938* [The Coptic Orthodox Seminary: Past and Present, 1893–1938]. Cairo: Jam'iyat al-Ta'āwun al-Iklīrīkī, 1938.

______. *Anāshīd Urthūdhuksiyah wa-tarānīm 'aqā'idiyah* [Orthodox Hymns and Dogmatic Songs]. Cairo: al-Lajnah al-'Āmmah li-Madāris al-Aḥḥad al-Qibṭiyah al-Urthūdhuksiyah, 1941.

______. *Hal min ṭalāq fī al-Masīḥiyah?* [Is There Divorce in Christianity?]. Cairo: Jam'iyat al-Ta'āwun al-Iklīrīkī, 1941.

______. *In'āsh al-ḍamīr fī tarānīm al-ṣaghīr* [Children's Hymns for Awakening the Conscience]. Cairo: al-Lajnah al-'Āmmah li-Madāris al-Aḥḥad al-Qibṭiyah al-Urthūdhuksiyah, 1941.

______. *Tarānīm wa-anāshīd rūḥiyah—li-madāris al-Aḥḥad wa-al-jam'iyāt al-Qibṭiyah al-Urthūdhuksiyah* [Spiritual Songs and Hymns—for Sunday Schools and Coptic Orthodox Societies]. Cairo, s.n., 1941.

______. *al-Wasā'il al-'amaliyah lil-iṣlāḥāt al-Qibṭiyah* [The Practical Means Toward Coptic Reform: Hopes and Dreams]. Cairo: Self-published, 1942.

______. *Naẓarāt rūḥiyah fī al-ḥayāt al-Masīḥiyah* [Spiritual Perspectives for Christian Living]. Cairo: al-Maṭba'ah al-Tijāriyah al-Ḥadīthah bi-al-Sakākīnī, 1946.

______, ed. *Sullam al-samā' wa-darajāt al-faḍā'il* [The Ladder of Heaven and the Stages of Virtues, by John Climacus]. Cairo: al-Maṭba'ah al-Tijāriyah al-Ḥadīthah bi-al-Sakākīnī, 1946.

______. *al-Dirāsāt al-Tarbawiyah li-madāris al-Aḥḥad al-Qibṭiyah al-Urthūdhuksiyah* [Educational Studies for Teachers of Coptic Orthodox Sunday Schools]. 6 vols. Cairo: al-Lajnah al-'ulyā li-Madāris al-Aḥḥad wa-Jāmi'at al-Shabāb al-Qibṭī, 1947.

______. *Iftiqād al-qaryah* [Visitations to the Village]. Cairo: al-Lajnah al-'Ulyā al-Markaziyah li-Madāris al-Aḥḥad al-Qibṭiyah al-Urthūdhuksiyah wa-Jāmi'at al-Shabāb al-Qibṭī bi-al-Kirāzah al-Murqusiyah, 1947.

______. *al-Manhaj al-'ām li-madāris al-Aḥḥad al-Qibṭiyah al-Urthūdhuksiyah bi-al-Kirāzah al-Murqusiyah* [The General Curriculum for Coptic Orthodox Sunday Schools at the See of St Mark]. Cairo: al-Lajnah al-'Āmmah al-Markaziyah li-Madāris al-Aḥḥad wa-Jāmi'at al-Shabāb al-Qibṭī, 1948.

______. *al-Ṣakhrah al-Urthūdhuksiyah* [The Orthodox Rock]. Cairo: Dār al-Nashr al Qibṭiyah, 1948.

______. *Iftiqād al-'āmm lil-qaryah* [General Visitations to the Village]. 2nd ed. Cairo: al-Lajnah al-'Ulyā li-Madāris al-Aḥḥad al-Qibṭiyah al-Urthūdhuksiyah, 1949.

______. *al-Qānūn al-asāsī li-madāris al-Aḥḥad al-Qibṭiyah al-Urthūdhuksiyah wa-Jāmi'at al-Shabāb al-Qibṭī bi-al-Kirāzah al-Murqusiyah* [The Fundamental Law for Coptic Orthodox Sunday Schools and the Coptic Youth League in the See of St Mark]. Cairo: al-Lajnah al-'Ulyā al-Markaziyah li-Madāris al-Aḥḥad al-Qibṭiyah al-Urthūdhuksiyah wa-Jāmi'at al-Shabāb al-Qibṭī bi-al-Kirāzah al-Murqusiyah [The Central Committee for Coptic Orthodox Sunday Schools and the Coptic Youth League in the See of St Mark], June 1949.

______. "Da'wah ilá al-waḥdah" [A Call to Unity]. *Majallat Madāris al-Aḥḥad* [Sunday School Magazine] 3.9 (November 1949): 1–3.

______. *al-Wasā'il al-'amaliyah lil-iṣlāḥāt al-Qibṭiyah* [The Practical Means Toward Coptic Reform: Hopes and Dreams]. 2nd ed. Cairo: Dār Madāris al-Aḥḥad al-Qibṭiyah, 1993.

______. "Reading the Holy Bible and Spiritual Books," translated by St Anthony Coptic Orthodox Monastery. *Coptic Church Review* 31.1 (2010): 3–7.

______. *Hal ta'raf? Asrār Kanīsatak al-sab'ah: Mulakhkhaṣah min kitāb asrār al-Kanīsah al-sab'ah* [Do You Know? The Seven Sacraments of Your Church: A Summary of the Book "Seven Sacraments of the Church"]. Cairo: Maktabat Jam'iyat al-Maḥabbah al-Qibṭiyah al-Urthūdhuksiyah, n.d.

______, ed. *Kitāb al-Khawlājī al-Muqaddas, ayy Quddās al-Qiddīs Bāsīliyūs ma'a mā yuqāl min Quddāsay al-Qiddīs Ighrīghūriyūs wa-al-Qiddīs Kīrullus* [The

Divine Liturgy of St Basil, Along with What Is Said from the Divine Liturgies of St Gregory and St Cyril]. 4th ed. Cairo: Maṭba'at 'Ayn-Shams, n.d.

______. *Min Dirāsāt at-Kitāb al-Muqaddas* [Some Biblical Studies]. 5 vols. Cairo: Maktabat al-Maḥabbah al-Qibṭiyah al-Urthūdhuksiyah, n.d.

______. *Muftāḥ al-anghām lil-tarānīm al-Urthūdhuksiyah* [A Key to the Tunes for Orthodox Hymns]. Cairo, s.n., n.d.

______. *Murshid al-madāris fī al-ṣalawāt wa-ḥuḍūr al-Kanā'is* [A School Guide for Prayers and Attendance at Churches]. Cairo: Maṭba'at al-Tawfīq, n.d.

______. *Ṣalawāt min turāth al-Ābā'* [Prayers from the Heritage of the Fathers]. Jabal Akhmīm: Dayr al-Sayyidah al-'Adhrā' Maryam, n.d.

al-Ṭayyib, Fr. Abū al-Faraj ibn, and Dāniyāl al-Ṣāliḥī. *al-Rawḍ al-naḍīr fī tafsīr al-Mazāmīr* [Interpreting the Psalms: A Flourishing Meadow]. Edited by Habib Girgis and Yūsuf Manqariyūs. Cairo: s.n., n.d.

Other Primary Sources

"A Coptic Layman" [pseudonym for Marcus H. Simaika]. "The Awakening of the Coptic Church." *Contemporary Review* 71 (1897): 734–47.

'Awaḍ, Jirjis Fīlūthā'us. *Dhikrá muṣliḥ 'aẓīm: li-maḍī khamsīn sanah li-wafāt rajul al-iṣlāḥ al-Shahīd al-Abbā Kīrulluṣ al-rābi', Abī al-iṣlāḥ al-Qibṭī; Tārīkh awwal bāriqah min bawāriq al-iṣlāḥ* [In Memory of a Great Reformer: The Passing of Fifty Years From the Departure of a Man of Reform, the Martyr Anba Cyril the Fourth, Father of Coptic Reform; History of the First Ray of the Rays of Reform]. Cairo: Maṭba'at al-Tawfīq, 1911.

______. *Tārīkh al-Īghūmānus Fīlūthā'us faqīd al-ummah al-Qibṭiyah: wa-man kān la-hu min mu'āṣirīh 'ilāqah bi-al-iṣlāḥ al-Qibṭī, aw tārīkh al-iṣlāḥ al-Qibṭī al-'aṣrī* [The History of the Late Hegumen Philotheos of the Coptic Nation, and Those of His Contemporaries Who Were Linked to Coptic Reform, or the History of Contemporary Coptic Reform]. Cairo: Maṭba'at al-Tawfīq, 1906.

Boktor, Amir. *School and Society in the Valley of the Nile*. Cairo: Elias Modern Press, 1936.

British Foreign School Society. *Manual of the System of Primary Instruction, Pursued in the Model Schools of the British and Foreign School Society*. London: Longman and Company, 1831.

Browne, George. *The History of the British and Foreign Bible Society, From Its Institution in 1804, to the Close of Its Jubilee in 1854*. 2 vols. London: Bagster and Sons, 1859.

Butcher, E. L. [A. L. Butshir]. *Kitāb tārīkh al-ummah al-Qibṭiyah* (wa-Kanīsatahā) [The Book of the History of the Coptic Nation (and Its Church)]. 3 vols. Cairo: Maṭba'at Miṣr, 1906.

______. *The Story of the Church of Egypt: Being an Outline of the History of the Egyptians Under Their Successive Masters From the Roman Conquest Until Now*. 2 vols. London: Smith, Elder, & Co., 1897.

Butler, Alfred Joshua. *The Ancient Coptic Churches of Egypt*. Oxford: Clarendon Press, 1884.

Demetrius II, His Holiness Pope. "Patriarchal Bull, Issued by the Patriarch of the Copts Against Protestantism." Translated by Gulian Lansing. *The Evangelical Repository and United Presbyterian Review* 6.6 (1867): 353–58.

dī Blīsī, Awjīn. "Muḥāḍarāt lāhutīyah" [Theological Lectures]. Translated from French by the Administration of the Theological College, unpublished manuscript, n.d.:

"al-Muḥāḍarah al-ūlá: Baḥth fī wujūd Allāh" [First Lecture: A Study on the Mystery of the Presence of God].

"al-Muḥāḍarah al-thāniyah: Baḥth fī ṭabī'at Allāh" [Second Lecture: A Study on the Nature of God].

"al-Muḥāḍarah al-thālithah: Baḥth fī ṭabī'at al-Insān" [Third Lecture: A Study on the Nature of Man].

"al-Muḥāḍarah al-rābi'ah: Baḥth fī al-diyānah" [Fourth Lecture: A Study on Religion].

"al-Muḥāḍarah al-khāmisah: Baḥth fī al-Waḥī" [Fifth Lecture: A Study on Revelation].

"al-Muḥāḍarah al-sādisah: Baḥth fī sumū al-diyānah al-Masīḥiyah" [Sixth Lecture: A Study on the Superiority of the Christian Religion].

"al-Muḥāḍarah al-sābi'ah: Baḥth fī ṣiḥḥat al-Injīl" [Seventh Lecture: A Study on the Correctness of the Gospel].

"al-Muḥāḍarah al-thāminah: Baḥth fī sirr al-Tathlīth" [Eighth Lecture: A Study on the Mystery of the Trinity]

"al-Muḥāḍarah al-tāsi'ah: Baḥth fī suqūṭ al-Insān" [Ninth Lecture: A Study on the Fall of Man].

Egypt. *Maṣlaḥat 'Umūm al-Iḥṣā'* [The Census of Egypt Taken in 1907]. Cairo: National Printing Department, 1909.

Egypt. *Maṣlaḥat 'Umūm al-Iḥṣā'* [The Census of Egypt Taken in 1917]. 2 vols. Cairo: Government Press, 1920.

El-Maqrizi, Taqi-ed-Din. *A Short History of the Copts and of their Church*. Translated by R. S. C. Malan. London: D. Nutt, 1873.

Fowler, Montague. *Christian Egypt Microform: Past, Present, and Future*. London: Church Newspaper Co., 1901.

Galt, Russell. *The Effects of Centralization of Education in Modern Egypt*. Cairo: American University at Cairo, Department of Education, 1936.

General Central Committee of Sunday Schools and the Coptic Youth League. *al Manhaj al 'ām li-madāris al Aḥḥad al Qibṭiyah al Urthūdhuksiyah bi-al-Kirāzah al Murqusiyah* [The General Curriculum for Coptic Orthodox Sunday Schools at the See of St Mark] (January 1, 1948). In Ṣalīb Sūryāl, "Tārīkh Madāris al Aḥḥad al Qibṭiyah al Urthūdhuksiyah bi-al-Jīzah" [The History of Coptic Orthodox Sunday Schools in Giza]. Giza: Kanīsat Mār Murqus, unpublished manuscript, n.d., vol. 4, section 10, appendix 2, 4.

Girgis, Habib. "Ghilāf al-sanah al-thāniyah" [The Cover of the Second Year]. *Majallat Madāris al-Aḥḥad* [Sunday School Magazine] 2.1 (1948): 40.

______. "Ilayka ayyuhā al-Wālid" [To You, O Father]. *Majallat Madāris al-Aḥḥad* [Sunday School Magazine] 2.2 (1948): 21.

______, ed. "Madāris al Aḥḥad al Qibṭiyah al Urthūdhuksiyah bi-Asyūṭ" [Report on Sunday Schools in Asyūṭ]. *al-Karmah* [The Vine] 10.2 (1924): 86–92.

______. "Madāris al Aḥad ta'mal" [Sunday School Performs]. *Majallat Madāris al-Aḥḥad* [Sunday School Magazine] 2.2 (1948): 37–9.

______. "al-Madrasah al Iklīrīkiyah" [The Clerical School]. *al-Karmah* [The Vine] 6.7 (1912): 305–8.

______. "al-Madrasah al Iklīrīkiyah: Māḍīhā wa-ḥāḍirhā wa-mustaqbalahā" [The Clerical School: Its Past, Present, and Future]. *al-Karmah* [The Vine] 9.9 (November 1923): 463–65.

______. "Qānūn al-Madrasah al Iklīrīkiyah al Qibṭiyah al Urthūdhuksiyah" [Statutes of the Coptic Orthodox Clerical School]. *al-Karmah* [The Vine] 6.7 (1912): 308–28.

Herbermann, Charles George, Edward Aloysius Pace, Conde Benoist Pallen, Thomas Joseph Shahan, and John Joseph Wynne. *The Catholic Encyclopedia: An International Work of Reference on the Constitution, Doctrine, Discipline, and History of the Catholic Church*. New York: Robert Appleton Co., 1907.

Heyworth-Dunne, J. "Education in Egypt and the Copts." *Bulletin de la Société d'Archeologie Copte* 6 (1940): 91–108.

______. *An Introduction to the History of Education in Modern Egypt*. London: Luzac, 1938.

Iskārūs, Tawfīq. *Nawābigh al-Aqbāṭ wa-mashāhīrahum fī al-qarn al-tāsi' 'ashar* [Coptic Geniuses and Celebrities in the Nineteenth Century]. 2 vols. Cairo: Maṭba'at al-Tawfīq, 1913.

al-Jam'iyah al-Khayriyah al-Qibṭiyah al-Kubrá [Great Coptic Philanthropic Society]. *al-Yūbīl al-dhahabī: Tārīkh al-Jam'iyah fī muddat al-khamsīn sanah, 1881–1930; wa-taqrīrahā min sanat 1931* [Golden Jubilee: The Fifty-Year

History of the Society, 1881–1930; Report in the Year 1931]. Cairo: Maṭba'at al-Ma'ārif, 1931.

Lane, Edward William. *An Account of the Manners and Customs of the Modern Egyptians*. Reprint from 5th ed. Vol. 1. Cairo: American University in Cairo Press, 1860.

Lansing, Gulian. *Egypt's Princes: A Narrative of Missionary Labor in the Valley of the Nile*. Philadelphia: William S. Rentoul, 1864.

Leeder, S. H. *Modern Sons of the Pharaohs: A Study of the Manners and Customs of the Copts of Egypt*. London: Hodder and Stoughton, 1918.

Macbrair, Robert Maxwell. *Sketches of a Missionary's Travels in Egypt, Syria, Western Africa, &c*. London: Simpkin, Marshall, and Co., 1839.

Mackenzie, Hettie Millicent. *Hegel's Educational Theory and Practice*. London: Longman, 1908.

Manqariyūs, Yūsuf. *al-Qawl al-yaqīn fī mas'alat al-Aqbāṭ al-Urthūdhuksiyīn* [The Last Word on the Coptic Orthodox Question]. Cairo: Maṭba'at al-Waṭan, 1893.

______. *Tārīkh al-ummah al-Qibṭiyah* [History of the Coptic People in the Last Twenty Years From 1893 to 1912]. Old Cairo: s.n., 1913.

Mikhail, Kyriakos. *Copts and Moslems Under British Control*. London: Smith Elder & Co., 1911.

Philips, H. E., and S. M. Zwemer. *A Survey of the Missionary Occupation of Egypt*. Cairo: Nile Mission Press, 1924.

al-Qummuṣ, Manassá. *Kitāb tārīkh al-Kanīsah al-Qibṭiyah* [The Book of the History of the Coptic Church]. Cairo: Maṭba'at al-Yaqẓah, 1924.

Starbuck, Charles Casey. "A General View of Missions, 2d ser., pt. 2: Egypt." *Andover Review* (Boston, MA) 11.65 (May 1, 1889): 529–39.

Watson, Andrew. *The American Mission in Egypt*. Pittsburgh, PA: United Presbyterian Board of Publication, 1898.

______. *The American Mission in Egypt, 1854–1896*. 2nd ed. Pittsburgh, PA: United Presbyterian Board of Publication, 1904.

Secondary Sources

Abbas Hilmi II. *The Last Khedive of Egypt*. Translated by A. Sonbol. Reading, NY: Ithaca Press, 1998.

'Abd al-Karīm, Aḥmad 'Izzat. *Tārīkh al-Ta'līm fī Miṣr (al-juz' al-awwal) 'Aṣr Muḥammad 'Alī* [A History of Education in Egypt (Part 1): The Time of Muhammad Ali]. Cairo: Maṭba'at al-Naṣr, 1938.

______. *Tārīkh al-Ta'līm fī Miṣr min nihāyat ḥukm Muḥammad 'Alī ilá awā'il ḥukm Tawfīq, 1848–1882* [A History of Education in Egypt From the End of

Muhammad Ali's Rule Until the First Years of Tawfiq's Rule, 1848–1882]. 3 vols. Cairo: Maṭba'at al-Naṣr, 1945.

'Abd al-Masīḥ, Mīnā 'Abd al-Nūr. *'Adhrā' Mahmashah bayn al-māḍī wa-al-ḥāḍir* [The Virgin of Mahmashah, Past and Present]. Cairo: Kanīsat al-Sayyidah al-'Adhrā' bi-Mahmashah, 2004.

'Abduh, Muḥammad. *al-Islām wa-al-Naṣrāniyah ma'a 'ilm wa-al-madaniyah* [Islam and Christianity with Science and Civility]. Cairo: Maṭba'at 'Alī Subayh, 1954.

Abu-Lughod, Lila, ed. *Remaking Women: Feminism and Modernity in the Middle East*. Princeton Studies in Culture/Power/History. Princeton, NJ: Princeton University Press, 1998.

Abu Salih the Armenian. *The Churches and Monasteries of Egypt and Some Neighbouring Countries*. Translated by B. T. A. Evetts. Piscataway, N.J.: Gorgias Press, 2001.

Afifi, Muhammad. "The State and the Church in Nineteenth-Century Egypt." *Die Welt des Islams* 39.3 (1999): 273–88.

Akhdary, Faheem Botrous Mikhail Attia. "A History of the Educational Emphases of the Major Religions of Egypt." Ph.D. diss., Boston University, 1955.

Akkari, Abdeljalil. "Education in the Middle East and North Africa: The Current Situation and Future Challenges." *International Education Journal* 5.2 (2004): 144–53.

Alayan, Samira, and Achim Rohde. *The Politics of Education Reform in the Middle East: Self and Other in Textbooks and Curricula*. New York: Berghahn Books, 2012.

'Alī, Ṣalāḥ Aḥmad Harīdī. *al-Ta'līm fī Miṣr fī al-qarn al-thāmin 'ashar* [Education in Egypt in the Eighteenth Century]. Alexandria: Dār al-Ma'ārif al-Jāmi'īyah, 1990.

American Friends Service Committee. "Popular Education." *American Friends Service Committee*. <https://afsc.org/resource/popular-education>, accessed January 11, 2014.

Anderson, Benedict. *Imagined Communities: Reflections on the Origin and Spread of Nationalism*. 3rd ed. London: Verso, 2006.

Antonius, George. *The Arab Awakening: The Story of the Arab National Movement*. Beirut: Librairie du Liban, 1969.

Armanious, Febe. *Coptic Christianity in Ottoman Egypt*. Oxford: Oxford University Press, 2011.

Assad, Maurice Mikhail. "Education in the Coptic Orthodox Church: Strategies for the Future." Ed.D. diss., Columbia University in New York, Teacher's College, 1970.

ʻAṭā'-Allāh, Wahīb. "al-Arshīdyākūn Ḥabīb Jirjis fi al-majlis al-millī al-ʻāmm" [Archdeacon Habib Girgis in the Lay Community Council]. *Majallat Madāris al-Aḥḥad* [Sunday School Magazine] 5.9–10 (November–December 1951): 34–38.

______. "Kalimat Madāris al-Aḥḥad fī ḥaflat al-Ta'bīn" [The Sunday Schools' Speech at the Commemoration Celebration]. *Majallat Madāris al-Aḥḥad* [Sunday School Magazine] 5.9–10 (November–December 1951): 26–33.

Atiya, Aziz Suryal, ed. *The Coptic Encyclopedia*. New York: Macmillan, 1991.

Axtell, James. "Lancaster, Joseph (1778–1838)." In *Encyclopedia of World Biography*, Gale Research, Inc. Detroit, MI: Gale, 1998. *Academic OneFile*. Accessed December 7, 2013.

Badr, Habib, Suad Abou el Rouss Slim, and Joseph Abou Nohra, eds. *Christianity: A History in the Middle East*. Beirut: Middle East Council of Churches Studies and Research Program, 2005.

Bailey, Ewing M. *May We Introduce ... Egypt*. Philadelphia, PA: United Presbyterian Board of Foreign Missions, c. 1954.

Bakewell, Joan, ed. *Chambers Biographical Dictionary*. London: Chambers Harrap, 2011. <http://www.credoreference.com/entry/chambbd/laubach_frank_charles>, accessed January 3, 2014.

Barclay, William. *Educational Ideals in the Ancient World*. London: Collins, 1959.

Baron, Beth. *The Women's Awakening in Egypt: Culture, Society, and the Press*. New Haven, CT: Yale University Press, 1994.

Barzun, Jacques, and Henry F. Graff. *The Modern Researcher*. 5th ed. Forth Worth, TX: Harcourt Brace Jovanovich College Publishers, 1992.

Basili, Fr. Boulos. "My Years with Habib Girgis." *Watani International* 43.2062 (August 26, 2001): 3.

Bates, Dennis, Gloria Durka, Friedrich Schweitzer, eds. *Education, Religion and Society: Essays in Honour of John M. Hull*. New York: Routledge, 2006.

Behrens-Abouseif, Doris. *Die Kopten in der ägyptischen Gesellschaft: von der Mitte des 19. Jahrhunderts bis 1923; Islamkundliche Untersuchungen*. Frieburg im Breisgau: K. Schwarz, 1972.

______. "The Political Situation of the Copts, 1798–1923." In *Christians and Jews in the Ottoman Empire: The Functioning of a Plural Society*. Edited by Benjamin Braude and Bernard Lewis, vol. 2, 185–206. New York: Holmes and Meier, 1982.

Bestawros, Adel Azer. "Coptic Community Council." In *The Coptic Encyclopedia*. Edited by Aziz Suryal Atiya, vol. 2, 580–82. New York: Macmillan, 1991.

Bishāy, Mukhtār Fāyiq, and Akram Rifʻat Ḥabīb, eds. "al-Kanīsah al-Qibṭiyah khilāl al-qarn al-ʻishrīn" [The Coptic Church During the Twentieth Century], *Majallat*

Madāris al-Aḥḥad [Sunday School Magazine] 54.9–10 (November–December 2000).

______, eds. "al-Kanīsah al-Qibṭiyah khilāl al-qarn al-'ishrīn 2." *Majallat Madāris al-Aḥḥad* [Sunday School Magazine] 55.9–10 (November–December 2001).

______, eds. "al-Kanīsah al-Qibṭiyah khilāl al-qarn al-'ishrīn 3." *Majallat Madāris al-Aḥḥad* [Sunday School Magazine] 56.3–4 (March–April 2002).

______, eds. *Majallat Madāris al-Aḥḥad* [Sunday School Magazine] 45.7 (September 1991).

Boojamra, John L. *Foundations for Orthodox Christian Education*. Crestwood, NY: St Vladimir's Seminary Press, 1989.

Boutros Ghali, Mirrit. "Clerical College." In *The Coptic Encyclopedia*. Edited by Aziz Suryal Atiya, vol. 2, 563–64. New York: Macmillan, 1991.

______. "Ethiopian Church Autocephaly." In *The Coptic Encyclopedia*. Edited by Aziz Suryal Atiya, vol. 3, 980–84. New York: Macmillan, 1991.

Burke, Jeffrey C. "The Establishment of the American Presbyterian Mission in Egypt, 1854–1940: An Overview." Ph.D. diss., McGill University, 2000.

Burton, Keith Augustus. *The Blessing of Africa: The Bible and African Christianity*. Downers Grove, IL: IVP Academic, 2007.

Buṭrus, Athanāsiyūs. "Bā'ith al-nahḍah al-rūḥiyah fī 'aṣrinā al-ḥadīth" [The Impetus of the Spiritual Revival in Our Contemporary Era]. *al-Karmah* [The Vine] 1.1 (January 2002): 30–31.

Cannuyer, Christian. *Coptic Egypt: The Christians of the Nile*. London: Thames and Hudson, 2001.

Carter, B. L. *The Copts in Egyptian Politics*. London: Croom Helm, 1986.

______. "On Spreading the Gospel to Egyptians Sitting in Darkness: The Political Problem of Missionaries in Egypt in the 1930s." *Middle Eastern Studies* 20.4 (1984): 18–36.

Chaillot, Christine. *The Coptic Orthodox Church: A Brief Introduction to Its Life and Spirituality*. Paris: Inter-Orthodox Dialogue, 2005.

______. "The Life and Situation of the Coptic Orthodox Church Today." *Studies in World Christianity* 15.3 (2009): 199–216.

Cleveland, William L., and Martin Bunton. *A History of the Modern Middle East*. 4th ed. Boulder, CO: Westview Press, 2009.

Cochran, Judith. *Educational Roots of Political Crisis in Egypt*. Lanham, MD: Lexington Books, 2008.

______. *Education in Egypt*. London: Croom Helm, 1986.

Cole, Juan Ricardo. *Colonialism and Revolution in the Middle East: Social and Cultural Origins of Egypt's 'Urabi Movement*. Cairo: American University in Cairo Press, 1999.

______. "Feminism, Class, and Islam in Turn-of-the-Century Egypt." *International Journal of Middle East Studies* 13.4 (1981): 387–407.

Corley, Bruce, Steve Lemke, and Grant Lovejoy. *Biblical Hermeneutics: A Comprehensive Introduction to Interpreting Scripture*. 2nd ed. Nashville, TN: Broadman & Holman, 2002.

Cross, F. L., and Elizabeth A. Livingstone, eds. *Oxford Dictionary of the Christian Church*. 3rd ed. Oxford: Oxford University Press, 2005.

Daily News Egypt, "Egypt's Illiteracy Rate Drops Slightly to 26 pct." *The Free Library by Farlex*, 2009. <http://www.thefreelibrary.com/Egypt's+illiteracy+rate+drops+slightly+to+26+pct.-a0212009019>, accessed February 1, 2014.

Daly, M. W., ed. *The Cambridge History of Egypt*. 2 vols. Cambridge: Cambridge University Press, 1998.

Daus, Timothy Daniel. "The Coptic Community in 19th Century Egypt." Master's thesis, University of Calgary, Department of Anthropology, 1986.

Davis, Allen F., ed. *For Better or Worse: The American Influence in the World.* Contributions in American Studies 51. Westport, CT: Greenwood Press, 1981.

Dodge, Bayard. "American Educational and Missionary Efforts in the Nineteenth and Early Twentieth Centuries." *Annals of the American Academy of Political and Social Science* 401.1 (1972): 15–22.

Dodwell, Henry. *The Founder of Modern Egypt: A Study of Muhammad 'Ali*. Cambridge: The University Press, 1931.

Doğan, Mehmet Ali, and Heather J. Sharkey, eds. *American Missionaries and the Middle East: Foundational Encounters*. Salt Lake City, UT: University of Utah Press, 2011.

Durka, Gloria. "A Course on Foundations in Religious Education, Lecture 2." Presented at Fordham University, New York, 2005.

Elder, Earl E. *Vindicating a Vision: The Story of the American Mission in Egypt, 1854–1954*. Philadelphia, PA: Board of Foreign Missions of the United Presbyterian Church of North America, 1958.

Elias, John L. *A History of Christian Education: Protestant, Catholic, and Orthodox Perspectives*. Malabar, FL: Krieger Pub. Co., 2002.

El Souriany, Makary. "Ancient and Contemporary Christian Education in the Coptic Church of Egypt." M. R. E. diss., Princeton Theological Seminary, 1955.

Erlich, Haggai. "Identity and Church: Ethiopian-Egyptian Dialogue, 1924–1959." *International Journal of Middle East Studies* 32.1 (2000): 23–46.

Estafanos, Samy. "Defying the Pharaohs: Contemporary Educational Challenges for the Evangelical Church in Egypt." *Christian Education Journal* 10 (October 2, 2013): 162–73.

Evangelical Theological Seminary in Cairo. "Our History." *Evangelical Theological Seminary in Cairo*. <http://www.etsc.org/new/our-history>, accessed January 4, 2014.

Fahmy, Khaled. *All the Pasha's Men*. Cairo: American University in Cairo Press, 2002.

______. "Women, Medicine, and Power in Nineteenth-Century Egypt." In *Remaking Women: Feminism and Modernity in the Middle East*. Edited by Lila Abu-Lughod, 35–72. Princeton, NJ: Princeton University Press, 1998.

Fanack Chronicle of the Middle East & North Africa: Egypt: Population. <https://chronicle.fanack.com/egypt/population/>, accessed April 15, 2016.

al-Faqī, Ḥasan. *al-Tārīkh al-thaqāfī lil-ta'līm bi-al-Jumhūriyah al-'Arabiyah al-Muttaḥidah fi al-qarn al-tāsi' 'ashar wa-al-'ishrīn* [The Cultural History of Education in the United Arab Republic in the Nineteenth and Twentieth Centuries]. Cairo: Dār al-Nahḍah al-'Arabiyah, 1966.

Farīd, Zaynab Muḥammad. *Min Tarikh al-ta'līm fī Miṣr* [From the History of Education in Egypt]. Cairo: Maktabat al-Anjlū al-Miṣriyah, 1975.

Ferguson, Everett, Michael P. McHugh, and Frederick W. Norris, eds. *Encyclopedia of Early Christianity*. 2nd ed. New York: Garland, 1997.

Fichte, Johann Gottlieb. *Addresses to the German Nation*. Westport, CT: Greenwood Press, 1979.

Franc, Jaroslav. "Vzdělávání v Koptské Církvi a tradice nedělních škol" [Education in the Coptic Orthodox Church and Tradition of Sunday Schools]. *Studia Theologica* 29 (January 1, 2007): 48–55.

Gabra, Gawdat. *The A to Z of the Coptic Church*. A to Z Guide Series 107. Lanham, MD: Scarecrow Press, 2009.

______. *Historical Dictionary of the Coptic Church*. Historical Dictionaries of Religions, Philosophies, and Movements 84. Lanham, MD: Scarecrow Press, 2008.

Ghiraldelli Jr., Paulo. "Educational Theory: Herbart, Dewey, Freire and Postmodernists. A Perspective from Philosophy of Education." *Encyclopaedia of Educational Philosophy and Theory* (2000). <http://eepat.net/doku.php?id=educational_theory>, accessed January 3, 2014.

Ghrīghūriyūs, al-Anbā. *al-Ta'līm al-dīnī wa-al-Kulliyah al-Iklīrīkiyah wa-madāris al-tarbiyah al-Kanasiyah* [Religious Education, the Theological College and Church Education Schools]. Mawsū'at al-Anbā Ghrīghūriyūs 36. Cairo: Jam'iyat al-Anbā Ghrīghūriyūs Usquf al-Baḥth al-'Ilmī, 2011.

Gibrael, Michael. *Archdeacon Habeeb Guirguis*. Translated by Shaheer Gobran. Sydney: Sunday School Central Committee, 1991.

______. *A Man of Vision: Archdeacon Habeeb Guirguis in His 40th Anniversary, 1951–1991*. Translated by Shaheer Gobran. Sydney: Sunday School Central Committee, 1991.

Glass, Dagmar, Geoffrey Roper, and Hrant Gabeyan. "Arabic Book and Newspaper Printing in the Arab World." In *Middle Eastern Languages and the Print Revolution: A Cross-Cultural Encounter; A Catalogue and Companion to the Exhibition*. Edited by Eva M. Hanebutt-Benz, Dagmar Glass and Geoffrey Roper, 177–226. Westhofen: WVA-Verlag Skulima, 2002.

Goldschmidt, Arthur Jr. *Biographical Dictionary of Modern Egypt*. Cairo: American University in Cairo Press, 2000.

______, and Lawrence Davidson. *A Concise History of the Middle East*. 8th ed. Boulder, CO: Westview Press, 2006

Gorman, Anthony. *Historians, State, and Politics in Twentieth Century Egypt: Contesting the Nation*. London: Routledge, 2003.

Habashy, Ragheb Moftah. "Coptic Music: Value and Origins." *Institute of Coptic Studies*. Last modified September 23, 2000. <http://www.coptic.org/music/valnorig.htm>.

Ḥāmid, Ra'ūf 'Abbās, ed. *al-Awāmir wa-al-mukātabāt al-ṣādirah min 'Azīz Miṣr Muḥammad 'Alī* [The Instructions and Records Issued by King of Egypt Mohammed Ali], vol. 1 Cairo: Dār al-Kutub wa-al-Wathā'iq al-Qawmiyah, 2005.

Hamilton, Alastair. *The Copts and the West, 1439–1822: The European Discovery of the Egyptian Church*. Oxford: Oxford University Press, 2006.

______. "Pilgrims, Missionaries, and Scholars." In *The Cave Church of Paul the Hermit at the Monastery of St. Paul, Egypt*, edited by William Lyster, 75–94. New Haven, CT: Yale University Press; Cairo: American Research Center in Egypt, 2008.

Hardy, Edward Rochie. *Christian Egypt: Church and People; Christianity and Nationalism in the Patriarchate of Alexandria*. New York: Oxford University Press, 1952.

Hasan, Sana'. *Christians Versus Muslims in Modern Egypt: The Century-Long Struggle for Coptic Equality*. Oxford: Oxford University Press, 2003.

Heikal, Mohamed. *Autumn of Fury: The Assassination of Sadat*. New York: Random House, 1983.

Henderson, Randall P. "The Egyptian Coptic Christians: The Conflict Between Identity and Equality." *Islam and Christian-Muslim Relations* 16.2 (April 2005): 155–66.

Hodgson, Peter Crafts. *God's Wisdom: Toward a Theology of Education*. Louisville, KY: Westminster John Knox Press, 1999.

Hogan, David. "The Market Revolution and Disciplinary Power: Joseph Lancaster and the Psychology of the Early Classroom System." *History of Education Quarterly* 29.3 (1989): 381–417.

Hourani, Albert. *Arabic Thought in the Liberal Age, 1798–1939*. Cambridge: Cambridge University Press, 1983.

Hulsman, Cornelis. "Renewal in the Coptic Orthodox Church; Notes of the Ph.D. Thesis of Rev. Dr. Wolfram Reiss." *Religious News Service from the Arab World* 46.23 (November 22, 2002). <http://www.arabwestreport.info/year-2002/week-46/23-renewal-coptic-orthodox-church-notes-phd-thesis-revd-dr-wolfram-reiss>, accessed January 5, 2014.

Hunter, F. Robert. "State–Society Relations in Nineteenth-Century Egypt: The Years of Transition, 1848–79." *Middle Eastern Studies* 36.3 (2000): 145–59.

______. *Egypt under the Khedives, 1805–1879*. Cairo: American University in Cairo Press, 1999.

Hyde, Georgie D. M. *Education in Modern Egypt: Ideals and Realities*. World Education series. London: Routledge and Kegan Paul, 1978.

Ibrahim, Vivian. *The Copts of Egypt: Challenges of Modernisation and Identity*. Library of Modern Middle East Studies 99. London: I. B. Tauris Academic Studies, 2010.

Īliyā, Vīktūr. *Shumūʿ muʿāṣirah: Ḥabīb Jirjis* [Contemporary Candles: Habib Girgis]. Shubrā, Cairo: Kanīsat Mār Mīnā, 1983.

Isaac, John. "Separate but Equal: Segregated Religious Education in Egypt's Public Schools." *International Journal of Progressive Education* 8.1 (2012): 6–21.

Iskandar, Rāghib Bik. "Ḥabīb Jirjis fi al-majlis al-millī al-ʿāmm" [Habib Girgis in the Lay Community Council]. *Majallat Madāris al-Aḥḥad* [Sunday School Magazine] 5.9–10 (November–December 1951): 42–46.

al-Iskandarī, *ʿUmar, and Salīm Ḥasan. Tārīkh Miṣr min al-fatḥ al-ʿUthmānī (ilá qubayl al-waqt al-ḥāḍir)* [The History of Egypt from the Ottoman Conquest (Until the Present Time)]. Safḥāt min Tārīkh Miṣr 6. Cairo: Maktabat Madbūlī, n.d.

Jamāl al-Dīn, ʿAbd al-ʿAzīz, ed. *Tārīkh Miṣr min bidāyāt al-qarn al-awwal al-Mīlādī ḥattá nihāyat al-qarn al-ʿishrīn* [The History of Egypt From the Beginning of the First Christian Century Until the End of the Twentieth Century]. 5 vols. Cairo: Maktabat Madbūlī, 2006.

al-Jamīʿī, *ʿAbd al-Munʿim Ibrāhīm, ed., Wathāʾiq al-taʿlīm al-ʿālī fī Miṣr khilāl al-qarn al-tāsiʿ ʿashar* [Archives of Higher Education in Egypt During the Nineteenth Century]. Vol. 1. Cairo: Dār al-Kutub wa-al-Wathāʾiq al-Qawmiyah, 2004.

Jayyid, Naẓīr, ed. "al-Arshīdyākūn Ḥabīb Jirjis: Bāʿith al-nahḍah al-Kanasiyah" [Archdeacon Habib Girgis: The Impetus for the Church's Revival]. *Majallat*

Madāris al-Aḥḥad [Sunday School Magazine] 5.9–10 (November–December 1951).

______, ed. *Majallat Madāris al-Aḥḥad* [Sunday School Magazine] 5.8 (September 1951).

______. "Thumma qāl Allāh li-yakun nūr … fa-kān nūr" [Then God said, 'Let there be light'... so there was light]. *Majallat Madāris al-Aḥḥad* [Sunday School Magazine] 5.9–10 (November–December 1951): 1–5.

Jirjis, Majdī [Magdi Girgis, or Magdi Guirguis]. "al-Adrāj al-Bābāwiyah li-Baṭārikat al-Kanīsah al-Qibṭiyah: Dirāsah wa-nashr li-adrāj al-Bābā 'Dīmitriyūs" [The Papal Decrees of the Coptic Patriarchs: A Study and Publication of the Pope Demetruis II's Decrees, 1862–1870]. *al-Majallah al-Tārīkhiyah al-Miṣriyah: Bulletin de la Société Égyptienne des études historiques* 41 (2002): 63–87.

______. "al-Niẓām al-siyāsī wa-ḥirāk al-ijtimā'ī lil-ṭā'ifah al-Qibṭiyah: Dirāsah muqāranah bayn al-'aṣr al-'Uthmānī wa-al-qarn al tāsi' 'ashar" [The Political Organization and Social Mobilization of the Coptic Community: A Comparative Study between the Ottoman Period and the Nineteenth Century]. In *al-Tārīkh al-muqāran lil-Sharq al-Awsaṭ: Ḥalaqah Baḥthiyah, 20–21 Māris 2002* [A Comparative History of the Middle East: Research Series, March 20–21, 2002]. Edited by Bītir Jarān and Ra'ūf 'Abbās, 95–109. Cairo: al-Majlis al-A'lá lil-Thaqāfah; Markaz al-Buḥūth al-Amrīkī bi-Miṣr, 2005.

______. "The Financial Resources of Coptic Priests in Nineteenth-Century Egypt." In *Money, Land and Trade: An Economic History of the Muslim Mediterranean*. Edited by Nelly Hanna, 223–243. London: I. B. Tauris, 2002.

______. "Idārat al-azamāt fī tārīkh al-Qibṭ: Namūdhaj min al-qarn al-thāmin 'ashar" [Administering Crises in the History of the Copts: An Eighteenth-Century Example]. In *Ḥawliyāt Islāmiyah* 33, 45–59. Cairo: al-Ma'had al-'Ilmī al-Faransī lil-Āthār al-Sharqiyah, 1999.

Jirjis, Majdī, and Pieternella van Doorn-Harder. *The Emergence of the Modern Coptic Papacy: The Egyptian Church and Its Leadership from the Ottoman Period to the Present*. The Popes of Egypt 3. Cairo: American University in Cairo Press, 2011.

Kaestle, Carl Frederick. *Joseph Lancaster and the Monitorial School Movement: A Documentary History*. Classics in Education 47. New York: Teachers College Press, 1973.

Kamal Mujani, Wan, and Napisah Karimah Ismail. "The Social Impact of French Occupation on Egypt." *Advances in Natural & Applied Sciences* 6.8 (2012): 1361–65.

Kamel, Adly, and Monier Attallah. *Foundations of Behavior and the Principles of Education in the Light of Christianity*. Edited by S. Nasim. Cairo: Institute of Coptic Studies, 1993.

Kamil, Jill. *Christianity in the Land of the Pharaohs: The Coptic Orthodox Church.* Cairo: American University in Cairo Press, 2002.

Kamrava, Mehran. *The Modern Middle East: A Political History Since the First World War*. Berkeley, CA: University of California Press, 2005.

Kedourie, Elie, and Sylvia Kedourie. *Modern Egypt: Studies in Politics and Society*. London: F. Cass, 1980.

Korany, Osama Mahmoud. "Reformative Changes in Educational Leadership in Post Revolutionary Egypt: A Critical Appraisal." *Educational Research* 2.10 (October 2011): 1553–64.

Lane, Edward William. *An Account of the Manners and Customs of the Modern Egyptians*. Reprint from 5th ed. Cairo: American University in Cairo Press, 1860.

______. *Description of Egypt*. Cairo: American University in Cairo Press, 2000.

Lane-Poole, Stanley. *A History of Egypt in the Middle Ages*. London: Methuen & Co., 1901.

Lorimer, Jack. *The Presbyterian Experience in Egypt, 1950–2000*. Denver, CO: Outskirts Press, Inc., 2007.

Lūqā, Malāk. *Aqbāṭ al-qarn al-ʻishrīn* [Copts of the Twentieth Century]. Cairo: Maṭbūʻāt Anjīlūs, 2009.

Lysons-Balcon, Heather. "Lancaster, Joseph." In *Dictionary of Canadian Biography*. Edited by Francess G. Halpenny, vol. 7 (1836 to 1850). Toronto: University of Toronto Press; Laval: Les Presses de l'Université Laval, 2003–. <http://www.biographi.ca/en/bio/lancaster_joseph_7E.html>, accessed December 8, 2013.

Malaty, Fr. Tadros Y. *The School of Alexandria*. Jersey City, NJ: St Mark's Coptic Orthodox Church, 1995.

Mansfield, Peter. *The British in Egypt*. London: Weidenfeld and Nicolson, 1971.

Markham, Donna. *Spiritlinking Leadership: Working Through Resistance to Organizational Change*. New York: Paulist Press, 1999.

Marlowe, John. *A History of Modern Egypt and Anglo–Egyptian Relations, 1800–1956*. 2nd ed. Hamden, CT: Archon Books, 1965.

Marsot, Afaf Lutfi al-Sayyid. *Egypt in the Reign of Muhammad Ali*. Cambridge: Cambridge University Press, 1984.

Martin, Maurice. "Jullien, Michel Marie." In *The Coptic Encyclopedia*. Edited by Aziz Suryal Atiya, vol. 5, 1382–83. New York: Macmillan, 1991.

Mārtīrūs, al-Anbā. *Nūr Ashraq fī al-ẓulmah: al-Qiddīs al-ʻaẓīm al-Arshīdyākūn Ḥabīb Jirjis* [The Light that Shone in the Darkness: The Great Saint, Archdeacon Habib Girgis]. Cairo: s.n., 2014.

Matthew, H. C. G., and Brian Harrison, eds. *Oxford Dictionary of National Biography*. Oxford: Oxford University Press, 2004.

McManners, John. *The Oxford Illustrated History of Christianity*. Oxford: Oxford University Press, 1990.

Megally, Fuad, and Sulayman Nasim. "Coptic Benevolent Societies." In *The Coptic Encyclopedia*. Edited by Aziz Suryal Atiya, vol. 2, 374–75. New York: Macmillan, 1991.

Meinardus, Otto Friedrich August. *Christian Egypt, Ancient and Modern*. 2nd ed. Cairo: American University in Cairo Press, 1977.

______. *Christian Egypt, Faith and Life*. Cairo: American University in Cairo Press, 1970.

______. *Christians in Egypt: Orthodox, Catholic, and Protestant Communities Past and Present*. Cairo: American University in Cairo Press, 2006.

______. *Two Thousand Years of Coptic Christianity*. Cairo: American University in Cairo Press, 1999.

Meyendorff, John. *Byzantine Theology: Historical Trends and Doctrinal Themes*. New York: Fordham University Press, 1979.

Miedema, Siebren, ed., *Religious Education as Encounter: A Tribute to John M. Hull*. Münster: Waxmann Verlag, 2009.

Milner, Viscount. *England in Egypt*. 13th ed. New York: Howard Fertig, 1970.

Mīnā, Tal'at Dhikrī. "al-Kulliyah al-Iklīrīkiyah ka-mā tamannāhā Ḥabīb Jirjis" [The Theological College as Habib Girgis Desired It]. *Majallat Madāris al-Aḥḥad* [Sunday School Magazine] 47.8–9 (October–November 1993): 30–33.

______. *Ḥabīb Jirjis wa-turāthih al-ta'līmī* [Habib Girgis and His Educational Legacy]. Cairo: Maṭba'at Madāris al-Aḥḥad, 1993.

al-Miṣrī, Īrīs Ḥabīb [Iris H. el-Masry]. *The Copts and Christian Civilization*. Salt Lake City, UT: University of Utah Press, 1979.

______. *A History of Eastern Christianity*. Millwood, NY: Kraus Reprint, 1980.

______. *Qiṣṣat al-Kanīsah al-Qibṭīyah, wa-hiya tārīkh al-Kanīsah al-Urthūdhuksīyah al-Miṣrīyah allatī assasahā Mār Murquṣ al-Bashīr* [The Story of the Coptic Church, i.e. the History of the Egyptian Orthodox Church Which Was Established by St Mark the Evangelist]. 9 vols. Cairo: Dār al-'Ālam al-'Arabī, 1988.

______. *The Story of the Copts: The True Story of Christianity in Egypt*. 2 vols. Newberry Springs, CA: St Anthony Coptic Orthodox Monastery, 1982.

Mitchell, Timothy. *Colonising Egypt*. Berkeley, CA: University of California Press, 1991.

Moreh, Shmuel. *Modern Arabic Poetry, 1800–1970: The Development of Its Forms and Themes Under the Influence of Western Literature*. Leiden: Brill, 1976.

Murqus, Samīr. "Tārīkh khidmat madāris al-Aḥḥad wa-atharahā al-ta'līmī fī al-fatrah min 1900-1950 Masīḥiyah" [A History of the Sunday School Ministry]. *Majallat Madāris al-Aḥḥad* [Sunday School Magazine] 38.9–10 (November–December 1984): 72–85.

Murray, Jocelyn. *Proclaim the Good News: A Short History of the Church Missionary Society*. London: Hodder and Stoughton, 1985.

Mustafa, Ahmed 'Abd al-Rahim. "The Hekekyan Papers." In *Political and Social Change in Modern Egypt*. Edited by P. M. Holt. London: Oxford University Press, 1968.

Mutawallī, Fu'ād Basyūnī. *Mujmal tārīkh al-ta'līm: Dirāsah li-tārīkh al-ta'līm al-'āmm wa-al-fann mundhu bidāyat al-qarn al-tāsi' 'ashar wa-ḥattá nihāyat al-qarn al-'ishrīn* [An Overview of Educational History: A Study of the History of Public Education and Art from the Beginning of the Nineteenth Century and Until the End of the Twentieth Century]. Alexandria: Dār al-Ma'rifah al-Jāmi'īyah, 1989.

Nasīm, Sulaymān [Sulayman Nasim, or Soliman Nassim]. *al-Aqbāṭ wa-al-ta'līm fī Miṣr al-ḥadīthah* [Copts and Education in Modern Egypt]. Edited by Bishop Ghrīghūriyūs and 'Azīz Sūryāl 'Aṭiyah. Cairo: Manshūrāt Usqufiyat al-Dirāsāt al-'Ulyā al-Lāhūtiyah wa-al-Thaqāfah al-Qibṭiyah wa-al-Baḥth al-'Ilmī, 1983.

______, ed., "al-Aqbāṭ wa-al-ta'līm wa-al-thaqāfah" [Copts, Education, and Culture]. In *Mawsū'ah min turāth al-Qibṭ* [Encyclopedia of Coptic Heritage]. Edited by Mūrīs As'ad and Samīr Fawzī Jirjis, vol. 4, 81–163. Cairo: Dār al-Qiddīs Yūhannā al-Ḥabīb lil-Nashr, 2004.

______. *al-Tarbiyah fī al-'aṣr al-Qibṭī: wa-al-Shakhṣiyah al-qawmiyah al-Miṣriyah* [Education in the Coptic Period: And the Egyptian National Character]. Cairo: Dār al-Thaqāfah, 1989.

______. "Coptic Education." In *The Coptic Encyclopedia*. Edited by Aziz Suryal Atiya, vol. 3, 931–33. New York: Macmillan, 1991.

______. *Tārīkh al-tarbiyah al Qibṭiyah* [The History of Coptic Education]. Cairo: Dār al-Karnak lil-Nashr wa-al-Ṭab' wa-al-Tawzī', 1963.

______. "Ḥabīb Jirjis (1876–1951)." In *The Coptic Encyclopedia*. Edited by Aziz Suryal Atiya, vol. 4, 1189. New York: Macmillan, 1991.

______. "Ḥabīb Jirjis wa-al-Iklīrīkiyah" [Habib Girgis and the Theological College]. *Majallat Madāris al-Aḥḥad* [Sunday School Magazine] 45.7 (September 1991): 20–25.

______."Rāḥilnā al-'Aẓīm" [Our Great One Who Has Departed]. *Majallat Madāris al-Aḥḥad* [Sunday School Magazine] 5.9–10 (November–December 1951): 85–88.

______, and Kamāl Ḥabib. *Fī al-tarbiyah al-Masīḥiyah* [Regarding Christian Education]. Cairo: Maktabat Majallat Murqus, 1964.

Naṣīr, ʻAbd al-Ḥalīm Ilyās. "Kalimat al-Majlis al-Milliyah" [The Speech of the Lay Community Council]. *Majallat Madāris al-Aḥḥad* [Sunday School Magazine] 5.9–10 (November–December 1951): 38–41.

Neill, Stephen. *Colonialism and Christian Missions*. London: Lutterworth Press, 1966.

Nurdogan, Arzu M. "Lord Shall be Taught to Egypt: The Girls' Boarding School in Babelluk (1892–1923)." *Education* 129.4 (Summer 2009): 770–87.

Ong, Walter J. *Orality and Literacy: The Technologizing of the Word*. London and New York: Routledge, 2002.

Oram, Elizabeth E. "Constructing Modern Copts: The Production of Coptic Christian Identity in Contemporary Egypt." Ph.D. diss., Princeton University, Department of Anthropology, 2004.

Patrick, Theodore Hall. *Traditional Egyptian Christianity: A History of the Coptic Orthodox Church*. Greensboro, NC: Fisher Park Press, 1996.

Pennington, J. D. "The Copts in Modern Egypt." *Middle Eastern Studies* 18.2 (April 1982): 158–79.

Petricioli, Marta. "Italian Schools in Egypt." *British Journal of Middle Eastern Studies* 24.2 (1997): 179–91.

Philips, H. E. *Blessed Be Egypt My People: Life Studies from the Land of the Nile*. Philadelphia, PA: Judson Press, 1953.

Philo of Alexandria, and David Winston. *The Contemplative Life, the Giants and Selections*. Classics of Western Spirituality. New York: Paulist Press, 1981.

Pikkert, Pieter. *Protestant Missionaries to the Middle East: Ambassadors of Christ or Culture?* Hamilton: WEC Canada, 2008.

Polk, William R., and Richard L. Chambers, eds. *Beginnings of Modernization in the Middle East: The Nineteenth Century*. Publications of the Center for Middle Eastern Studies 1. Chicago, IL: University of Chicago Press, 1968.

Porter, Stanley E. *Dictionary of Biblical Criticism and Interpretation*. London: Routledge, 2006.

Qāmūs al-Tarājim al-Qibṭiyah [Coptic Biographical Dictionary]. Alexandria: Jamʻiyat Mār Mīnā al-ʻAjāyibī lil-Dirāsāt al-Qibṭīyah, 1995.

Raflah, Jirjis. *Min Ṭarā'if al-Arshīdyākūn Ḥabīb Jirjis* [Some Anecdotes Regarding the Archdeacon Habib Girgis]. Cairo, n.d.

Reid, Donald M. "Archaeology, Social Reform, and Modern Identity Among the Copts, 1854–1952." In *Entre reforme sociale et mouvement national: identité et modernisation en Égypte, 1882–1962*. Edited by A. Roussillon, 311–35. Cairo: Centre d'Études et de Documentation Économiques, Juridiques et Sociales (CEDEJ), 1995.

______. "Turn-of-the-Century Egyptian School Days." *Comparative Education Review* 27.3 (1983): 374–93.

______. *Whose Pharaohs? Archaeology, Museums, and Egyptian National Identity From Napoleon to World War I*. Berkeley, CA: University of California Press, 2002.

Reiss, Wolfram. *Erneuerung in der Koptisch-Orthodoxen Kirche: die Geschichte der koptisch-orthodoxen Sonntagsschulbewegung und die Aufnahme ihrer Reformansatze in den Erneurungsbewegungen der Koptisch-Orthodoxen Kirche der Gegenwart*. Studien zur orientalischen Kirchengeschichte. Hamburg: LIT Verlag, 1998.

Richmond, J. C. B. *Egypt 1798–1952*. New York: Columbia University Press, 1977.

Roper, G. *Arabic Printing in Malta 1825–1845: Its History and Its Place in the Development of Print Culture in the Arab Middle East*. Durham: University of Durham Press, 1988.

Rūfaylah, Ya'qūb Nakhlah. *Tārīkh al-ummah al-Qibṭiyah* [The History of the Coptic People]. 2nd ed. Cairo: Mu'assasat Mār Murqus li-Dirāsāt al-Tārīkh al-Qibṭī, 2000.

Russell, Mona L. "Competing, Overlapping, and Contradictory Agendas: Egyptian Education under British Occupation, 1882–1922." *Comparative Studies of South Asia, Africa and the Middle East* 21.1–2 (2001): 50–60.

______. *Creating the New Egyptian Woman: Consumerism, Education, and National Identity, 1863–1922*. New York: Palgrave Macmillan, 2004.

Ryzova, Lucie. *The Age of the Efendiyya: Passages to Modernity in National-Colonial Egypt*. Oxford Historical Monographs. New York: Oxford University Press, 2013.

Saad, Saad Michael. "al-Dīmūqrāṭiyah al-Kanasiyah fī fikr al-Arshīdyākūn Ḥabīb Jirjis" [Ecclesiastical Democracy in the Thought of Archdeacon Habib Girgis]. *Majallat Madāris al-Aḥḥad* [Sunday School Magazine] 46.1 (January 1992): 32–36.

______. "al-Majlis al-millī fī fikr al-Arshīdyākūn Ḥabīb Jirjis" [The Lay Community Council in the Thought of the Archdeacon Habib Girgis]. *Watani* 41.1967 (September 5, 1999): 5.

______. "Archdeacon Habib Girgis: His Dreams, Struggles and Shining Light." *Watani International* 43.2040 (March 25, 2001): 2.

______. "Habib Girgis: A Theologian and Reformer," In "The Coptic Church, History and Liturgy: Papers Presented at the First St Shenouda the Archimandrite Coptic Symposium." *Bulletin of Saint Shenouda the Archimandrite Coptic Society* 4 (1997–98):

______. "Habib Girgis and the Revival of Coptic Patristic Theology." *Watani International* 43.2062 (August 26, 2001): 3.

______. "Habib Girgis: The Revival of Coptic Patristic Theology." *Watani International* 55.2696 (August 25, 2013): 2.

______. "Min turāth al-Arshīdyākūn Ḥabīb Jirjis: 'Amal al-Rūḥ al-Qudus fī al-Majma' al-Muqaddas" [From the Legacy of Archdeacon Habib Girgis: The Work of the Holy Spirit in the Holy Synod]. *Watani* 43.2059 (June 10, 2001): 15.

______. "St Archdeacon Habib Girgis: The Revival of Coptic Patristic Theology." *Watani International* 55.2696 (August 25, 2013): 2.

Sabagh, Georges, and Gustave E. von Grunebaum Center for Near Eastern Studies. *The Modern Economic and Social History of the Middle East in Its World Context* [Tenth Giorgio Levi Della Vida Biennial Conference]. Giorgio Levi Della Vida Conferences. Cambridge: Cambridge University Press, 1989.

Ṣādiq, 'Ādil Shukrī. "Khamsūn 'āmman 'alá intiqāl bā'ith al-nahḍah al-Kanasiyah: al-Arshīdyākūn Ḥabīb Jirjis" [Fifty Years From the Passing of the Impetus for the Church's Revival: The Archdeacon Habib Girgis]. *Majallat Madāris al-Aḥḥad* [Sunday School Magazine] 55.7 (August 2001): 24–28.

Ṣādiq, Rāmī 'Aṭā. "al-Arshīdyākūn Ḥabīb Jirjis: Karmah Mushtahāh" [The Archdeacon Habib Girgis: A Satisfying Vine]. Unpublished manuscript, 2014.

Safran, Nadav. *Egypt in Search of Political Community*. Cambridge, MA: Harvard University Press, 1961.

al-Sahm, Sāmī Sulaymān Muḥammad. *al-Ta'līm wa-al-taghyīr al-ijtimā'ī fī Miṣr fī al-qarn al-tāsi' 'ashar* [Education and Social Change in Egypt in the Nineteenth Century]. *Tārīkh al-Miṣriyīn* [History of the Egyptians] 165. Cairo: al-Hay'ah al-Miṣriyah al-'Āmmah lil-Kitāb, 2000.

Salāmah, Jirjis. *Athar al-iḥtilāl al-Brīṭānī fī al-ta'līm al-qawmī fī Miṣr, 1982–1922* [The Impact of British Occupation on National Education in Egypt, 1882–1922]. Cairo: Maktabat al-Anjlū al-Miṣriyah, 1966.

______. *Tārīkh al-ta'līm al-ajnabī fī Miṣr fī al-qarnayn al-tāsi' 'ashar wa-al-'ishrīn* [A History of Foreign Education in Egypt in the Nineteenth and Twentieth Centuries]. Cairo: al-Majlis al-A'lá li-Ri'āyat al-Funūn wa-al-Ādāb wa-al-'Ulūm al-Ijtimā'iyah, 1963.

Salmoni, Barak A. "Women in the Nationalist-Educational Prism: Turkish and Egyptian Pedagogues and Their Gendered Agenda, 1920–1952." *History of Education Quarterly* 43.4 (2003): 483–516.

Samir, Khalil. "Barlam and Yuwaṣaf." In *The Coptic Encyclopedia*. Edited by Aziz Suryal Atiya, vol. 2, 346–7. New York: Macmillan, 1991.

Sawaie, Mohammed. "Rafi al-Tahtawi and his Contribution to the Lexical Development of Modern Literary Arabic." *International Journal of Middle East Studies* 32.3 (2000): 395–410.

Sawicki, Marianne. "Historical Methods and Religious Education." *Religious Education* 82.3 (1987): 375–89.

Sāwīrus Ibn al-Muqaffa‘, Bishop. *Tārīkh al-Baṭārikah* [The History of the Patriarchs]. Edited by Mīkhā’īl Maksī Iskandar. Silsilat al-Turāth al-Qibṭī al-Qadīm [Ancient Coptic Heritage Series]. Cairo: Maktabat al-Maḥabbah, 2004.

Sayed, Fatma. H. *Transforming Education in Egypt: Western Influence and Domestic Policy Reform*. Cairo: American University in Cairo Press, 2006.

Schaff, Philip. *History of the Christian Church*. 3rd ed. 8 vols. Peabody, MA: Hendrickson Publishers, 1996.

______, and Henry Wallace, eds. *Eusebius Pamphilius: Church History, Life of Constantine the Great, Oration in Praise of Constantine*. Nicene and Post-Nicene Fathers, 2nd ser., vol. 1. New York: Cosimo Classics, 2007.

Sedra, Paul D. "Class Cleavages and Ethnic Conflict: Coptic Christian Communities in Modern Egyptian Politics." *Islam and Christian-Muslim Relations* 10.2 (1999): 219–35.

______. "Ecclesiastical Warfare: Patriarch, Presbyterian, and Peasant in Nineteenth-Century Asyut." In *The United States and the Middle East: Cultural Encounters*. Edited by A. Amanat and M. T. Bernhardsson, 290–314. New Haven, CT: Yale Center for International and Area Studies, 2002.

______. *From Mission to Modernity: Evangelicals, Reformers and Education in Nineteenth Century Egypt*. London: I. B. Tauris, 2011.

______. "John Lieder and his Mission in Egypt: The Evangelical Ethos at Work Among Nineteenth-Century Copts." *The Journal of Religious History* 28.3 (October 2004): 219–39.

______. "Missionaries, Peasants, and the Protection Problem: Negotiating Coptic Reform in Nineteenth-Century Egypt." In *US–Middle East Historical Encounters*. Edited by Abbas Amanat and Magnus T. Bernhardsson, 77–100. Gainesville, FL: University Press of Florida, 2007.

______. "Observing Muhammad ‘Ali Paşa and His Administration at Work, 1843–1846." In *The Modern Middle East: A Sourcebook for History*. Edited by Camron Michael Amin, Benjamin C. Fortna, and Elizabeth Frierson, 39–42. Oxford: Oxford University Press, 2006.

______. "Schooling for a Modern Coptic Subjectivity in Nineteenth-Century Egypt." In *North African Mosaic: A Cultural Reappraisal of Ethnic and Religious Minorities*. Edited by Nabil Boudraa and Joseph Krause, 196–213. Newcastle: Cambridge Scholars Publishing, 2007.

______. "Textbook Maneuvers: Evangelicals and Educational Reform in Nineteenth-Century Egypt." Ph.D. diss., New York University, Graduate School of Arts and Science, 2006.

______. "Writing the History of the Modern Copts: From Victims and Symbols to Actors." *History Compass* 7.3 (2009): 1049–63.

Seikaly, Samir Menas. "Coptic Communal Reform: 1860–1914." *Middle Eastern Studies* 6.3 (January 1970): 247–75.

______. "The Copts under British Rule, 1882–1914." Ph.D. diss., University of London, 1967.

Serapion, Bishop. "A Lover Missionary to Egypt: A Short Record of the Life and Work of W. H. T. Gairdner (1873–1928)." Unpublished manuscript, n.d.

Seymour, Jack L. "The Future of the Past: History and Policy-Making in Religious Education." *Religious Education* 81.1 (1986): 113–33.

Sharkey, Heather J. *American Evangelicals in Egypt: Missionary Encounters in an Age of Empire*. Princeton, NJ: Princeton University Press, 2008.

Shārūbīm, Mīkhā'īl Bik. *al-Kāfī fī tārīkh Miṣr al-qadīm wa-al-ḥadīth* [The Complete History of Egypt, Ancient and Modern]. Edited by 'Abd al-Wahhāb Bakr. Vol. 5, parts 1–2. Cairo: Dār al-Kutub wa-al-Wathā'iq al-Qawmiyah, 1998.

Shenouda III, His Holiness Pope. "al-Iḥtifāl bi-murūr arba'ūn 'āmman 'alá niyāḥat al-Arshīdyākūn Ḥabīb Jirjis" [The Commemoration of the Fortieth Anniversary of the Death of Archdeacon Habib Girgis]. *Majallat al-Kirāzah* 19.29–30 (August 16, 1991): 1.

______. "Ḥabīb Jirjis: Rā'id al-ta'līm al-Masīḥī" [Habib Girgis: A Pioneer of Christian Education]. *Majallat al-Kirāzah* 18.31–32 (September 7, 1990): 1, 7–9.

______. *Holy Zeal*, translated by Glynis Younan. Cairo: Dar El Tebaa El Kawmia, 1990.

______. "Light in the Darkness: Life of Archdeacon Habib Guirguis (1876–1951)." *Watani International* 43.2062 (August 26, 2001): 2.

______. "Our Teacher Archdeacon Habib Girgis." *Watani International* 43.2062 (August 26, 2001): 2.

______. "Our Teacher Archdeacon Habib Girgis: Pioneer of Religious Education in Modern Times," translated by Saad Michael Saad. *Watani International* 55.2696 (August 25, 2013): 2.

______. "Ustādhunā al-Arshīdyākūn Ḥabīb Jirjis" [Our Teacher Archdeacon Habib Girgis]. *Majallat al-Kirāzah* 18.29–30 (August 24, 1990): 1.

Shulman, Lee S. "Disciplines of Inquiry in Education: A New Overview." In *Methods for Research in Religious Education*. Edited by R. M. Jaeger. 3–29. Washington, DC: American Educational Research Association, 1997.

Starrett, Gregory. *Putting Islam to Work: Education, Politics, and Religious Transformation in Egypt*. Comparative Studies on Muslim Societies. Berkeley: University of California Press, 1998.

Steppat, Fritz. "National Education Projects in Egypt before the British Occupation." In *Beginnings of Modernization in the Middle East: The Nineteenth Century*. Edited by W. R. Polk and R. L. Chambers, Publications of the Center for

Middle Eastern Studies 1, 281–97. Chicago, IL: University of Chicago Press, 1968.

Suriel, Bishop. *Christian Education in the Church of Alexandria in the First Five Centuries*. Melbourne: St Athanasius Press, 2002.

______. *Interview with His Holiness Pope Shenouda the Third Regarding His Memories with Habib Girgis*. New York: Digital Audio, 2005.

Sūryāl, Riyād. *al-Mujtama'al-Qibṭī fī Miṣr fī al-qarn al-tāsi' 'ashar* [Coptic Society in Egypt During the Nineteenth Century]. Cairo: Maktabat al-Maḥabbah, 1984.

Sūryāl, Ṣalīb. *Tārīkh Madāris al-Aḥḥad al-Qibṭiyah al-Urthūdhuksiyah bi-al-Jīzah* [The History of Coptic Orthodox Sunday Schools in Giza]. 4 vols. Giza: Kanīsat Mār Murqus, n.d.

al-Suryānī, Fr. Thī'udusyūs. "'Ann al-Kashf al-mu'jizī li-rifāt al-arshīdyākūn Ḥabīb Jirjis" [On the Miraculous Discovery of the Relics of Archdeacon Habib Girgis]. *Majallat al-Kirāzah* 22.17–18 (May 13, 1994): 19.

Szyliowicz, Joseph S. *Education and Modernization in the Middle East*. Ithaca, NY: Cornell University Press, 1973.

Taft, Robert F. *Beyond East and West: Problems in Liturgical Understanding*. Rome: Edizioni Orientalia Christiana, 2001.

Tagher, Jacques. *Christians in Muslim Egypt: An Historical Study of the Relations Between Copts and Muslims from 640 to 1922*. Altenberge: Oros Verlag, 1998.

Tamura, Airi. "Ethnic Consciousness and its Transformation in the Course of Nation-Building: The Muslim and the Copt in Egypt, 1906–1919." *The Muslim World* 75.2 (April 1985): 102–14.

Tāwaḍrūs, Ṣamū'īl. *Tārīkh Bābāwāt al-Kursī al-Iskandarī 1809–1971 Masīḥiyah* [History of the Popes of the Alexandrian See (AD 1809–1971)]. Dayr al-Suryān: Maṭbū'āt Dayr al-Suryān, 2002.

Tuchman, Barbara W. *Practising History*. London: Papermac, 1985

van Doorn-Harder, Pieternella. *Contemporary Coptic Nuns*. Columbia, SC: University of South Carolina Press, 1995.

______. "Finding a Platform: Studying Copts in the 19th and 20th Centuries." *International Journal of Middle East Studies* 42.3 (2010): 479–82.

______, and K. Vogt, eds. *Between Desert and City: The Coptic Orthodox Church Today*. Oslo: Institute for Comparative Research in Human Culture, 1997.

Vatikiotis, P. J. *The Modern History of Egypt*. New York: Frederick A. Praeger, 1969.

Vliet, Jacques van der. "The Copts: 'Modern Sons of the Pharaohs'?" *Church History and Religious Culture* 90.1–3 (2009): 279–90.

Vrame, Anton C. *The Educating Icon: Teaching Wisdom and Holiness in the Orthodox Way*. Brookline, MA: Holy Cross Orthodox Press, 1999.

Wakin, Edward. *A Lonely Minority: The Modern Story of Egypt's Copts*. New York: Morrow, 1963.

Walter, Alissa. "A Minority Within a Minority: A History of Women in the Egyptian Coptic Orthodox and Evangelical Churches (1854–Present)." Master's thesis, Georgetown University, Graduate School of Arts and Sciences, 2011.

Warburg, Gabriel R., and Uri M. Kupferschmidt. *Islam, Nationalism, and Radicalism in Egypt and the Sudan*. New York: Praeger, 1983.

Watson, John H. *Among the Copts*. Brighton: Sussex Academic Press, 2000.

Werff, Lyle L. Vander. *Christian Mission to Muslims: The Record, Anglican and Reformed Approaches in India and the Near East, 1800–1938*. South Pasadena, CA: William Carey Library, 1977.

Williams, James. *Education in Egypt Before British Control*. Birmingham: Press of Frank Juckes, Ltd., 1939.

Winter, Michael. *Egyptian Society under Ottoman Rule, 1517–1798*. London: Routledge, 2004.

Worrell, William H. *A Short Account of the Copts*. Ann Arbor, MI: University of Michigan Press, 1945.

Yanney, Rodolph. "Light in the Darkness: Life of Archdeacon Habib Guirguis (1876–1951)." *Coptic Church Review* 5.2 (1984): 47–52.

Yousef, Hoda. A. "Reassessing Egypt's Dual System of Education Under Isma'il: Growing ʿIlm and Shifting Ground in Egypt's First Educational Journal." Rawdat Al-Madaris, 1870–77." *International Journal of Middle East Studies* 40.1 (2008): 109–30.

Zaalouk, Malak. *The Pedagogy of Empowerment: Community Schools as a Social Movement in Egypt*. Cairo: American University in Cairo Press, 2006.

Zaqlamah, Nash'at. *al-Khādim al-Amīn: al-Arshīdyākūn Ḥabīb Jirjis* [The Faithful Servant: The Archdeacon Habib Girgis]. Cairo: Maṭbaʿat Madāris al-Aḥḥad, n.d.

______. *Rajul al-bannā' al-ʿaẓīm: al-Arshīdyākūn Ḥabīb Jirjis* [The Great Builder: The Archdeacon Habib Girgis]. Cairo: Maṭbaʿat Madāris al-Aḥḥad, 2010.

Index

Note: Page numbers in **bold** refer to illustrations. An 'n' after a page number, e.g. 21n4, refers to a note on the page.

Praise for *Habib Girgis*

This is a groundbreaking study that adds considerable depth and complexity to our understanding of Habib Girgis's long career and the Coptic Church's educational reforms over the first half of the twentieth century. It is an engaging, nuanced examination of Girgis's aspirations, frustrations, and enduring legacy.

Maged S.A. Mikhail, *Professor of History, California State University at Fullerton*

This meticulously researched and beautifully written study examines the inspiring life of Habib Girgis, who believed that everybody deserved an education and who made it his life's work to enrich Coptic communities with learning. In the face of limited resources and considerable challenges, Habib Girgis strove to expand educational opportunities for villagers, Sunday School students, seminarians, and others. Historians of modern Egypt generally, and of Coptic Orthodox and other Egyptian Christian communities more specifically, will appreciate this study for its sensitive yet rigorous treatment of a great twentieth-century educator who, in the words of Bishop Suriel, helped Egyptians "to give meaning to their own struggles . . . [and] to look within to understand their lives and to think of what lay beyond."

Heather J. Sharkey, *Associate Professor of Middle Eastern & Islamic Studies, Department of Near Eastern Languages & Civilizations, University of Pennsylvania*

At a time when internal and external turmoil seemed to rip the Coptic Church apart, a self-effacing teacher had the brilliant insight that educating the children was the way forward. Overcoming practical, theoretical, social, and cultural obstacles, Habib Girgis created curricula and projects that aimed at restoring the Church to its original glory. Nowadays, the Sunday schools he started are considered to be the foundation of Coptic renewal. However, up to now very little was known about Habib Girgis' life. This book presents the first comprehensive study that places his life, work, and strategies within their historical, religious, and educational context. Based on primary texts, educational curricula, Church archives, and historical sources, it presents a compelling and insightful story that is a must read for students of Coptic history and Church life.

Nelly van Doorn-Harder, *Professor of Religion, Wake Forest University*